PRAISE FOR *ADVANCING STRATEGY THROUGH BEHAVIOURAL PSYCHO*

T0289698

Too often, we try to control the hyperactive world of business with staid and passive strategies, enshrined in documents and presentation materials rather than in hearts and minds. Pontus Wadström's excellent book on active, behaviourally engaged strategy is a welcome antidote to this passivity, and offers a scintillating take on making strategy a living, breathing thing, without turning it into something convoluted and verbose. It outlines the future of behaviour-sensitive strategizing for an ever more complicated world, and will be a powerful tool for any executive trying to develop smart, straightforward strategies.
Alf Rehn, Professor and Head of the Department of Technology and Innovation, University of Southern Denmark

This book has been a great source of inspiration for our company's strategy work and was read by our entire management team. It has helped us de-dramatize and concretize the concept of 'strategy' and clearly demonstrates how long-term goals are achieved by prioritizing shorter-term goals, and by continuously driving and developing behaviour linked to such priorities. Pontus' book can be highly recommended.
Lars Bergh, Vice President and CFO, Elgiganten Logistik

In this book Wadström presents a truly crucial link between strategy and behavioural science as well as sharp and concrete advice to everyone who wants to make strategies come alive in business. This book is an 'Aha!' experience that inspires one to action.
Elisabeth Wahlström, Business Development Manager, Manpower Group Sweden

Pontus describes, in a truly accessible way, how organizations can work to realize strategies in practice. This book is, in my opinion, one of the few management books that can really make a difference in your organization.
Peter Hjelmze, Head of Project Management, AFRY

Pontus Wadström presents an intelligent combination of the usually separated domains of strategy and behavioural psychology. It is a tangible and hands-on guide to how to actually realize your strategy, which is achieved only by fully understanding and affecting the behaviour of the organization.
Daniel Resh, Business Development Manager, Volvo Cars

I hope that many will read this book, it makes such an important point! Truly great strategies can be perfectly formulated and yet be a total waste of time since it is not clear how they should be realized by the individuals of the organization. Pontus Wadström has clearly and credibly captured the essentials of psychology and management to present how strategy must be linked to behaviours if we are to improve our organizations. This book is therefore as relevant to the CEO, the board and the management team as it is to the psychologist in occupational healthcare or anyone trying to develop an organization and its members. Pontus' background in both academia and practice shines through as he presents in a simple, understandable and theoretically substantiated way both organizations' strategy realization challenges and pitfalls, and how to manage them in real life. This captured me as a reader.
Carin Dannert, Founding Partner, Heartpace Söderberg & Partners

In today's turbulent time, finding the 'right' strategy is not enough: excellence in realization has become an utterly critical imperative. By introducing the behavioural dimension of strategy work, this book presents a powerful complement to existing management books. Wadström's own practical experience from leading change processes in major firms, in combination with deep insights into relevant research, makes this text a must read for people interested in strategizing processes in organizations.
Matti Kaulio, Professor and former Head of the Department of Industrial Economics and Management, KTH Royal Institute of Technology

This truly usable book is a must read for all organizations trying to create competitive edge and value for their customers. Its methods built on science and proven experience will help you thrive in today's changing, challenging and fluctuating markets. Clearly presented and to the point in each chapter, Pontus Wadström forms a system and recipe for company success at all levels. Your clients, staff and colleagues will thank you, and your competitors will gasp and wonder what happened.
Mattias Magnell, Leadership Development Manager, Skanska and Chairman of the board of Swedish Chartered Institute for Standards (SIS) Human Resource Management committee

An inspiring and accessible one-stop-shop for change makers in search of understanding and accessing the sweet spot where successful strategy execution moves beyond just plans and metrics into a place of people-centric continuous evolution of learning, changing and adaptation.

Åsa Åberg, Head of Executive and Member Office, Plan International

Wadström strives to create a common leadership language of behavioural psychology that would make an organization continuously eager and self-sufficient, with empowered people moving in the right direction; a behavioural strategy to engage within. This is a book worth reading, to understand and to utilize in any organization today. It is well and clearly written but tough to implement.

Jan-Erik Nordström, Business Development Manager Innovation, Neste

Advancing Strategy through Behavioural Psychology

*Create competitive advantage
in relentlessly changing markets*

Pontus Wadström

KoganPage

Publisher's note

Every possible effort has been made to ensure that the information contained in this book is accurate at the time of going to press, and the publishers and authors cannot accept responsibility for any errors or omissions, however caused. No responsibility for loss or damage occasioned to any person acting, or refraining from action, as a result of the material in this publication can be accepted by the editor, the publisher or the author.

First published in Sweden as *Strategi är ett verb* in 2014 by Liber.
Revised English edition published in Great Britain and the United States in 2022 by Kogan Page Limited.

2nd Floor, 45 Gee Street	122 W 27th St, 10th Floor	4737/23 Ansari Road
London	New York, NY 10001	Daryaganj
EC1V 3RS	USA	New Delhi 110002
United Kingdom		India
www.koganpage.com		

Kogan Page books are printed on paper from sustainable forests.

© Pontus Wadström 2022

The right of Pontus Wadström to be identified as the author of this work has been asserted by him in accordance with the Copyright, Designs and Patents Act 1988.

ISBNs

Hardback	978 1 3986 0487 2
Paperback	978 1 3986 0482 7
Ebook	978 1 3986 0486 5

British Library Cataloguing-in-Publication Data

A CIP record for this book is available from the British Library.

Library of Congress Control Number

2021946243

Typeset by Integra Software Services, Pondicherry
Print production managed by Jellyfish
Printed and bound by CPI Group (UK) Ltd, Croydon CR0 4YY

To my father, for his profound knowledge of the principles of human behaviour and his dedication to help me apply them in order to understand 'the world'.

CONTENTS

LIST OF FIGURES

ABOUT THE AUTHOR

Pontus Wadström works as an independent strategy advisor, lecturer and researcher. He has previously worked as strategy consultant and as head of various strategy, business development and change departments, portfolios and projects in publicly listed companies and in start-ups.

His expertise is how organizations strategize – doing strategy for real and in practice – and the impact this has on their ability to adjust, to change and, in the long run, to become more successful, regardless of how success is defined. Over the years he has worked with publicly listed multinationals, privately held companies, start-ups, municipalities, governmental bodies, unions and NGOs; he has clients in manufacturing, real estate, engineering and construction, telecom, finance, professional services, IT, logistics, education, health and social work.

Alongside his practice he is an affiliate researcher at the Department of Industrial Economics and Management at KTH Royal Institute of Technology in Stockholm, Sweden. This is also where he earned his PhD. He also holds an MBA, a BSc in International Management and a BSc in Behavioural Science from Linköping University.

Pontus' ability to draw on extensive practical experience as well as deep theoretical knowledge from domains that typically may not be associated with each other enables him to provide an alternative viewpoint on how organizations can become successful in changing times.

PREFACE

A while ago, I saw a documentary about one of my favourite hip-hop groups, A Tribe Called Quest. In the documentary, one of the group members, Phife, is wearing a T-shirt that says, 'Peace is a verb'. I liked the ambiguity of the message. Grammatically speaking, peace is a noun. I also liked the way you can interpret the message itself. My interpretation is that if we are to have peace, nice words and plans are not sufficient. We need to act. I was in the middle of writing this book and was immediately struck by the message's similarities to the main idea behind this book. Just like peace, strategy is a verb. We will not get anywhere if we don't do something. Strategies are never realized unless people act. No goals are reached unless people 'behave'. And as strategy is involved with precisely that – deciding where you want to go and making sure you actually get there – in its purest sense strategy is behaviour.

In many cases, organizations overlook a number of aspects that research unequivocally argues are needed in order to create a successful organization. When we discuss strategy, there are many words and expressions that we throw around without knowing what they really mean. My strategy map still has plenty of blank spots. This book is an attempt to fill in a couple of those blank 'strategy spots'.

Briefly put, the ambition is to describe strategy, and its relation to performance and to change, and to explain how to work with these – how to strategize – to turn such actions, or behaviours, into a competitive advantage, and in the long term, success. I want to do this in ways that are as concrete as possible, which I will accomplish by explaining them using the language found in behavioural psychology.

To make this accessible, we need a common language. As the book is about strategy, performance, change and behavioural psychology, we need to learn more about these fields. What is behavioural psychology and how does it affect strategy and performance? How and why do we learn or not learn new behaviour – behaviours that are crucial if we are to develop? If the strategy is for organizations to reflect an ever-changing world, the strategy of organizations also needs to imply change – so how do we make sure of that? And how do we change behaviour to bring it in line with or, better yet, to accelerate a strategy?

Creating a truly high-performance and thriving organization requires systematic work that combines strategy and change. Innovation, adaptation and learning need to be ingrained so deeply into the core of the organization that they come as naturally as working with customers, production, marketing or human resources. According to Jack Welch, former CEO of General Electric, and one of the most legendary business leaders of modern times, 'an organization's ability to learn, and translate that learning into action rapidly, is the ultimate competitive business advantage'.[1] I think this is beautifully put and it sets the scene for what I am aspiring to address with this book.

My wish is that this book contributes knowledge that enables more employees to focus on creating successful and thriving organizations by applying principles drawn from behavioural and learning psychology to strategy and change. I hope that the book will give leaders and employees the tools to seriously tackle behaviour and really drive through change to help them hone their business.

> This book is aimed at readers who question the effectiveness of management platitudes and who wish to strengthen behaviour that leads to actual results.

If you are a leader in an organization, a consultant who works with strategic management, performance management, governance or change – or if you are a project manager, development manager, business controller, HR manager or any other employee, executive or non-executive, who really wishes to create an organization that performs well through changing times – then this book is for you.

Note

1   R Slater (1998) *Jack Welch and the GE Way: Management insights and leadership*, p 12, McGraw-Hill, New York

ACKNOWLEDGEMENTS

It is said that, to hold a course on something that fits on a sheet of paper, your knowledge would need to fill a whole table-top. By the same logic, writing a book would require many tables. In the process of writing this book I assimilated knowledge from articles, books, conversations with colleagues and clients, structured interviews in research projects, lectures and seminars at conferences, reports and my own scribblings over the years. The only thing I can say with certainty is that this book is actually the 'creation' of many people in addition to myself.

This book would never have come about were it not for a number of people who have contributed in one way or another.

First and foremost, I would like to thank my father – he is by far the most knowledgeable person I know of when it comes to applied behaviour analysis, and he basically taught me everything I know about it. If I had not been schooled in operant conditioning and behavioural psychology principles from childhood, and if I had not had access to your knowledge and encouragement, I would not have come to look at strategy and management – and for that matter, 'the world' – the way I do. Second, the next person who was absolutely critical in the realization of this book is my wife, Karin. Your having put up with my endless scribbling is admirable, to say the least. Your ability to see that I need to balance my arguments when I stray into dogmatism or armchair theory is amazing. Perspective is of infinite value. Third, I also want to thank my mother, who helped me simplify matters whenever I became entangled in long and winding arguments. Your ability to present difficult matters in a simple way is admirable.

I would also like thank my good friend and fellow researcher Jan Lindvall at Uppsala University. He is the epitome of a well-read and wise person, and luckily we share an interest in the well-being of organizations. Conversing with you is a true pleasure. Someone else I owe a big thank you to is my undergraduate strategy professor, Per Åman, at Stockholm School of Economics. Credit where credit is due: Per developed the 'big, best, fast and beautiful' framework and taught it during my Master, some 20 years ago.

Lastly, although extensively referred to throughout the book, three – in my opinion – truly great thinkers of our time deserve a special acknowledgement. This book would not have come to be if I had not discovered the writings of B F Skinner, Herbert Simon and Henry Mintzberg.

Prologue
Realizing strategy

How can we ensure success tomorrow while delivering today? The outside world is changing ever faster, which has altered the circumstances under which organizations operate. Historically, to become competitive and hence successful, it has been enough to focus on economies of scale, customization, innovation or brand building – exploiting competitive advantages by being big, best, fast or beautiful. The real challenge, since the turn of the millennium, is being able to change enough things fast enough, while at the same time getting through the day; and this challenge has been substantially accentuated by the financial crisis in 2008 and the spread of the COVID-19 pandemic in 2020. Yet changing much and fast requires clear focus, and that's where strategy comes into play. These days, strategy has to be more about acting and adapting and less about analysing and planning. Organizations need to abandon the prevailing mindset that strategy making is something done by senior management. Strategy and change are so tightly intertwined that both must permeate the entire company. A good strategy is one that is realized. The realization of the strategy is what determines competitiveness and success, not the planning of it. Involving more people from different levels and functions in strategizing makes it easier to set relevant goals and strategies that more people understand and want to get behind, which considerably improves the likelihood of realization.

Organizations are populated by people. All of the value created in an organization is created by employee behaviour. Times change. Markets change. People's behaviour changes in every new context. But the laws that govern human behaviour remain constant. We use behaviour that has worked in the past.

An organization's strength in being able to repeat a past success can therefore also become a weakness. Today's truths are at risk of stagnating in the changed landscape of tomorrow. In order to create an innovative climate inclined toward change, organizations need to find ways to question the prevailing norms in the industry or organization.

Feedback in all forms drives behaviour. By focusing on behaviour, and on reinforcing behaviour that creates actual results, it is possible to create an organization with a climate where employees perform because they want to – not because they have to. A lack of feedback is also a form of feedback. It is all too common for organizations to fail to consciously work to actively reinforce the 'right' behaviour. 'Everything's all right if no one says anything' is a common attitude that can easily lead to a punitive culture.

My experience from several hundred organizations tells me that organizations spend far more time on planning, defining and sending out signals to the organization about what needs to be done than they do on follow-up, analysing reasons for certain results, drawing lessons from this, providing feedback to the organization and adjusting courses of action. Extensive behavioural research shows that the balance to strike if we want to affect behaviour is the inverse.[1] By completely rethinking the split and dedicating more of our time to follow-up, learning and feedback we can create an organization that becomes more adaptable to its environment and achieves better results.

Long-term success requires organizations to work with a behaviour focus. By shifting parts of the responsibility for developing the organization on to its employees, we create a willingness on the part of employees to contribute to their organization's future. Encouraging employees to ask questions, to try out new ideas and take certain risks, providing opportunities for them to dedicate some of their working hours to projects in other parts of the organization and setting up working methods to systematically manage new ideas – that is how we create an organization that harnesses the potential of the entire organization while improving the chances of identifying new business opportunities and becoming successful in the long term.

Note

1 See, e.g., B F Skinner (1966) *Science and Human Behavior*, The Free Press, New York; M Sundel and S Sundel (1999) *Behavior Change in the Human Services: An introduction to principles and applications*, 4th edn, SAGE Publications, London; B Sulzer-Azaroff and G Meyer (1991) *Behaviour Analysis for Lasting Change*, Wadsworth/Thomson Learning, Belmont

A theory of everything

Every truth has relation to some other. And we should try to write the facts of our knowledge so as to see them in their several bearings. This we do when we frame them into a system. To do so legitimately, we must begin by analysis and end with synthesis.

WILLIAM FLEMING

In order to understand strategy from a behavioural perspective, we need to have a common understanding of certain concepts and promote an overall comprehension of how people actually work.

IN THIS PART

This part will discuss the following issues:

- What is behavioural strategizing?
- What are the basic assumptions of behavioural strategizing?
- How can we view the science of behaviour as a truly important part of managing a business?
- What is meant by 'a theory of everything' in this context?

01

Introduction to strategy and behaviour

A quote often attributed to Charles Darwin is about the survival of the fittest. It reads: 'It is not the strongest of the species that survives, nor the most intelligent that survives. It is the one that is most adaptable to change.' Although it is a great synopsis of Darwin's thoughts on evolution, he never actually said this. Instead, an American management professor called Leon C Megginson allegedly said this in a speech at Louisiana State University in 1953. His main reason for using natural selection as an example was arguably that he believed change is a natural law and adaptation by individuals, institutions and societies is a must if we want to escape a quick demise.

How do organizations become successful in both the short term and the long term? How do companies seize competitive advantage? What principles can organizations apply in order to increase the degree of goal achievement? How can an organization ensure that every truly good and viable idea that is born, is also realized? How can organizations work in order to develop and realize strategies and achieve set goals in a systematic way? How do organizations become successful by drawing on: size – big; tailoring customer unique solutions – best; gaining temporary monopoly – fast; and exploiting the strength of their brand – beautiful? How do they become successful by continuously learning how to improve – being adaptable?

The truth is that there is scope for nearly all organizations to function better. Strategy is about considerably more than just formulating a plan. Above all, it's about realizing an idea or ambition and achieving set goals. Far too many companies fail to live up to their full potential. Far too many organizations fail to utilize their resources in an optimal, or even near optimal, way. Most organizations have the potential to function better, make more money and have more satisfied customers and more satisfied employees. They have the potential to be quicker to adapt.

By applying principles to strategizing that have been drawn from behavioural psychology, organizations can get considerably better at achieving their goals and fulfilling their purpose – at *realizing strategy*. In these simplified, concise terms, this is hardly news. It's about shifting the focus of strategizing from talking about how something *should be done* to focusing on how it was *actually done*, learning from it, and making adjustments to find a better way forward.

The brain has a number of functions that have developed over the course of human evolution and that make it impossible to lead organizations using the customary, established models that are taught in, e.g., business schools and that many rely on when managing an organization. The human survival instinct makes us prone to getting stuck in a rut. It's built into our DNA. The orbital cortex – the 'scaredy brain' – is always warning us of potential dangers. This has been a benefit to mankind through all the stages of what we call evolution. But the dangers were easier to recognize and predict during early human development – such as a dangerous animal or a cold winter ahead.

In a world that is changing ever faster and with a business environment that is becoming harder and harder to anticipate, ingrained ways of thinking pose problems for organizations that want to be at the forefront. To avoid getting stuck in a rut, they need to learn to develop their own future while at the same time delivering in today's market. Organizations need to make an effort to question and change the existing structures and ideas more often, continuously and in a systematic way. This requires both courage and competence.

There are more than 100 years of research findings about what affects human behaviour and how people learn, that can help organizations get better at adapting and developing – results that extremely few companies harness in their organizations. There is often a lack of understanding of the principles that govern human behaviour in organizations. And hence, those that understand and apply them stand a good chance of taking up an attractive position in the market of the future.

There are various ways to create sustainable, high-performance organizations. All organizations can perform better, achieve their goals and reach their full potential – whether this is a matter of creating a better capital base by increasing the return on invested capital, reducing workplace accidents, building a stronger brand, creating a more innovative product development process or providing better service at the same cost.

Besides these options, the organization's way of strategizing can become a lasting competitive advantage in and of itself. A good way of starting such a journey is to become behaviour-oriented.

02

A common language for strategy and behaviour

Through its strategy, every organization can map out a direction and create a competitive advantage for itself. The strategy, however, cannot be written in stone but should adapt to circumstances in the outside world. The outside world is changing, societies and technologies develop, branches of industry flourish and fade, and customers' needs change. This means that the strategy and the organization need to change with it. Change is thus necessary if we are to make sure that we will achieve our goals. Employee behaviour is what produces results in an organization. So, in order to realize strategy, we need to understand what behaviour is, how we learn new behaviour and what makes us behave in a certain way. We need proper words.

Author Mark Twain was a master with words. Allegedly, he wrote: 'The difference between the almost right word and the right word is really a large matter – 'tis the difference between the lightning-bug and the lightning.'[1] Naturally, Twain's ingenious explanation is transferable to the context of organizations.

Organizations need to deliver today while at the same time ensuring that they will remain competitive tomorrow. To do this, change is a prerequisite. This means that the organization needs to bridge the gap between strategy and change – it needs to bring about a more change-inclined or innovative climate to achieve the goals, present and future. More precisely, this has to do with behaviour as a lever in strategy, with how we can utilize the principles of behavioural psychology in order to realize strategies for continuous change and adaptation.

Consequently, theoretically this book is at the crossroads of two major knowledge domains: management and behavioural psychology. Within management the emphasis lies in *strategic management*, but a critical component for evaluating success is also *performance measurement and management*. In addition, if organizations are to be successful, changing continuously is a must, and therefore ideas from *change management* and *innovation* are also drawn upon. Since embracing new principles and methods for managing an organization includes changing the existing ways of how the organization is led, *management innovation* is also a discipline where I have found inspiration. Regarding behavioural psychology, that focus is narrower: the absolute main point of reference is *applied behaviour analysis* and, as applied to organizations, *organizational behaviour management*.

What I get at the nexus of these domains is an interdisciplinary way of managing an organization's way of strategizing to continuously learn and adapt to become more successful, regardless of how success is defined. I call this *behavioural strategizing*. Behavioural strategizing is thus a way of managing an organization to ensure long-term success through continuous learning, change and adaptation. Two of its characteristic features are that the whole organization's way of 'behaving managerially' is based on principles drawn from behavioural psychology, and that the focus of attention in strategizing is on behaviour.

In many aspects, this reasoning is similar to the foundation of behavioural economics, which studies the effects of psychological and social factors on decision-making, rather than traditional economic factors. Or, even closer, the field of *behavioural strategy* that argues for the incorporation of strategic management with behavioural economics. However, while both of these streams' emphasis is on the *behavioural theory of the firm*, or possibly psychology in a wide sense in relation to economics and strategic management, my foundation is *behaviourism* and my focus is behavioural psychology, principles of learning and applied behaviour analysis.

What we share, though, is a conviction that by combining traditionally separated areas of expertise, we can view things from new perspectives, and hopefully learn something new about how long-term organizational success can be achieved. My ambition with this book is to provide a broader approach, with more perspectives considered important to matters of organizational performance and success than in traditional strategic management. Simultaneously, I also hope it provides more precision about what creates such performance and success, what strategy in its essence is about – doing 'things', as behaviour is always the focal point.

> Organizations that strategize behaviourally focus on driving continuous learning and adaptation by drawing on the laws of human behaviour. They become successful by getting better at learning and adapting their behaviour to changing circumstances faster.

There is a 'plan' for nearly every organization – some type of strategy, some kind of idea about what the organization should do. This is what a strategy is, to some extent. But as part of management, entrepreneurship and organizational science, strategy is a relatively young discipline. It's been around since the early 1960s. In addition, strategy has traditionally been a theoretical subject. There are basically as many definitions of strategy as there are people who have tried to define it, which makes it hard to be specific when discussing the term. And yet on an overarching level, most would agree – both practitioners and researchers – with the following: strategy has to do with some kind of describing of how to set and achieve goals – it is a description of a course chosen to try to get to a future desired position.

Now we will shift over to looking at development and change. Is there any difference, or are they the same thing? Development has acquired a more positive connotation and change possibly a more negative one. I want to view them as synonymous for the sake of simplicity. Not many people want to change for change's sake, but everyone wants to improve something.

Change can be seen as occurring on two levels – that of the organization and that of the individual. The organizational level includes changes in the organization's structures, processes, systems or product portfolio, for example. But realizing change in the organization's structure does not necessarily mean that there will be any real change in how the business operates. The object of organizational change should therefore always be to change behaviour. Real change takes place at the individual level – we need to change employee behaviour. There is no real change without behavioural change, and this takes place on an individual level.

If we look at change from a behavioural perspective, we might describe it as a new, altered or alternative way for someone to perform a task – a change in a behaviour that the person has in his or her behavioural repertoire.

Note

1 M Twain (1890) *The Art of Authorship: Literary reminiscences, methods of work, and advice to young beginners,* compiled and edited by George Bainton, pp 87–88, D. Appleton and Company, New York

03

Behaviour as the least
common denominator

Physics has attempted to arrive at a *theory of everything* (ToE). This is the pursuit of a theory that will explain everything from the smallest fragments of matter that we know of today – quarks, leptons, bosons and so on – to the biggest thing we know of today – the universe. Behavioural psychology is my 'theory of everything' when it comes to strategy and change. It forms the basis of what I refer to as behaviour strategizing and is a prerequisite for creating adaptable organizations.

The issue of being successful in bringing about change and becoming more innovative is discussed both in the research world and in the corporate sector. We often read about things like 'change-oriented corporations', 'innovative organizations' or a 'high-performance culture', and how we can achieve these things. Indeed, it is important for companies both to be innovative and to be perceived as being innovative. Throughout the last decades companies have used slogans to allude to change and innovation.[1] Renault's slogan during the 2010s was 'Driving the change'. Mitsubishi Electric's is, and has been since 2001, 'Changes for the better' and Ericsson's 'Taking you forward' was evocative of being at the forefront. Another classic example is Apple's 'Think different' that was launched in 1997, a phrase that was partly seen as a response to IBMs 'Think'.

Throughout the several hundred organizations I have worked with, and several thousand managers I have met over the years, nearly everyone mentions that one of the most difficult tasks is to 'reach all the way out' with desired changes. And bringing about significant strategic change seems to be the most difficult, bar none. It is natural that this should present a challenge in a large organization, but it is in fact a challenge in all organizations.

Simply put, we typically all say that we want progress and development but very few of us really want to change our personal behaviour if it is not necessary.

No wonder we can't manage to reach all the way out. Change is hard. Think of how hard it is to change yourself. Have you tried to lace your fingers together the 'wrong' way, so that your right thumb ends up on top? Or the left one? There is, however, a body of knowledge about influence and change that we are not fully utilizing. We use descriptions like customer-focused, innovative and service-oriented, businesslike and driven. But who can explain exactly what these terms really mean? Does everyone in the organization have the same picture, and is it sufficiently clear for a new hire to understand it? Is it sufficiently clear for everyone in the organization to understand what is demanded of them to behave in such a way?

Most of the books, advisors, experts and even so-called 'gurus' in management use words without specifying their meaning. Possibly such words can serve as a framework. Organizations then have to fill this framework with their own meaning. However, if we cannot agree on a more or less common description of what we want to achieve, how then are we to expect that others in the organization who were not on board from the start and involved in all the discussions will understand? Muddled descriptions make the goals, i.e. what we want to achieve or change in order to make the organization more successful, more 'fuzzy', confusing even.

My 'theory of everything' boils down to more clearly defining what we wish to achieve or change in order to clarify what we actually mean by, for example, 'customer-focused', thereby giving the organization a chance to live by it. This is something that far too many organizations today fail to do. Those that are able to pull it off will be the winners in the market of the future.

In school we learn to do fractions using the *lowest common denominator* or LCD. The LCD is used to simplify what appears to be a difficult task by breaking down something big and hard to grasp into something smaller and easier to work with. When it comes to the realization of strategy and organizational change, change of leadership or of corporate culture, the LCD has to do with behaviour. Complex concepts need to be reworked in order to make them manageable. They need to be expressed in behavioural terms – what people have to do.

What, then, is a behaviour? At this stage, it is sufficient to say that behaviour is what people do, think and feel. In grammatical terms, we might say that behaviours are closely related to verbs. They describe something that someone does; how someone behaves.

> Concretely speaking, realization of strategy is about how we can influence behaviour to achieve a change or a goal. No results are created and no goals are achieved if employees do not do anything – that is to say, behave in some way. The organization itself is merely the arena.

In other words, employee behaviour is what realizes strategy. To understand strategy, we need to understand behaviour; to understand an organization we need to understand people; to understand development and change, we need to understand what it is that makes people do what they do and how we can influence this. We need to understand human behaviour and the laws that govern it.

It's not enough for an organization to know that profitability is low, or that customers are dissatisfied, or that there are too many workplace accidents and that they are too serious. In order for the organization to be able to improve, it must learn how to identify the concrete behaviour that underlies all this. Is the low profitability due to excess investments, or to the fact that a certain work process is taking too long? Is the customer dissatisfaction due to the fact that we are insufficiently competent when we perform our needs analysis, or to our inability to deliver what they are actually demanding? Are the workplace accidents due to poor compliance with safety regulations, or to the fact that we actually engage in workplace behaviour that is inappropriate?

Behaviour analysis describes evolution on a behavioural level. Evolution happens no matter what we think of it. The lion does not care whether its prey is an injured gazelle or a healthy one. Likewise, an object falls to the ground if the laws of gravity dictate that it must. It doesn't matter whether we use Newton's or Einstein's explanatory model. The object still falls to the ground. The same thing goes for human behaviour. We do not always care about why we do things the way we do. We may not care whether we 'understand' why we drink a glass of water. If the water has the intended effect – for example, if it quenches our thirst – we will probably drink a glass of water the next time we feel thirsty. Regardless of whether or not we understand what is governing the behaviour. Natural selection operates on human behaviour; our consciousness of that fact varies.

Behaviour analysis is a model that provides an understanding of why we do the things we do and how we can influence our behaviour.

Chaos, order, disorder and anti-disorder

Hardly a day passes without me reading or hearing something about how developments in the outside world are constantly accelerating, making it hard for organizations to anticipate the next crisis or opportunity. Yet one thing is certain. Those who manage to keep up with developments better than their competitors have a clear advantage in the market of tomorrow.

In simplified terms, chaos theory conceives of chaos as the impossibility of predicting the next event. If a prediction is impossible, this is referred to as a state of chaos or disorder. If there is some kind of structure that makes it possible to predict what will happen, it is no longer a state of chaos. People have always attempted to make assessments about the future as a survival strategy. We have done so with the help of various models and theories. From listening to soothsayers like Nostradamus, gazing into a crystal ball, relying on horoscopes or reading tea leaves – these practices have all had as their aim to yield a picture of what the next day may bring.

All snowflakes are unique, but they follow certain universal structures. They consist of water, they occur only below a certain pressure and below a certain temperature, they always have seven points, etc. These universal structures create something that might be referred to as anti-disorder. It is not chaos, since there are a number of factors that make it possible to predict when they will occur, what they look like, etc. Nor is it order in the strict sense: we do not know exactly what the next snowflake will look like, or when it may appear. On the other hand, we may have an idea of when it will form and about certain of its distinctive features. There is an underlying structure that makes certain predictions possible.

In many ways, the world is unstructured: things happen without us being aware of them or having an opportunity to anticipate them. In many cases, people are irrational from our own perspective, and appear to behave illogically. If we follow this thought through to the end, the whole world can seem like complete chaos. As is true of snow, however, there is an overall structure when it comes to the way people behave as well. This structure is called the law of human behaviour.

Sometimes, what can help create order amid the disorder, and increase understanding, is called an *attractor*. Behavioural psychology, behaviour analysis, and therefore also behavioural strategizing are means of increasing our understanding of what people do. The law of human behaviour can therefore be seen as an attractor. It is difficult to fully predict what a person will do, but within certain bounds it is possible for us to say what they will not do, and we can have some idea of what they will do based on history. Indeed, the world and organizations may be perceived as chaotic. One way of sorting out this chaos is to apply the principles of behaviour analysis.

The more relevant experience and information I have about a certain phenomenon, the better my chances of minimizing the feeling of chaos. Behavioural strategizing is a model for trying to understand the conceivable and inconceivable things that people in organizations will do in a given situation. It is a way for organizations to become more successful, no matter how success is defined.

Note

1   Renault Group. Renault and the French: A passion story expressed through advertising, 2015, https://group.renault.com/en/news-on-air/news/renault-and-the-french-a-passion-story-expressed-through-advertising (archived at https://perma.cc/FV8V-RNGA); Mitsubishi. History of our corporate logo, www.mitsubishielectric.com/en/about/history/logo/index.html (archived at https://perma.cc/565E-LGFY); Ericsson. Global brand campaign, 1998, https://ericssoners.wordpress.com/2011/07/29/global-brand-campaign-make-yourself-heard/ (archived at https://perma.cc/494J-55LJ); D Sull (2003) *Revival of the Fittest: Why good companies go bad and how great managers remake them*, Harvard Business Review Press, Cambridge

KEY POINTS

Part One: A theory of everything

What is behavioural strategizing?

Behavioural strategizing is a way of managing an organization to ensure long-term success through continuous change and adaptation. Two of its defining features are that the whole organization's way of behaving is based on principles drawn from behavioural psychology, and that the focus in strategizing is on behaviour.

What are the basic assumptions of behavioural strategizing?

Behavioural strategizing is based on two disciplines: management and behavioural psychology.

How can we view the science of behaviour as a truly important part of managing a business?

More than 100 years of research have been done on how to influence behaviour. The knowledge yielded by this research is rarely applied in the organization. By applying principles drawn from behavioural psychology, organizations can get better at achieving their goals and at creating long-term success.

What is meant by 'a theory of everything' in this context?

Times change. Markets change. People's behaviour changes in every new context. But the laws that govern human behaviour remain constant. All the results in an organization come from human behaviour. The laws of human behaviour can therefore be viewed as an organization's theory of everything.

PART TWO

Arbitrariness is over

Nature!... She is the only artist; working up the most uniform material into utter opposites; arriving, without a trace of effort, at perfection, at the most exact precision, though always veiled under a certain softness!
JOHANN WOLFGANG VON GOETHE

The world does not work the way it did 50 years ago, or even 10 years ago. The pace of change is increasing, and the strategy challenges facing organizations today cannot be handled using yesterday's methods. New ways of managing organizations are needed.

IN THIS PART

This part will expand on the following ideas:

- Why are the old ways of leading an organization not good enough?
- How can we understand organizations in order to better develop them?
- Why are measurement and evidence important parts of leading organizations?
- What does it mean to say that 'arbitrariness is over'?

04

Old management principles
are no longer good enough

No organization is better than its employees. Employees are people, and people are formed by their surroundings and the situations they find themselves in. In order to create a successful organization, we need to understand what it is that makes people do what they do and understand how to create the conditions that allow them to achieve peak performance.

The survival of the most adaptable. Darwin's reasoning that whoever fails to adapt will have a hard time surviving applies to organizations, products and employee behaviours alike. But the analysis doesn't stop there. If there is one thing that is important to an organization, it's not who the employees are, but above all what they do – what behaviour they engage in.

History is full of examples of phenomena that have died out because they failed to adapt. They had no function. How many people have bought a DVD player over the last 10 years? In a classic televised interview from 2007, Microsoft CEO Steve Ballmer laughed at the first iPhone and said that it would never be appreciated by business people, as it did not have a keyboard. How many smartphones today have keyboards? Organizations that adapt to their market fare better than those that do not adapt.

People who adapt to their surroundings fare better than those who do not adapt. Behaviour that has proved successful in similar contexts in the past is reinforced and perpetuated, increasing the likelihood that it will be used in the future. Success reinforces the habits. This is usually referred to as *path dependence*[1] – that is to say, a kind of dependence on the path you are already on. From a behavioural psychology perspective, this could be referred to as *automated behaviour*: we do what we have done previously, because it saves us from wasting energy on trying something new or unfamiliar. In somewhat simplified terms, we can refer to this as habit.

Based on this, it is easy to understand the way many organizations are lulled into a (possibly false) sense of security and are unwilling to take large risks. But what is to say that what worked yesterday will work tomorrow? Not taking any risks today can lead to even bigger risks in the long run.

There are countless examples of companies that at one time were the most profitable in their industry, only to find themselves on the brink of ruin just a few years later. This goes for big and small companies alike. Kodak, at one time the United States' most profitable company and with a 132-year history, filed for bankruptcy in the spring of 2013. Kodak was the first to introduce digital photo technology back in 1975. Many people considered them and their 'new thinking' to be the Apple or Google of the 1970s. Then what happened? Dell, one of the world's biggest PC vendors, was in the process of going bankrupt because they refused to adapt their concept to changed market realities. IBM was on the brink of bankruptcy in spite of having been by far the world's largest computer company for several decades. The reason in their case was also an unwillingness or inability to change and adapt.

It is easy for organizations and the employees in them to get stuck in a rut. 'Don't change a winning concept' is an expression that reflects this. I would like to venture the opposite. Sooner or later, we will need to change even a winning concept. What was winning yesterday will probably not be winning tomorrow. If the pace of change outside our organization is faster than that on the inside, we risk falling behind. This requires a process of continually questioning whether our winning concept will continue to be a winning one tomorrow.

People and organizations choose to do what has led to success in the past, but not necessarily what will be successful in the future. To be perfectly honest, experience is mostly beneficial if the future looks the same as the past. I don't mean that experience is unimportant – just that there are a number of qualities ascribed to it that are not always as favourable to organizations as is commonly believed. Organizations that want to become successful should be aware of this.

Rule governance and contingency shaping

In philosophy, we encounter the terms normative ethics and consequentialism. When we act on the basis of normative ethics, we do what we usually do. Whereas consequentialism is when we do something based on the consequence it will reasonably have. Behavioural psychology refers to these two approaches as *rule governance* and *contingency shaping*, respectively. The rules are synonymous with, e.g., standards, policies, strategies, goals and culture. Contingency-shaped behaviour is related to the consequences – what is likely to happen if we run our business, behave, in a certain way.

Sometimes rules and consequences go hand-in-hand, but what happens when they don't? What do we do when an internal policy runs counter to a huge business opportunity? Sometimes we stick to the standard and say, 'We don't do that at this company.' Sometimes we let the consequence prevail even if it goes against the standard.

Too many companies are led by normative ethics – that is, relying on rule governance. They are governed by policies, traditions and culture. 'This is what we've always done!' is a common approach. Many organizations could be considerably more profitable, successful, well-reputed or healthy if they were to more frequently question why they do what they do, and if they were to instead let themselves be guided by what the action actually leads to – the *consequences*.

Organizations that want to become more successful should frequently ask themselves this fundamental question: What might an alternative way of leading our organization look like?

The better things are going for an organization, the greater the risk of being lulled into a (possibly false) sense of security and of being content with the way things are. What happens is that we create ways of working that run directly counter to development and adaptability, and there is an obvious risk that employees' capacity and initiative will remain underutilized. The expression 'fat and happy' exists for a reason.

> The better things are going for a company, the worse off it is. This is a
> significant paradox that can be avoided by applying behavioural strategizing,
> thereby making the organization adaptable and, in the long term, successful.

Success definitely breeds numerous opportunities, but not necessarily more success in the long run. In far too many cases, success breeds decline over the long term. Organizations can get better at adapting to changing circumstances, realizing strategies, and thus also better at achieving their goals. Instituting innovation and adaptation at the very core of the organization, along with strategic and systematic management of change and development, is fundamental. A first step in this direction is to dare to see the world the way it actually is and let that challenge our own conceptions.

Today's conditions are not the same as yesterday's

The complex environment that emerged at the end of the 20th century means that old methods of running companies no longer work.[2] French management expert and academic Hervé Sérieyx refers to these developments as 'the Big Bang of the organizations'.[3] This Big Bang includes the information revolution, the globalization 2.0 phenomenon, where the BRIC countries (Brazil, Russia, India and China) are growing and becoming more powerful, the collapse of major ideologies, and worldwide news reporting. All of these factors together really do make the whole world a small village where virtually everyone has access to 'all the world's information' at the same time, and all at the stroke of a key. Many researchers and futurists, including the American innovator and futurist Raymond Kurzweil, claim that the rate of change in evolutionary systems is exponential.[4] This basically means that in 25 years from now the changes will be as great as the ones we have seen in the last 100 years. What does that mean for our organizations?

We have only just grown comfortable with the notion of the BRIC countries as new economic powerhouses. And then a new concept pops up: *Next 11*, or *N-11*, was launched by the same person who coined the term BRIC[5] – British economist Jim O'Neill, at the time a senior executive at Goldman Sachs. We've only just grasped the extent of the new global society – the importance of China, India, Brazil and Russia – before their growth rate begins to flag and we turn our attention to the next squad. The new global growth locomotives are Bangladesh, Egypt, Indonesia, Iran, Mexico, Nigeria, Pakistan, the Philippines, Turkey, South Korea and Vietnam. And who knows what changes will be brought in the wake of the COVID-19 pandemic that has hit our societies.

Facebook, a phenomenon that that was launched 2004, has over two and a half billion active users every month in 2021.[6] If Facebook were a country, it would have roughly as many inhabitants as China, the USA and the European Union combined. The first commercial text message was sent in December 1992. In the spring of 2021, the number of text messages sent each day – app-to-app messaging excluded – exceeds the total number of people on earth doubled. It is estimated that 2.5 quintillion bytes (2.5*1030) of unique new information is created every day.[7] In the last two years, 90 per cent of the world's data has been created.[8] No deeper analysis is required to understand that this has consequences in terms of how we live our lives and how we lead our organizations.

In May 2018 Netflix surpassed Disney as the highest-valued media company in the world. And in May 2021 giants Discovery and Warner media (spun off from AT&T) merged to take on both Netflix and Disney. Google and Amazon are often portrayed as the most valuable companies in the world. These companies are barely 25 years old. Their worth is often accredited to their incredible amount of information. But is information worth anything? We generally say that we are now in a knowledge economy, as opposed to an information economy. A major difference between the two is that in the information economy, information has a worth; it might help us gain a competitive advantage. In the knowledge economy, everybody has access to 'too much' information, and it is the ability to transform information into knowledge and actions that creates competitiveness.

It is employees that may achieve such transformations. With allowances for individual country variations, today's university students will typically have had 10 different jobs before reaching the age of 40; only a quarter of all employees have been with their employer for more than a year, and one employee in two has been in their current role for less than five years. In short, we change jobs frequently and, it seems, increasingly often. These conditions place high demands on organizations, and on us as individuals – on how quickly we can learn new tasks and behaviour so as to become more efficient and productive. It also places high demands on the way organizations need to work with their human and structural capital. Not least in terms of the process of creating learning that helps in adapting to changing environments.

In a so-called knowledge economy, value is a more fuzzy and hard-to-explain concept than in the past and making assessments about the future is becoming increasingly difficult. We cannot peer into 'the fog of the future', as MIT senior lecturer and former London Business School professor Donald Sull so eloquently puts it.[9] Our knowledge of the future is essentially provisional. We do not know what will happen in the future. There are too many variables affecting how organizations perform: legislation, technology and access to capital, raw materials and skills. Each of these factors is uncertain in itself, and they also interact in ways that we cannot fathom. The only thing we know for sure is that what we think we know about the future is wrong.

The change that our society is now undergoing is more extensive than any we have been through in the past, yet we insist on leading our organizations based on old principles.

Notes

1 G M Hodgson (1993) *Economics and Evolution: Bringing life back into economics*, University of Michigan Press, Ann Arbor

2 E Brynjolfsson and A McAfee. Big Data: The management revolution, *Harvard Business Review*, 2014, 90, 61–68; F Ferraro and B Cassiman. Three trends that will change how you manage: Globalization, digitization and politicization, *IESE – Insight Magazine*, 2014; D Franklin and J Andrews (2012) *Megachange: The world in 2050*, The Economist, London; J Manyika, M Chui, B Brown, J Bughin, R Dobbs, C Roxburgh and A HungByers. Big Data: The next generation for innovation, competition and productivity, 2011, www.mckinsey.com/business-functions/mckinsey-digital/our-insights/big-data-the-next-frontier-for-innovation (archived at https://perma.cc/VZF3-6A7V); P Weill and S Woerner. Thriving in an increasingly digital ecosystem, *MIT Sloan Management Review*, 2015, 56, 26–34

3 H Sérieyx (1994) *Le Big Bang des organizations: Quand l'entreprise, l'Eta, les régions entrent en mutation*, Paris, CalmannLévy

4 R Kurzweil (1999) *The Age of Spiritual Machines*, Viking, New York

5 J O'Neil. Building better global economic BRICs, Goldman Sachs, 2021, www.goldmansachs.com/insights/archive/archive-pdfs/build-better-brics.pdf (archived at https://perma.cc/T4DV-3VGP); S Lawson, D Heacock and A Stunytska. Beyond the BRICs: A look at the 'Next 11', Goldman Sachs, 2007, www.goldmansachs.com/insights/archive/archive-pdfs/brics-book/brics-chap-13.pdf (archived at https://perma.cc/7CDM-YKU8)

6 H Tankowska. Facebook: Number of monthly active users worldwide 2008–2021, Statista, May 2021, www.statista.com/statistics/264810/number-of-monthly-active-facebook-users-worldwide (archived at https://perma.cc/93SM-9X6G)

7 Domo. Data never sleeps 6.0, 2018, www.domo.com/solution/data-never-sleeps-6 (archived at https://perma.cc/9CDK-GSWS)

8 SINTEF. Big Data, for better or worse: 90 per cent of world's data generated over last two years, ScienceDaily, 22 May 2013, www.sciencedaily.com/releases/2013/05/130522085217.htm (archived at https://perma.cc/57S6-GGVJ)

9 D Sull. Strategy as active waiting, *Harvard Business Review*, 2005, 83 (9), 120–29

05

The organization, its development and lack of development

The Industrial Revolution in the middle of the 19th century created an unprecedented climate for companies in the Western world. New types of organizations were developed. Sole proprietorships grew into large industries. Due to increased competition, new tariffs, new technology and the rapid growth of the large organized workplaces and industries, it became more important to organize and structure the work. The goal was to influence employee behaviour and thus become more efficient in order to be able to stand up under the stiffening competition.

This willingness to structure and organize work is clearly evident in Frederick Taylor's ideas on rationalization from the late 19th and early 20th century.[1] These ideas later came to be called *Taylorism* and have come under heavy criticism for their allegedly rigid bureaucracy. Rationalization increased awareness of the importance of organizational structure. A company's productivity and efficiency, and the quality of its products, became crucial factors for continued survival. These three factors are largely dependent on employee competency.

In order to really understand what productivity, efficiency and quality are, organizations need to turn to their employees and find out what they are doing. Productivity, efficiency and quality need to be built into working methods and behaviour. If the organization's least common denominator – behaviour – is not influenced, how are we supposed to influence productivity, efficiency and quality? We lose all our credibility if we apply a 'stamp' of quality after the fact. If we want increased quality, the people doing the work need to learn ways of doing the job that make quality higher.

During the 1930s and 1940s, scientists began to take an interest in the work environment. The basic assumption was that the companies would be able to boost their performance by enhancing the well-being of the individual. One of the best-known examples of this is the *Hawthorne study*, which was conducted from 1927 to 1932. The study was initiated due to growing dissatisfaction among the employees at an electronics factory, and it involved implementing changes in order to improve employees' physical working conditions. The result of the study can be summed up as the meaning of the work to employees is more important than the traditional idea that they only want to earn more money. Indeed, the improvements that were implemented were not what contributed to increased employee satisfaction – it was the very fact that they were asked about their conditions and felt that they were listened to. Other drivers in the work apart from money, primarily social ones, are of great importance. We sometimes talk about the 'latent content of the work'.

In the 1950s and 1960s, these theoretical contributions were then developed into a more 'human' organization. Among other things, a discrepancy was noted between individual preferences and needs versus the structure of the company. The organizations often treated their employees like children, which meant that the employees would be unable to reach their full potential.

These arguments were used to articulate a number of ideas about how to increase organizational efficiency and productivity. There is an extensive body of research on organizational performance. Pertinent disciplines include work environment, organizational structure, work design and reward systems. Last but not least, a great deal of work has been done to understand how goals and strategy affect how an organization performs. What is often done is that companies try to establish new conditions that are conducive to productivity or efficiency. However, they often forget to define what behaviour actually results in increased productivity or efficiency. The change they are trying to bring about is on the organizational level, but they forget the behavioural one.

Since the early 1990s, a shift has begun from a situation where power was concentrated at the top of organizations and societies. Consumers and employees are gaining more and more power. And, with that, those who know and understand consumers or employees are able to gain power as well. One concept used is 'blog storm'. This was something the lock company Kryptonite suffered from. In just over one week in September 2006 reports in social media on how many people could pick a Kryptonite lock with a Bic pen went from zero to more than 5 million. These ten devastating days cost the company approximately $10 million.[2] The term 'blog storm' thus refers to the power that social media gives consumers, one that makes it impossible for rogue companies (and good honest ones) to 'hide'. Other concepts, including 'a buyer's market' and 'happy capitalism', place completely different demands on today's organization than in the past. A surge of peer-to-peer platforms that enable individuals to have direct conversations shortcuts many businesses. What is happening out in the world is also happening in our organizations, it just isn't always as clear.

This nullifies the rules of the game, rendering yesterday's way of leading organizations outdated in one stroke. In short: everything has changed, but in general we're still leading organizations in the same old way.

> Continuous renewal and adaptation have traditionally been viewed as particularly important in the service sector, where companies are directly dependent on staff competency if they are to be competitive. This is crucial in all types of organizations. Ultimately, staff behaviour is what is most critical for achieving success, regardless of the type of organization.

Knowledge and intellectual resources

Contemporary research in the fields of strategy, change, organization and leadership make it clear that, just as effectiveness of leadership in terms of physical resources determined a company's success in the past, effectiveness of leadership in terms of intellectual resources will determine organizational success in the future. Henry Mintzberg, one of the great strategy and management thinkers of all time, also stresses how the traditional and clear organizational structures that were a great part of yesterday's success stories need to be replaced by adhocracies, as these are clearly the structures of tomorrow.[3] This applies to all companies. Everyone wants to improve efficiency, productivity and quality. By adhocracy, Mintzberg means this capacity for flexibility, adaptation and learning, and the knowledge needed to handle things ad hoc, i.e. for a particular purpose.

Another term for a similar phenomenon is *organizational ambidexterity*.[4] Ambidextrous comes from the Latin word for two-handed (ambi = both and dexter = right) and in this context it is supposed to symbolize organizations that are able to handle delivering in today's market even as they create the opportunities of the future. A company that is to survive in the long run needs to be able to deliver today while simultaneously creating its future.

Telecommunications company Ericsson was long at the forefront of tech-nological developments in the mobile telephony industry. They developed one of the first analogue mobile systems, which led to a huge global expan-sion. Yet their impressive sales figures concealed costs that were too high and an organizational structure that had grown too big. At its apex, Ericsson had around 30,000 employees in its research department alone. Ericsson was devoting so much attention to its delivery in the now that it forgot to prepare for the future. So, when the telecom industry crashed, as one part of the dot-com bubble, the consequences for Ericsson were greater than for companies that had prepared. In the year 2000, Ericsson had 110,000 employees, but in the following years they were forced to lay off half their workforce owing to sales declines. In 2001, Ericsson posted a loss of €3 billion (equivalent to $3.5 billion).[5]

In the long run, the performance and success of an organization depend on learning and adaptation. Human beings are born with a curiosity and a will to learn and explore. It is up to organizations to harness this ability. Agile and resilient are current buzzwords; they both emphasize being good at adapting to the prevailing and changing circumstances. Using this defini-tion, one agile or resilient skill could mean learning how to learn.

Employees in high-performance organizations need more than profound professional expertise. They need to be able to foresee changes, adapt to new circumstances, and come up with new solutions and ideas for 'doing business'. Adapting means changing our behaviour to better fit its environment.

Awareness of a need: The first step towards change

Organizations need to go from being unaware of what is happening to becoming predictive – being able to control what is going to happen. Companies often say that they want to go from being reactive to becoming more proactive. They want to 'react to changes faster'. For many of them, it's about more than going from being reactive to being proactive – the leap is bigger than they suspect. It's often about going from being unaware of their full potential, to creating their own future if they truly want to be successful. Who doesn't want to create and control their market?

So, how do we do that? The more people there are who contribute their knowledge and come up with ideas for how the business can improve, the better our chances of adapting the business to the prevailing trends in the outside world. The greater the range and diversity of employee thought, the better our chances of understanding and thus influencing our market.

If we are to create organizations that perform and succeed, this means that we need to involve more people in order to understand how different parts are connected, and we need to question the status quo. How else are we supposed to develop? If we wish to achieve a result other than the one we have today, we need to do something differently.

Let's say we have a bank that wants to increase the quality of its risk analysis. As long as the employees run the calculations they usually do, double-check the information using exactly the same sources, and do their peer review for important cases based on exactly the same checklist, it's unlikely that their analysis will get any keener.

To really develop the analytical process, the employees need to ask themselves: which other sources can we double-check? They need to ask themselves what potential risk perspectives they have not included in the existing checklist, so that they can update it and use the new one. Development and the enhancement of quality and efficiency, as well as results of other kinds, all presuppose that someone questions the current situation, suggests new ideas, learns and applies new behaviour. And for such new behaviour to truly make an impact on the organization's results, it needs to be spread across the organization.

What is an organization?

Sometimes when I lecture on strategy, or work with an organization, there is need to clarify what an organization is. Otherwise, how do we know how to share, spread and scale our best practices? I'll then ask those present what an organization is and ask them to come up with a definition. The answers I get are often similar, which feels natural.

They almost always mention three things:

1   An organization comprises several people who are constituent parts of the same whole.

2   An organizations has some kind of structure and order in terms of relationships and responsibilities.

3   An organization has some type of common goal or purpose.

This is a good definition. If we look at the historical development of modern organizations, we can see that they have undergone major changes during their almost 200 years of existence, yet the above definition still works every step of the way. There is a strength in this definition, but it also harbours a weakness when we want to develop our way of leading the organization.

If we want to develop an organization, this description does not provide much guidance. My take on an organization is that it is a group of people who work interdependently and have some kind of common purpose or goal. Achieving this common goal requires some type of orderly interaction, meaning that employees have to communicate and collaborate in a structured manner. Communication and collaboration entail behaviour. Once again, behaviour is the lowest common denominator.

The strategy challenges organizations have faced through time

An exposé of the history of organizations shows that they have been exposed to various challenges at different times (see Figure 5.1). This has led to somewhat different ways of leading them and the development of a number of different strategic ideas (basic conceptions about how a business may be successful). However, we have failed to develop our organizations and our ways of leading them in step with the changes that have come to pass in the outside world since the early 1990s.

Viewing this history, we have gone from being an *agrarian* society to a knowledge-based one, and industrial revolutions have affected how different organizations are structured. There is a plethora of different types of organization, which of course also means that the challenges they face are different. A multinational organization with over 100,000 employees cannot have the same solution to a particular problem or working method as a sole proprietorship. Yet we persist in leading organizations in a fairly similar way.

It was during the latter half of the 19th century that organizations in our sense of the term actually started to be built. From a situation where everyone worked their own piece of land, we started coordinating the work in different types of industries. During the first half of the 19th century railways were opened in most Western countries. This ushered in sweeping changes in terms of how business was conducted. All the conditions of organizational logistics were changed in one stroke. All of a sudden, organizations were able to plan their transportation in a whole new way.

FIGURE 5.1 Organizations' development over time

	First railways 1840s	Black Thursday 1929	Oil crisis 1973	Internet launched 1991	IT bubble 2001	Financial crisis 2008
Significant events						
Society	Agriculture	Industry	Post-industrial	Information	Post-information/knowledge	Changing
	Compulsory education	Growth of organizations	Dependence on outside	Stock market crash 1987	Uncertainty	Fourth Industrial Revolution
	Industrial Revolution	States emerge	Growth not a given	Creation of the internet	Individualistic society	Digitalization, AI, IoT
	Organizations created	Cooperation in Europe begins	International work	Access to information	Global society	Sustainability
Strategic idea		Big	Best	Fast	Beautiful	Smart
		Volume	Segmentation	Innovation	Symbolic value	Continuous learning
		Mass production	Customer focus	Research and development focus	Brand	Disruptive changes
		Economies of scale	Service	Core competency	Experience, many senses	Unclear boundaries of industries and/or organizations
		Market leader	Best at what you do	Temporary monopolies	Design and aesthetics	Co-opetition
		Planning	Positioning	Creating your market	Co-creation of brand	

SOURCE Original model

During the middle and second half of the 19th century many Western societies introduced compulsory schooling. This also had consequences for companies. The short-term effect was that large parts of the workforce disappeared because they were forced to attend school. In the longer term, the effect on organizations was that they gained access to more advanced skills, or other types of skills.

After Black Thursday and the stock market crash in New York in 1929, we had a society that was *industrial*, and enterprise was mainly about growth. Things really took off after the Second World War. States began to take shape and industrialization increased. There was a market for everything that was produced, and the entire Western world saw phenomenal rates of growth as a result. The most important strategic issue was how organizations were to get hold of resources and how they could utilize their existing resources a little more efficiently. The challenges they faced were handled by planning, organizing and structuring the operations. The biggest company was the most successful company.

This changed drastically in the early 1970s. Unrest in the Middle East led to an oil crisis. *Post-industrial* is a shorthand way of describing the society that emerged after that. Organizations discovered – in a way that they had not previously seen – that they were dependent on their surroundings. All of a sudden, they found that resource shortages could manifest in a different way. Simply put, there were now limitations to deal with, such as a lack of oil. Organizations were forced to learn how to cope with altered circumstances and a situation where growth was no longer a given. They began to collaborate across national borders, and more multinational corporations were formed. Increased risk awareness and an elevated focus on understanding the outside world and its needs were considered more important than in the past. By focusing on what the outside world wanted, the hope was that companies could avoid poor results in the event of another crisis. The organizations that became best at tailoring products to the customer's unique needs were not as badly hit by economic downturns.

The World Wide Web was launched in 1993. This is usually considered the watershed marking our entry into the *information society*. People recognized early on that the internet and the increased access to information it allowed would make it easier to predict crises at an early stage. The increased access to information also made it possible for organizations to build up unique knowledge. Those that were innovative and fastest to market with new products and services had an opportunity to be successful. Among other things, this led to tech companies inventing new technologies, creating needs that had previously been completely unknown, and growing at a breakneck pace. When the bubble burst in 2001, having access to information was no longer considered enough to provide a competitive edge.

After 2001, society became more individualistic, while at the same time becoming more global. This meant that people no longer necessarily worked in the nearest town or city. People were able to live, work and create a unique identity on the internet, digitally. The slightest event on another continent, entirely outside my sphere of influence, could now have a major impact on me as a person and on my life. Amid the ever-increasing quantity of information and noise, it became progressively important for organizations to become more visible. It became more important to have a strong brand. Showing consumers that the organization was known and recognized allowed them to be seen and to become successful as a result.

The financial crisis hit in September 2008. Yet in 2021 many countries in the Western world are still struggling to get their economies running at speed. And just recently we have learned how vulnerable our global society is. In 2020, the spread of COVID-19 shut down entire organizations, cities, regions and countries, forcing completely new ways to live and work, and thereby completely new ways to operate a business. Not least, the digitalization of our lives has taken huge leaps forward. And with digitalization comes information.

We have more information than ever, but we are still more uncertain than ever about what is to come. We used to say that we live in a *post-information* society, or a knowledge society. We entered this new era when we realized that more information does not add any value in and of itself. What determines development is the transformation of information into knowledge. However, as a result of significant and increasing changes in our surroundings, sometimes referred to as the Fourth Industrial Revolution,[6] we might suggest that we have left the knowledge society, since all our knowledge is provisional anyway, and that we have entered a changing society.

For most organizations it is no longer enough to be *big*, as was the case in the post-war period. Nor is it enough to be the *best* at tailoring products and services, like it was the 1970s or 1980s. It's not enough to have unique knowledge or to be *fast* at bringing new inventions to market, as was the case during the dot-com boom of the 1990s. Having a strong brand and being *beautiful* is important, but even that is not enough. Since the entrance into the changing economy, roughly around 2008, one of the most important behaviours in an organization is the ability to find good information, to interpret it and to use it in order to learn to adapt faster to changing circumstances. We have to be *smart*.

Paradoxes of management in organizations

Different types of organizational structures are needed for different types of organizations under different conditions. A knowledge-intensive organization with 10 specialists operating in a local geographical market cannot be viewed from the same perspective as a multinational industrial conglomerate with over 200,000 employees. Yet there is a common point of contact, a lowest common denominator – employee behaviour. All results, no matter the organization, stem from what the employees do.

The world most organizations operate in is now so complex that it needs to be simplified using models if we are to understand it. To simplify things, our brain tends to set up two opposites and force an issue to one of the two sides. When it comes to strategy, management and change, however, issues are rarely black or white. Nothing is 100 per cent good or 100 per cent bad. Organizations that succeed do not limit themselves by forcing themselves into 'either or' – they are 'both'. The traditional view, according to which flexibility leads to chaos, has long been refuted by both researchers[7] and practitioners. An organization that is too loosely structured has a hard time achieving change and development. Innovation in itself needs to be one of a company's most structured processes. But despite the fact that structure is in itself a prerequisite for creativity and adaptation, it is not enough. An excessively structured organization inhibits learning and creativity. Once again, nothing is 100 per cent good or 100 per cent bad.

By looking at how we lead organizations through the lens of opposites, we can understand the difficulties of leading an organization and the strategic balances that all organizations need to strike.

Control vs chaos
It is not reasonable to believe that a company should try to maintain full control of everything that is happening. It is not a good idea to exercise full control over everything, as this inhibits learning and innovation. Nor can we say that an organization should let go entirely, as this inhibits the benefits of being coordinated.

Collaboration vs internal competition
Many major organizations, such as Audi and 3M, have clear ideas about how they want different units within the organization to collaborate. Collaboration confers a number of advantages on an organization, but always collaborating on every issue results in a lack of internal pressure in the organization, reducing the influx of knowledge and inhibiting the organization's development.

Logic vs creativity

A logical approach to how we make decisions is needed if we are to avoid making ones that are incorrect. On the other hand, if we only make what we believe are logical decisions, we will quickly go astray. The world is so complex that it is not possible to weigh every factor into a decision, even if we were able to identify them all.

Planning vs emergence

In a world where more and more things are moving, mutable and uncertain, it does become important to think and plan ahead. On the other hand, if we plan too carefully, there is a tendency not to have time left over for anything other than re-planning in response to all the rapid changes occurring in the outside world.

Revolution vs evolution

All companies are constantly changing. Certain change initiatives come from the top of the organization and have a formal mandate and purpose. Other changes occur from below, without there being a structured project or initiative behind them. Both are needed and need to be encouraged if we are to create a competitive organization.

As we can see above, it is not possible to say that an organization should be strictly one way or the other. Both perspectives are important in all cases; it's about being aware of the fact that nothing is black or white. All organizations are somewhere on a line – a continuum – between these opposites. To make it clear what these strategic positions mean for employees, they need to be broken down into something more concrete – behaviour.

There is no answer key in strategic management and change. The sooner organizations learn this and deal with the complexity it entails, the sooner they will be able to make wise decisions to realize strategy and to adapt.

Organizational metaphors

In his book *Images of Organization*, Gareth Morgan, a British/Canadian researcher, clarifies the different ways in which organizations use metaphors.[8] Metaphors allow us to better explain how an organization actually works. Naturally, this influences the way the organization strategizes. The metaphors are meant to emphasize certain characteristics and to downplay less important ones. The four metaphors are machine, system, organism and brain.

Organizations as machines

One apt metaphor for the generic traditional company with a rational view of human beings is that of the machine – as so brilliantly depicted in Charlie Chaplin's 1925 film *The Gold Rush*.

In this type of organization, the business is essentially seen as being logical and linear, and the thinking is that there is always a naturally planned sequence in which tasks should be performed. The business is regarded as rational and as being controllable and governable. It can be followed up on and planning is always possible. Nothing can go wrong, if only we plan carefully enough. These are the typical and distinctive features of a machine.

A number of fully automated machines on a production line whose task is to drill holes in a sheet and then bend the sheet into shape can be programmed in an optimal manner, at least in theory. As long as someone makes sure to maintain the machines and supply the raw material, there is no need to worry. They will always deliver what they are programmed to deliver for as long as they hold up. There is no need to worry about feelings, illnesses, crises or cooperation. But the robots themselves will not let us know that they can perform their work operations in a different, significantly better way, unless they possess fairly advanced artificial intelligence and machine learning. But also, on such occasions, someone, at least in the very beginning, writes the code. The strategizing behaviours that become important in a business reminiscent of a machine are planning, optimization and programming.

However, the social and technical developments that have occurred since the *big bang of organizations* have made it more difficult to view organizations as machines. Organizations consist of more than just machines whose work we can program and plan out. The planning-oriented model according to which the top of an organization does the thinking and the bottom acts accordingly has to yield to a more integrated type of thinking, planning and execution. As noted earlier, the strategizing needs to include both planning and execution, development and realization, in order for the organization to get more adaptable and be better able to predict what is to come. The more people contribute good ideas, the better the organization's chances of identifying unique gems. We need to take advantage of all good ideas based on the conditions that prevail today.

An important part of this act of integration is decentralizing the organization. The degree to which information, control and decision-making within an organization are decentralized affects the transmission and application of new knowledge. Learning has to do with change. Spontaneous learning becomes impossible in an organization where the majority of change is centrally determined.

The degree of *centralization* within an organization depends on how much structure it has that centralizes decision-making. In an excessively structured organization, management presumes that the behaviour of the organization's members can be determined by rules, instructions, procedures and detailed work plans. Excessively strong structures slow down employee development by inhibiting the ability to work creatively, thus thwarting opportunities for learning. An insufficiently structured organization is not conducive to learning, either. In such an organization, rules, work descriptions and responsibilities are too vague, making employees cautious and tentative in their behaviour. Nobody wants to make a mistake. The thinking is that by doing nothing, at least you're not doing the wrong thing. No one dares to do anything, and no one learns anything either, as failure is a natural part of learning.

An industrial organization I once worked with was extremely under-structured. They did have defined best-practice processes, but almost no one took advantage of them. They also had tools for all processes, but almost no one used them. There were no job descriptions or role descriptions. It was difficult for employees to know what to do. There was no lack of initiative at the individual level – the employees at the company worked hard. What the company suffered from was a lack of new ways of doing the work. Responsibilities were unclear and there was insufficient organizational buy-in to the working methods, with the result that no one dared to take independent initiatives to try out new ideas. People did whatever the person who had the job before them had done and did not come up with any new methods. The result was that people did what they had always done. In 2008 the company had a market share of about 22 per cent – when we started working together in 2015 it had shrunk to less than 13 per cent. In 2020, after five years of hard work to build structures and processes bottom-up, with an additional method to knowingly challenge the existing ways of working, the market share is up to 17 per cent again. To sum up, it comes down to creating a structure that does not inhibit learning and that creates opportunities for trying out new methods.

Combining a great deal of structure with very little structure is one way of balancing the need to try to do both. It is possible to strike a good balance by allowing a framework on an overall level to be extremely clear while simultaneously allowing latitude for movement within the framework. And if the framework itself is able to reinforce the positive, critical questioning of the status quo, we start to act smart.

Another important aspect of adaptation in organizations is *fragmentation*. Fragmentation refers to the splitting up of organizations into specialized units. This phenomenon frequently coincides with excessive structuring and limits the ability of employees to see their work as part of a greater whole. To promote understanding and initiative with regard to a greater whole, the organization needs to reinforce cooperation across boundaries. The situation is very similar to what applies to innovation. Real learning takes place in the borderland between different disciplines. A successful organization manages to chart a course between different operations in its collaboration, thereby creating understanding and knowledge for the entire organization. At the end of the day, this enables both cost and growth synergies.

Organizations as systems

Organizations are in some sense systems. A system can be exemplified by looking at an organization whose entire business is a quarry. The quarry consists of various resources, such as mountain, machinery and staff. Employees use dynamite and machinery to remove large stone blocks from the mountain. The stone blocks are placed in a crusher and sorted into different sizes and types of stone, gravel and sand. The raw material has been refined for onward sale. If there is money left over after the products are sold and all the other bills have been paid, the company has made a profit. Companies are economic circuits – systems.

When it is difficult to draw a clear line between what affects the system (the organization, in this book) and what does not, we usually say that these are *open systems* to differing degrees. It is rarely possible to draw a distinct boundary when it comes to organizations. An organization is always affected by what is happening outside the organization – outside the 'system' – no matter how the company is organized or what the ownership structure is like. All organizations are therefore open systems.

One of the world's leading construction companies hires subcontractors in its construction projects. These sometimes account for 60 per cent of total costs. In the production of an average car, raw material and auto parts make up almost as much. Where does the border of the construction or car manufacturing company's organization run? Where do we draw the border in terms of where results are generated in their organization? Where do we draw the border in terms of what affects how the organization's goals are achieved? A good question for everyone who wants to understand their organization as an open system is to ask which external factors are decisive in terms of goal achievement. From this perspective, strategizing behaviour needs to be related to network strategy – how and with whom we collaborate.

Organizations as organisms

If we view organizations as organisms, we obtain a better understanding of the organization's relationships to the outside world. Once we accept that individuals, groups and organizations have a close relationship to what is happening outside the organization, we can understand that the outside world is of importance to organizational performance.

Traditional management and leadership models view the organization as a closed system where internal systems are the subject of study. This typically results in planning orientation. By viewing the organization as an open system, we can focus on relationships with customers and suppliers rather than on internal departments and snapshots in the form of a balance sheet. Viewing the organization as an open system prioritizes the outside world – the market, the customers – as important and indeed crucial parts of the organization. Now there is an opportunity to become predictive and adaptable. Of course, the organization that is able to 'prophesy' the market correctly stands a good chance of creating its own market.

To do so we must put our customers first. Customer-centric is one term used for this quality. This does not have to mean providing exactly what they are asking for. Rather, it means providing what they actually need. How are we supposed to make our customers satisfied if they are not put first? How are we to understand an outside world and a market if we do not prioritize this issue? How are we to create a future market if we cannot be bothered to look at how the market affects our own organization?

Successful organizations are increasingly utilizing external partners in their development efforts. This, and similar approaches, is sometimes referred to as *open innovation*. Arguments for increased participation are also true for issues of a strategic nature, such as product development, brand building and partnership, and this is often referred to as *open strategy*. Not everyone takes it for granted any longer that someone needs to lose in order for me to win. Perhaps we can win together? This is common in the fashion industry. Karl Lagerfeld was head designer at Chanel while simultaneously developing a brand of his own. In a similar vein, Tom Ford used to be a designer for Gucci and Yves Saint Laurent while also creating his own brand and build his own company around this. H&M brings in renowned artists and designers (e.g. Simone Rocha, Sabyasachi Mukherjee) and allows them to lend a hand in the creation of shared success. How can companies in other industries learn from the fashion industry?

> Organizations that adapt to their surroundings stand a better chance of surviving in an ever-changing world. No matter how illogical behaviour in organizations seems to be, it is simply the result of the interplay between the organization and its outside world.

The sooner we accept that organizations and their employees are affected by outside forces, such as family, crises, customer needs, illnesses, natural disasters or traffic jams, and that we need to adapt and live with this, the better our chances are of becoming successful.

Organizations as brains

Another metaphor that can be used for an organization is that of the brain. Viewing the organization as a brain has to do with understanding the importance of learning and intelligence and seeing the organization as a living system in which a high degree of flexibility and innovation is necessary.

Large parts of organizational management are based on behaviour related to communication and decision-making. While mechanical organizations (cf. the machine) have clearly defined procedures for how this behaviour should be performed, along with a belief in rationality, organic organizations (cf. the brain) have a looser structure that is more adapted to different situations.

No matter how rationally and how well information, communication and decision-making processes are structured, organizations are only partially rational. Nobel laureate Herbert Simon argues that people need to act on the basis of incomplete information.[9] They only have the ability to examine a limited number of options and are incapable of linking the right values to results. What this means is that a traditional view of the organization, in which rationality and logic prevail, is obsolete. Individuals and organizations only behave on the basis of a *bounded rationality*. We need to deal with this if we are to succeed.

Simon's reasoning is supported by psychologists and brain researchers. The brain's ability to handle large volumes of information is limited. Cognitive psychologist George Miller at Harvard University suggests that our brain is able to take seven, plus or minus two, factors into consideration when we make decisions.[10] That means that even if we had access to all conceivable information, we still would not be able to factor it all into an assessment.

I once aided in the analysis of a European company in the travel industry that was going to buy a small hotel chain. The investment was huge by the company's standards, and the investment was no sure thing. It was impossible to get an overview of every factor that could potentially affect whether the deal would end up being profitable or not. The bulk of the hotel chain's revenues came from Asia. Asia's future economic development was uncertain at the time. This was back in 2008. Both the management team and the board of directors had difficulties in making a well-founded decision when the time came. The management team performed a thorough analysis and weighed in everything from macroeconomic reports, market analyses, statements by regulatory bodies and guarantees, to their own cultural and social, demographic analyses, etc, to be sure. In other words, there was proper due diligence and they provided recommendations of a good business opportunity.

However, one limitation was that management felt they did not have all the information they wanted, and they were forced to make a decision based on information that was limited and, according to some, insufficient. Based on all the analyses, they developed a gigantic calculation model to help them try to make the decision rationally. Despite having so much information, they only included three or four parameters in their decision. Many of these were actually more based on gut feeling than analysis. They did not feel capable of evaluating additional parameters. This was the second limitation. In a sense, they simply got caught up in what is sometimes referred to as *analysis paralysis*.[11]

In the end, the company opted not to buy the hotel chain due to the perceived uncertainty that the investment entailed and the consequences it would have for the company if the deal soured. Even before the COVID-19 pandemic hit their industry in 2020 the travel company was really struggling. The hotel chain, on the other hand, is profitable. They even bought a company resembling the travel company that wanted to buy them. It's easy to say so with the benefit of hindsight, but the travel company most probably missed out on a good deal.

No matter how much information we have access to when making a decision, we do not have all the information. Even if we did have all the information, it is impossible to weigh in every factor and come to a decision on this basis. All difficult decisions are based on 'insufficiencies'.

Notes

1   F Taylor (1911) *The Principles of Scientific Management*, Harper & Brother, New York

2   See, e.g., D Kirkpatrick. Why there's no escaping the blog, Fortune, 10 January 2005, https://money.cnn.com/magazines/fortune/fortune_archive/2005/01/10/8230982/index.htm (archived at https://perma.cc/WQ8S-L2R3)

3   H Mintzberg (1989) *Mintzberg on Management: Inside our strange world of organizations*, Free Press, New York; H Mintzberg (1983) *Structure in Fives: Designing effective organization*, Prentice Hall, Hoboken.

4   See, e.g., S Raisch and J Birkinshaw. Organizational ambidexterity: Antecedents, outcomes, and moderators, *Journal of Management*, 2008, 34, 375–409; M Tushman and C O'Reilly. Ambidextrous organizations: Managing evolutionary and revolutionary change, *California Management Review*, 1996, 38, 8–30; J March. Exploration and exploitation in organizational learning, *Organization Science*, 1991, 2, 71–87

5   See, e.g., S Kapner. Ericsson's 2001 loss is first in 50 years, *New York Times*, 26 January 2002, www.nytimes.com/2002/01/26/technology/ericssons-2001-loss-is-first-in-50-years.html (archived at https://perma.cc/SKJ5-U6K2)

6   K Schwab. The Fourth Industrial Revolution: What it means, how to respond, World Economic Forum, 2016, www.weforum.org/agenda/2016/01/the-fourth-industrial-revolution-what-it-means-and-how-to-respond (archived at https://perma.cc/3TU9-LFG5); K Schwab. The fourth industrial revolution, Forum, 2016, www3.weforum.org/docs/Media/KSC_4IR.pdf (archived at https://perma.cc/CV3M-K5FC)

7   M Lewis. Exploring paradox: Toward a more comprehensive guide, *Academy of Management Review*, 2000, 25, 760–76; M S Poole and A H Van de Ven. Using paradoxes to build management and organizational theories, *Academy of Management Review*, 1989, 14, 562–78

8   G Morgan (1986) *Images of Organization*, SAGE Publications, London

9   H Simon (1997) *Administrative Behaviour: A study of decision-making processes in administrative organizations*, 4th edn, The Free Press, New York; H Simon (1957) *Models of Man, Social and Rational: Mathematical essays on rational human behavior in a social setting*, Wiley, Hoboken

10 G A Miller. The magical number seven, plus or minus two: Some limits on our capacity for processing information, *Psychological Review*, 1956, 63 (2), 81–97

11 See, e.g., C R Schwartz. The return-on-investment concept as a tool for decision making, General Management Series Pamphlet no 183, American Management Association, 1956, 42–61; H I Ansoff (1965) *Corporate Strategy: An analytic approach to business policy for growth and expansion*, McGraw-Hill, New York

06

Evidence and measurement

One way to remedy the uncertainty and insufficiencies in an organization is to plan, to structure, and to try to manage the organization as if it were a machine. Another way is to measure what is happening in the organization. Many organizations have made use of this. Yet it is important to ask what is to be measured and what can be measured properly. Just as it is common for traditional organizations (cf. the machine) to be excessively structured, there is a tendency to measure everything.

Within most organizations, there is a clear link between a given strategy and the person or people who led the company at a certain time. This can take the form of a period characterized by the acquisition of various companies, the diversification of business operations, the narrowing of operational focus, reorganizations, the division of responsibilities, or the entry into new markets. Renowned business executive Percy Barnevik implemented a number of streamlining programmes during his time at the Swiss-Swedish industry group, ABB. He unveiled the T50 initiative (a programme aimed at cutting costs and lead times in half) and after he had served for a time as chairman of the board of Skanska, a global engineering and construction company, they introduced an initiative called 3T, which was not dissimilar to T50.[1]

A great deal of a company's corporate culture is built by one or a couple of able and charismatic managers who lead the organization for a period of time. All actions taken by leaders are taken with the aim of achieving the goals set by the organization, and the results of such actions depend on the decision-makers' perception of what is best. Much of the strategy and strategizing that predominated during a given period of time can be linked to one person's, or at most a handful of people's, way of looking at strategy, organization, goals, etc.

Behavioural strategizing is a way of managing an organization to ensure long-term success through continuous change and adaptation. New management ideas are sometimes regarded as a set of tools that are easy to use. As a result, many of them gain popularity for a period of time; a good example is *Lean*, which has been popular since the 1990s. Behavioural strategizing, or other ways of leading organizations for that matter, should not be reduced to a set of tools that the 'next guy' can copy and use. Their potential is deeper than that. We have to let the entire business be permeated by an underlying approach, so that every behaviour in the organization is governed by something that might be referred to as *central ideas*.

For instance, adaptability demands openness and objectivity on all accounts. Shell was early to embrace working with future scenarios in order to get its decision-makers to question their own ideas. This increased their preparedness for change. All models are simplifications of reality and are therefore incomplete, but they can help us see things from different perspectives. As noted, there are almost always several ways to look at complex issues. Nothing is purely good or bad.

It is good to see reality as an ally. By behaving with curiosity and doing what we can to understand the way things actually are, by striving to learn more and by actively seeking knowledge, we can create an organization that makes sound decisions and becomes successful. A basic approach within behavioural strategizing is therefore to start from the data to determine what the reality 'is', but the data by itself is not enough. We need to have the right data, not just a lot of data, and we need to do something active with the information to transform it into knowledge and competence (i.e. the ability to compete).

Information, data and level of detail

Big Data is at the centre of a debate in which virtually all world-leading universities and consulting firms are involved. A number of possibilities emerge in the wake of technical solutions that enable the recording, storage and retrieval of information in IT solutions. Thanks to this development, there are such tremendous amounts of information available that it is much easier to get an accurate picture of almost anything in 2020 than it was in 2015. The logical argument for the benefit of Big Data is that whoever manages to collect, analyse and understand information, and transform it into knowledge that can be used, can gain a competitive edge. By amassing a lot of information and gaining an understanding of what the outside world looks like, we can possibly agree on 'one truth'. With this truth in hand, we can then all agree on what the situation is today, which creates a good starting point for agreeing on a way forward.

It is relatively unusual to see organizations managed and governed on the basis of verified results (evidence). The reason for this may be that hierarchies are flattened when data and knowledge replace formal authority and prestige. The leader is no longer the obvious hero. Leaders who like shooting from the hip and who feel that they have all the answers have a hard time adapting to the new circumstances. Another reason is that a culture in which everyone is looking to make fact-based decisions requires self-discipline and courage. Not only must we want to listen to inconvenient truths, we must encourage employees to communicate them and reinforce them when they do.

Organizations that have proven themselves successful over an extended period of time do not simply ignore whatever runs contrary to their beliefs. They try to find out what they know and what they do not know, and to act on the basis of the knowledge they actually have. Wisdom is knowing what you know and what you don't know, and knowing when to ask for help. This is extremely important for organizations that want to be successful. The majority of psychological studies show that in nearly every field most people believe that their performance is above average; we typically also have a higher idea of our own performance than our managers do.[2] If performance cannot be measured objectively, there is an imminent risk that many employees will believe that their managers do not appreciate their behaviour and denigrate their performance.

Historically, organizations have looked at the aggregate result at the top of the organization. It was not possible to get a more granular measure than the average. The average conveyed whether the organization was successful. As a result, organizations engaged in a kind of *management by averages*. As more data is available, we know this leads to below-average performance. In nearly every industry, this is no longer enough. At a company with two stores that are basically identical but whose performance differs, we want to be able to learn from the best one in order to develop our organization. The important information needs to be captured further down in the organization, and organizations need to get better at coming up with the right data. If the best store produces sales of €100,000 per day (approximately

$120,000) and the worst one generates €50,000 per day, the stores generate average daily sales of €75,000. If we want to develop our organization, it is not enough to know that the organization generates average daily sales of €150,000 and that the average daily volume per store is €75,000.

This is sometimes referred to as the *granularity* of information. An organization that works properly with information learns how to retrieve data at the right level and does not settle for management by averages. As information is stored with greater granularity, we have the opportunity to access information that previously did not exist. We can also present information in an educational way and allow it to serve as a decision support and policy instrument in the context of various business intelligence tools.

A friend of mine, currently professor in management at Uppsala University in Sweden, worked as a controller at Phillips for some time during the 1980s. Phillips sold calculators, among other things. Sales were important of course, and management monitored the performance of the respective sales offices. The office that most often posted the best sales figures was the Södermalm office in Stockholm. Their high sales figures sparked the organization's interest, and management wondered what this office's 'secret sauce' was. They started from the premise that because this office had the highest sales, they were logically doing something better than everyone else. However, it turned out that the real reason for the office's outperformance was that the Swedish Tax Agency had its offices in the building next door. Known as *Skatteskrapan*, it had almost 20,000m^2 of offices on 25 stories (equivalent to more than 1.8 million square feet), and the offices' need for calculators was so great that the Södermalm office was able to make a major sale to them. The conditions were so favourable that the office generated the most sales, regardless of the effort they put in.

The biggest challenge in the post-war period was getting hold of resources. Whoever got hold of resources – whether in the form of people, capital or raw materials – went on to win the race. The current situation is such that we are facing a lack of competency, not of capital or raw materials. Overall, the situation is one of overcapacity in nearly all industries. This means that we need better systems for measuring our business and marketing our products. Streamlining and killer ad campaigns have been the means of choice for a long time. Those are relatively easy to measure. But measuring a sound business? How do we measure performance that is not financial? How do we measure competency? How do we measure an innovative climate? How do we measure the magnitude or rate of change? One way, the one brought forward in this book, is to measure behaviour.

Experiences and interpretation

'Without data you're just another schmuck with an opinion!' is a favourite expression of mine. It is sometimes attributed to Alan Greenspan, chair of the Federal Reserve of the United States between 1987 and 2006, and sometimes to the behaviour science professor Chris Andersson. Just as data is important if we are to gauge progress within a research project, it is also important in organizational management and development. Behavioural strategizing is in this sense like research. The basic idea is to use facts to underpin our decisions and to evaluate whether this brought about the expected result, and then formulate a way forward based on what was successful.

We see, experience and interpret the world in different ways. Our own way of understanding the world differs from that of others. We apply labels and expressions to things based on our own interpretations – interpretations that are sometimes different from those made by others. Divergence of interpretation does not mean that one interpretation is right and the other one is wrong. What it does mean, however, is that interpretations make it difficult for organizations to achieve their objectives if they cannot be agreed upon. The less clear a goal is, the more difficult it is to know when the goal has been achieved, how to achieve it, or what behaviour leads to the goal being achieved.

To test our perception, we can use something called an 'awareness test'. One example of an awareness test is to screen a film showing two groups of people. One group has black clothes and the other white. The teams throw a ball to each other within the group. The test is based on counting how many times the black group passes the ball to each other. When a group watches the film and is given the task of counting the number of passes, they typically arrive at anything between 11 and 15 throws. The film is only one minute and 30 seconds long, the task is clearly delimited and hard to misinterpret. And yet we get different answers. This shows that we perceive things in different ways, despite the fact that we are focusing for so brief a period of time. Spoiler alert: The right number of passes in this case is 13. This is beautifully described in the book *The Invisible Gorilla*, by psychology researchers Christopher Chabris and Daniel Simons.[3]

During the film, someone wearing a bear costume also wanders into the frame and moon walks. Some notice it, others don't. This shows that we pay attention to different things when we concentrate and make individual interpretations of what is important. Some people are good at counting the number of passes. Some are good at seeing what is out of place, and others understand how things are connected. Talking about realizing strategy, the goals we want to achieve and how to go about doing so creates an educational challenge.

Clarity and instructional value

In behavioural psychology, we sometimes talk about *instructional value*. What this means in short is that I understand, based on an instruction, what something means and what to do. The clearer we can be with, for example, our goals, the less room there is for interpretation and the better our chances of accomplishing what we set out to do. To give an example: I tell you to be funny. The goal is for me to think that you are funny. Do you know how to act? Probably not. On the other hand, if I tell you to stand on one leg, look up at the ceiling and put your right forefinger on your nose while singing a tune, that's the funniest thing I know. Then you know how to act; how to behave.

The opportunity to express things clearly instead of leaving them open to interpretation is important if we are to be able to communicate or convey a clear objective, while also dramatically increasing the chances of realizing a given strategy.

Researchers, for instance American psychologist Judith Komaki, have looked at how long it takes for different types of managers at various enterprise levels to communicate a wish, an assignment, or something else they want done.[4] The best ones succeeded in communicating simple tasks in a few seconds, whereas the worst ones needed over a minute. To some extent, realizing strategies has to do with describing what needs to be done, by when it should be done, and, sometimes, how it should be done. Instructional value is important in the context of assignment descriptions, in management systems and in strategy or target documents.

We cannot describe everything we want down to the smallest detail, and of course we don't want to either, as this inhibits local power of initiative. But it is important to think about the interpretation. There is an overlooked difference between being specific and precise and being detailed. Being specific and precise does not necessarily require a detailed explanation. 'Focus on the right customers' is a vague statement. 'Don't do assignments for anyone other than our A customers and B customers under any circumstances.' That is clear, but not detailed.

A person who wants to influence someone else has a responsibility to make sure that the recipient understands what is being influenced. The responsibility for presenting something in a clear way lies with the person who wants something done. That's part of leadership and governance. A high instructional value helps.

The brain and thinking in new ways

Up to now, the outside world has not forced organizations to become specific and precise. Management by averages, that is, looking at a result at an overall level and not diving deeper into the numbers, has in many cases been sufficient to lead an organization. We have looked at figures on an aggregate level. When the outside world is complex, we learn to resort to simplifications and generalizations. Evolution has forced us to see simplified connections in order to survive. We have to do this because it is impossible to describe everything that is happening around us in detail. As the world we live in is complex, it is indeed difficult to understand how things relate to each other, we generalize and apply labels and descriptions to various phenomena in order to understand them. This is the brain's way of simplifying.

Dangerous animals have had approximately the same appearance to all people at all times. Generalizations have helped us understand which animals are dangerous and which we should therefore avoid. This is concrete and does not require any abstract thinking. But what does a 'dangerous' market situation look like? Is it a new product being launched by a competitor? Is it a regulation that hits our services? Is it a new foreign player entering the market? Is it an economic downturn? Maybe it's all of these at the same time? A common mistake that the brain makes due to evolution is to proceed from the 'last time' things happened a certain way, and to take action on this basis. This means that most organizations still think that the market is a dangerous animal that they will be able to recognize in the same way each time. And the medicine for the symptom 'dangerous market' will then be the same every time.

The brain wants to simplify, and therefore generalizes. Generalizations have helped us survive, but they can cause problems. The brain automatically seeks out things that reinforce our own, existing opinions. Coming across something that runs directly contrary to our own opinion requires significantly more effort. It is difficult to question our own knowledge, our own ideas and set ways of thinking about how businesses become profitable and what makes for a business that works well.

Most managers I meet see intuition as being an important part of driving organizations into the future. Intuition can indeed be necessary and can yield success. But human intuition is not very reliable. It is coloured by a person's past experience and knowledge, knowledge that is not necessarily relevant to the current situation. Although no correct answer can be found, analytical thinking supported by data is necessary if we are to avoid the emotional interpretation of information. A clear disadvantage to drawing on experience, however, is that it often locks us into certain ways of thinking. Old habits die hard. When new types of problems arise, new ways of solving them are needed. This makes experience as much an enemy as an ally.

So, on the one hand, logical and analytical reasoning may aid us in making good decisions. On the other, we should also be a bit careful. One difficulty with logic and rationality is that humans are limited by three factors, cognitively speaking:

1 The ability of humans to retrieve information is limited. It is impossible for a person to be everywhere at all times, which imposes limitations on the ability to understand what is actually going on.

2 Humans have a limited capacity to process information. We find it hard to think our way to a solution when problems have many variables, complex correlations and large amounts of data.

3 Humans have a limited capacity to store information. We are worse than we think at remembering things and at logical reasoning, and sometimes we make memories of things we only believe we have experienced.

These limitations cause people to generalize. We use what are referred to as *cognitive maps*[5] to simplify things. Our generalizations are shaped by our experiences. People in a company, family, industry, city, country or even a continent share cognitive maps to some extent. This is then manifested in different cultures – societal culture, industry culture, corporate culture, etc – where certain factors are considered to be more important than others.

Intuition is not infrequently the result of a culture. If the purpose of strategizing is to develop new ideas and ways of leading the organization, it is easy to understand that intuition based on experience and culture can throw up obstacles in our path.

Intuition can be a good thing. Intuition is based on generalizations based on memories. Experience as such is often beneficial. Yet research indicates that we often misremember things and unconsciously make others' memories into our own.[6] The effect of this *bias* can range from being beneficial to completely devastating for organizations. There are not many managers and strategists who take into account their own cognitive biases that serve to undermine strategic decision-making. Some common sources of such biases are selective memory, telescoping, attribution, and exaggeration. These are by no means detached from experience. It is therefore crucial for organizations to recognize their own biases. In several studies of strategic decision-making over the last decades, managers were asked about the quality of the strategic decisions in their organization. In most studies, well over 50 per cent felt that bad decisions were just as common as good ones.[7] And often the greatest weakness was the lack of consideration for evidence, or facts.

Daniel Kahneman, an Israeli psychologist, economist and recipient of the Sveriges Riksbanks Prize in Economic Sciences in Memory of Alfred Nobel, coined the terms *System 1* and *System 2* to describe two different ways of thinking.[8] System 1 thinks quickly, instinctively and emotionally, while System 2 thinks slowly, intentionally and logically. One of his theses is that too many important decisions are made using System 1. In System 1, the brain is good at drawing rapid conclusions and making decisions that are more likely to be based on preconceptions and beliefs rather than on facts. System 2 requires more effort and is therefore more unusual: the human brain is a *cognitive miser,*[9] meaning it takes shortcuts whenever it can. This is how evolution has shaped our brain. When it comes to strategizing, one way to address this may be to introduce a proper decision-making process. A good decision-making process often involves a good analysis, but a good analysis does not automatically entail a good decision-making process. Having a good process where facts need to be brought up for discussion and where various sides are forced to discuss their biases when important decisions are to be made is therefore a hygiene factor for an organization that wants to make sound decisions.

Organizational leaders often talk about daring to think differently and daring to think bigger. 'Out of the box' is an expression I hear a lot and would certainly not miss if it disappeared. The brain has a built-in weakness when it comes to thinking in new ways and understanding connections. This makes it hard for us to see a development potential or a need for change that is too far removed from our own perceptions. It is easier to go on thinking what we thought before and to do what worked before than it is to think in a way that is 'unthought of' and uncertain.

There is a story that effectively illustrates the brain's inability to see the whole picture. It is about the farmer who invented the game of chess and the emperor of the land in which the farmer lived. The emperor wanted to reward the farmer for the invention. The emperor asked the farmer to tell him what he wanted. The farmer then asked for a grain of rice for the first square on the chessboard. For the second square he asked for two grains, and that the number of grains should then be doubled for every square on the board. The emperor agreed to the farmer's price. If you do the maths, this means that the farmer was owed over 18 trillion (million billion) tonnes of rice for the last square on the chessboard. That would be the equivalent of burying the entire planet under a meter-thick blanket of rice. By way of comparison, global rice production in 2020 is estimated to just above 500 million tonnes.

This example shows how easy it is to be fooled when we are convinced that something is true. Studies show particularly how exponential growth is particularly difficult to understands for us humans.[10] However, many things do change exponentially in our environments. If we fail to see these connections in our own business – which we ought to know well, after all – how are we supposed to cope with the outside world? How do we ensure that we have taken the right path and not just the easiest one?

Several years ago, I did a project to create a more change- and innovation-inclined climate in an industrial organization. As part of my assignment, I worked with two site managers at two different plants. One of them needed to get better at delegating so that the employees could take more individual responsibility and stop asking questions they knew the answers to. In turn, the plan was for them to use the time previously lost answering unnecessary questions to instead reinforce 'good behaviour', i.e. employees taking their own initiative without asking. The other manager had the impression that he was getting too few new ideas from his employees and wanted to reinforce those who presented new ideas.

I asked the two managers to make a note in a software program every time they were asked a question and every time a new idea was brought to them, respectively, and how many times they reinforced 'good behaviour' and new ideas.

After four weeks we held the first follow-up meeting. Both managers were of the opinion that 'not much had happened'. They were still answering questions and being shown too few new ideas. But when we sat down to look at the data the managers had recorded, we could see that something had happened. The first manager had gone from answering 35 'unnecessary questions' per week down to 19. He had also increased the frequency with which he reinforced workers taking independent responsibility from two times a week to six. In other words, he had managed to achieve something. The figures were about the same for the second manager.

One of the lessons here of course is that if we focus and take action in an area, it will produce results. Another is that we should not trust our gut feeling but should validate it with measurements. Looking at real data is a powerful tool for driving a project forward. Looking at the results we achieve gives us the opportunity to celebrate wins, wins we may not have known about. It also helps us to properly reflect and learn how to proceed.

What to measure

There is a certain amount of truth in the saying 'What gets measured gets done'. We get what we measure. But it is not entirely true, and I will revisit this issue later on. At this point, we can note that organizations measure everything conceivable (and inconceivable): market share, quality, profitability, return, costs, efficiency, productivity, customer base, backlog, time to launch, number of patents awarded, satisfied customers, satisfied employees, leadership, media coverage and much more. This does not mean that they get what they want out of the organization in these areas.

Sometimes the things that get measured are called *key performance indicators* (KPIs). I once worked with an engineering and construction company that was part of a publicly listed group of companies. In their operations I identified 273 KPIs. At a department of a major car manufacturer, I identified 178. It's a good thing to measure, of course, but how are we supposed to keep track of so many indicators? Can they all really be equally important? The answer is both yes and no, as long as each individual has a limited number of goals. Research tells us between 10 and 20 is appropriate.[11]

A large organization can of course have many of them, but we should keep in mind that working towards goals is a zero-sum game.

It is important to consider how many key figures someone can actually keep track of. As noted, opinions differ here, but when we say 'key' it should be understood to mean that the indicator is important or critical. Given Miller's research about the brain's limited capacity, we should use a limited number of KPIs. Like I said, the brain is thought to be able to include about seven factors in our decision-making process.

In addition, the time that an organization has to work towards goals is limited. The result is that the more goals there are, the less time is dedicated to achieving any given one. He who tries to control everything ends up controlling nothing.

Rumour has it that Percy Barnevik, former CEO and chairman of the Swiss-Swedish industrial conglomerate ABB, was a fan of measurement. His opinion was that different things had to be measured at different levels. At his level, which was the absolute pinnacle, what he measured was his subordinates' measurement of their operations. In short, do you have control of the measurements in your business? Often, measurement gets an undeserved reputation of being focused on details and tying up a lot of resources because everything has to be measured – yet this need not be the case. Barnevik's example is proof that measurement does not need to concern itself with the nitty-gritty *or* be extremely exhaustive, and that it can still yield valuable information.

> When realizing strategy, we are interested in influencing employee behaviour as early as possible. We want to get early indications so that we can avoid risks and harness opportunities as quickly as possible. This is why it is important to know how different results are created – often even more important than knowing what the result actually was.

Traditionally, financial data has been the main source of key figures and these are usually considered to be KPIs. In the 1990s, the American professors and business leaders Robert Kaplan and David Norton came up with the concept of *the balanced scorecard* as a result of organizations trying to lead their businesses based on financial information.[12] Their aim was to find a way of getting at what leads to financial results and to bring about more proactive 'steering' of an organization.

The framework they launched has four perspectives that are equally important to measure and follow up on. In addition to financials, these perspectives are customer, internal processes, and innovation and learning. The balanced scorecard is one of the most common tools used to break down a strategy into things to measure. Some examples of companies that use or have used balanced scorecards are Volkswagen, Citibank, Philips, Apple, FBI and Tetra Pak. There are also many municipalities and government organizations that use balanced scorecards to follow up on their operations.

A related term sometimes also emerges in the debate: *key result indicator* (KRI).[13] For me, the difference is that a KPI is 'leading' and a KRI is 'lagging'. What I mean by that is that a KPI is a measurement that shows us where the KRI may end up. A KPI points to and hopefully leads to a certain KRI. Many economic key figures are result indicators that indicate something that has already become a definite result, meaning that they should be classified as KRIs and not KPIs. In other words, this can be seen as a clarification of the roles played by the various perspectives in the balanced scorecard with respect to each other.

Engineering and construction conglomerate Skanska's scorecard is heavily influenced by what is referred to as 'The success model'. In highly simplified terms:

- Good leadership results in satisfied employees (learning and growth).
- Satisfied employees do a good job (internal business processes).
- Good work leads to good products and thus satisfied customers (customer).
- Satisfied customers are more likely to return, which results in predictable profitability (financial).[14]

There is nothing remarkable about this, but it does clearly show where they think the result comes from and thus what might be classified as KPIs and KRIs, respectively.

How to measure

If we want to strengthen our business by trying to look at the outside world as objectively as possible, measurement becomes an important area of focus.

Measuring, however, is not the easiest thing to do properly. Below I therefore demonstrate how a few high-performing companies measure their performance:

- Start with a baseline measurement so we know where we stand. Generally speaking, percentages are a poor indicator of change, and are hard for our brains to relate to. There was a company that went from having one woman on the management team to two. That is a 100 per cent increase. If the target had been the proportion of women on the management team, which is a state, it would have been fine to use a percentage. But if what they wanted to accomplish was an increase in real numbers, then 'appointing two more women to the management team' would have been a better target.

- Measure one factor at a time, that way we don't confuse leading and lagging indicators. It is important to determine what leads to what. People sometimes use the terms independent and dependent variables. If we fail to identify what influences what, it is easy to get stuck in the statistical weeds. There is a well-known example of a statistical correlation, one that has been validated by all the rules of the craft, between ice cream sales and the number of drownings. If we take a level-headed look at this, we realize that something is off. What the statistics miss is the variable that influences both of them, namely hot weather. Ice cream sales do not affect the number of drownings, or vice versa.

- Measure factors several times to determine what the trend is. If we only measure on two occasions, we can certainly draw a straight line between these points and see some kind of direction, but it is hard to know for sure. It is possible that the third point will deviate entirely from what we thought was the trend. The more measuring points, the easier it is to see a trend. And trends are more important than snapshots when managing an organization.

- Measure factors at different levels, preferably at the individual level, the team level and the organizational level(s), to see how they are correlated. If we only measure at the organizational level, the result is management by averages, and that is not enough in the changing and super-competitive markets of the 2020s. Organizational initiatives have effects on various levels. If there are numerous hierarchical levels in the organization, we need to make sure that we have a spread among the levels. Things that can be seen clearly further down in the organization have a tendency to 'fade' with every level we move up the hierarchy.

- Run a pilot test and evaluate how things went before proceeding on a larger scale. This is particularly pertinent if we are going to implement something 'new'. When we want to perform a change, it is hard to know what result the change actually has. It is extremely difficult to isolate influencing factors in studies outside a laboratory setting.

- Use both test groups and placebo groups. We need to measure the 'group', department, business unit, etc, where we are implementing an actual initiative, and then also measure a group where we do nothing in order to verify that our initiative has an effect. Changes often involve investments. If we want to ensure that our investment has the intended effect, we should evaluate it.

- Always question the results of measurements. Think twice to make sure they seem reasonable. It's easy to take figures and statistics for granted. If we want to work properly with measurements, we have to create a process for questioning the figures produced by our measurement. The number 150,000 says nothing if we do not also include the fact, for example, that it refers to the number of group employees worldwide, or to customers that left a telecommunication operator for a direct competitor over the last month, or if it is an increase in sales from last month.

Notes

1 See, e.g., Affärsvärlden. Epoken Barnevik, Affärsvärlden, 30 January 2002, www.affarsvarlden.se/artikel/epoken-barnevik-6752297 (archived at https://perma.cc/2VH9-DJA8); Skanska AB. *Annual Report 1992*, Skanska, 1993 https://group.skanska.com/4ae901/siteassets/investors/reports-publications/annual-reports/1992/annual_report_1992.pdf (archived at https://perma.cc/X8BF-NYX7)

2 See, e.g., H Meyer. Self-appraisal of job performance, *Personnel Psychology*, 1980, 33 (2), 291–95; D J Campbell. Self-appraisal in performance evaluation: Development versus evaluation, *The Academy of Management Review*, 1998, 13 (2), 302–14

3 C Chabris and D Simons (2011) *The Invisible Gorilla: How our intuitions deceive us*, Harmony, New York

4 J Komaki (1998) *Leadership From an Operant Perspective*, Routledge, New York

5 See, e.g., E C Tolman. Cognitive maps in rats and men, *Psychological Review*, 1948, 55 (4), 189–208; C Eden. On the nature of cognitive maps, *Journal of*

Management Studies, 1992, 29 (3), 261–65; C M Fiol and A S Huff. Maps for managers: Where are we? Where do we go from here? *Journal of Management Studies*, 1992, 29 (3), 267–85

6 E F Loftus and J E Pickrell. The formation of false memories, *Psychiatric Annals*, 1995, 25 (12), 720–25

7 J Pfeffer and R I Sutton (2006) *Hard Facts, Dangerous Half-Truths and Total Nonsense*, Harvard Business School Press, Cambridge, MA

8 D Kahneman. The big idea, *Harvard Business Review*, June 2011, 50–60; D Kahneman (2011) *Thinking, Fast and Slow*, Farrar, Straus and Giroux, New York

9 S Fiske and S Taylor (1984) *Social Cognition*, McGraw-Hill, New York

10 See, e.g., M H Bazerman. The relevance of Kahneman and Tversky's concept of framing to organizational behavior, *Journal of Management*, 1984, 10 (3), 333–43

11 S Melnyk, U Bititci, K Platts and B Andersen. Is performance measurement fit for the future? *Management Accounting Research*, 2014, 25, 173–86; R Chenall. Integrative strategic performance measurement systems, strategic alignment of manufacturing, learning and strategic outcomes, *Accounting, Organizations and Society*, 2005, 30, 395–422; M Bourne, J Mils, M Wilcox, A Neely and K Platts. Designing, implementing and updating performance measurement systems, *International Journal of Operations and Production Management*, 2000, 20, 754–71

12 R Kaplan and D Norton. The balanced scorecard, *Harvard Business Review*, 1992, 70, 71–79

13 D Parmenter (2007) *Key Performance Indicators: Developing, implementing, and using winning KPIs*, John Wiley & Sons, Hoboken

14 See, e.g., P Samuelsson, Integrated measurement and assessment of performance in large organizations: The case of a Swedish construction company, PhD Dissertation, 2006, Chalmers Technical University, Gothenburg.

KEY POINTS

Part Two: Arbitrariness is over

Why are yesterday's management philosophies not good enough anymore?

The world has changed dramatically since the beginning of the 1990s. The rapid rate of change in the outside world means that our way of leading organizations is also in need of an update. Yet many organizations insist on leading their businesses based on the same old principles. Organizations that aim to achieve long-term success need to integrate new ways of thinking into their way of leading and must always be responsive to changes in the outside world.

How can we look at organizations in order to better develop them?

It is impossible to control and govern every aspect of an organization. Planning is still important, but it is of limited utility at a time when changes are so far-reaching and quick that the landscape will have changed entirely by tomorrow. Organizations are open systems that learn from their own business operations and develop as they learn. Organizations do not have business operations that are entirely logical and sequential, which means that it is not possible to control them completely based on a defined plan.

Why are measurement and evidence important parts of leading organizations?

If we are to know that we have achieved our goals, that our initiatives have had an effect, or that we are on the right path, we need to measure and follow up. It is not professional to lead an organization arbitrarily. Who would want to be treated by a doctor who does not use scientifically proven surgical methods or medications? No one would dream of presenting an annual report without providing income statement and balance sheet metrics for the year. But we are suddenly less careful when it comes to measuring the factors that generate these results, e.g. behaviour, learning, competence.

What does it mean to say that 'arbitrariness is over'?

Anyone who wants to achieve sustained success cannot rely on their gut feeling. Strategy is realized through employee behaviour. Goals are achieved by employees doing something – behaving in some way. Behaviour is what creates results. Some behaviours have a greater impact on organizational results than others. Some are absolutely vital. Yet others do not contribute to the survival or success of the organization at all and are thus completely unnecessary. All behaviour is not equal. To be successful, we need to pay attention to what behaviours are important, and try to influence them. Accordingly, these are the behaviours that need to be measured and evaluated.

PART THREE

Unexpected simplicity

Human subtlety... will never devise an invention more beautiful, more simple or more direct than does nature, because in her inventions nothing is lacking, and nothing is superfluous.

LEONARDO DA VINCI

By looking at the world through the lens of behaviour, we can understand why people do what they do – in organizations and in society at large. Adopting a behavioural focus can help organizations become high-performing and successful in the long run.

IN THIS PART

This part includes discussions on the following areas:

- What is behaviour?
- What affects behaviour?
- Why are consequences crucial if an organization is to perform?
- How can behaviour analysis help create higher-performing organizations?
- What does 'unexpected simplicity' have to do with behaviour?

07

Behaviour

The foundation of everything

Physics and mathematics are in agreement: beauty takes the form of unexpected simplicity, and it is lovely to behold. The simpler it is, the more beautiful it is. For Greek philosopher and mathematician Pythagoras, the integer was the most beautiful thing. He considered that the whole world was made up of integers and music. Economist E F Schumacher wrote that 'Any intelligent fool can make things bigger and more complex... It takes a touch of genius – and a lot of courage – to move in the opposite direction.'[1] To me, the simplicity of the behavioural perspective is beautiful. Everything people do is a behaviour. Behaviour is the foundation of all creativity.

This chapter will address one of the most basic concepts in behavioural strategizing: the behaviour as such. Behaviour is the first of three components in what is referred to as the *contingency of reinforcement*.[2] The other two components are activators and consequences and these will be discussed later. Reinforcement contingency is the 'here and now situation' – the context in which the behaviour occurs – describing the link between a behaviour, its activators (what starts it) and its consequences (what happens after it).

How do we recognize behaviour? How do we define different behaviour? How do we ensure that behaviour is formulated with sufficient precision to be able to work with and refine it? Since behaviour is an organization's lowest common denominator, we can always break down strategy, overall goals or culture into behaviours. Nothing happens in an organization without someone doing something.

Often when reading about leadership and leadership studies we are told that there are more or less successful behaviours for leaders. To summarize much of the literature we could conclude that four common successful 'behaviours' for leaders are being: (1) social; (2) motivating; (3) charismatic;

and (4) honest. We can all agree that these attributes are important in managers and leaders. As we shall see, however, they are not behaviours in my book. And since there are different views on what a behaviour is, this needs to be discussed.

Behaviour and personality

The hard thing for someone who wants to work in a structured way to influence and change behaviour is understanding what they need to change in order to become 'motivating' or 'charismatic'. These aren't behaviour. Behaviour is much more clearly defined than that.

B F Skinner, an American psychologist and one of the most influential researchers in the field of behaviour, and psychology for that matter, defined behaviour as all organismic events, i.e. the processes of all organisms.[3] In other words, learning theory holds that behaviour is more than just what we do.

Behaviour is both external and internal. Actions, and to some extent bodily reactions and emotions too, are observable from the outside, whereas thoughts and feelings can rarely be observed from the outside. Internal behaviour is often difficult to distinguish, since emotions, thoughts and bodily reactions are closely related.

Behaviour in a broad sense can be defined as a complex pattern of thoughts, emotions, bodily reactions and actions. Two American researchers, Martin Sundel and Sandra Sundel, define behaviour as any observable or measurable movement or activity in an individual, visible or invisible, verbal or non-verbal.[4] This is, of course, a technical definition that is hard to use in everyday life, but it does provide a clear indication of what is important. Observability is important, as are measurability and activity.

As I mentioned earlier, in order to accomplish a strategic shift or change, the behaviour of the employees in the organization needs to change. One common reason that organizations fail to bring about the shift they set out to accomplish is that they fail to define the behaviour they want to influence in a sufficiently clear manner, and they fail to perform a behaviour analysis and impact assessment. More customer-focused, more social, more confident or more sustainable – these are not behavioural traits.

One common approach found in the management and leadership literature is to look at people based on how we perceive them as 'being'. We see people as something set and ready. There is an idea to the effect that we are controlled by our traits, or that we have a personality that remains constant. This means that, by definition, people are unable to change very much.

Many of these arguments are based on the outdated psychodynamic theory of Sigmund Freud and Carl Gustav Jung from the beginning of the 20th century. One of the premises of this theory is that there is a personality, and that the first years of life are absolutely critical in determining how someone will be for the rest of their lives. This line of reasoning argues that great leaders are born that way. You are either born a leader, or you aren't. You are either born driven, or you are aren't. You are either born the world's best bass clarinet player, or you aren't.

This view is alien to a learning theorist. We know fairly well that people learn their entire lives and are changeable. There is a certain *genetic predisposition* that creates conditions, but it accounts for a relatively small part of what might be called the 'personality'. A behavioural perspective on learning argues that the situation we are in, as well as our prior experience, are highly significant as well. My take on behavioural psychology is that it is characterized by a 'pedagogical optimism', which means that there are always opportunities to influence behaviour for the better. People do have some basic characteristics, but it is always possible to influence their behaviour.

Under the behavioural perspective, we assume that most of our behaviour is automated and that it is only occasionally preceded or controlled by a conscious thought. We are called on to think, above all, in unknown situations. Changing our thoughts does not always mean changing our 'practical' behaviour – what we do. Thinking is not enough in order for things to turn out differently. Action is crucial. Behaviour is a tool for achieving a given goal, and learning is how we acquire new and better behaviour and improve our toolbox.

Behaviour, situations and arbitrariness

In somewhat simplified terms, *situational contingency* means that a person's behaviour is chosen in the specific situation. It is often said that behaviour is *contextual*. We learn how to behave in various contexts. From personal experience, I can be social or motivating in one context, but reserved and lazy in another. We are all 'behavioural chameleons'.

The situation and the influence brought to bear by the outside world have a critical effect on how we behave. This has been found over and over again in studies, both in behavioural psychology and in social psychology. In spite of extensive research showing that different situations cause people to behave in different ways, we insist on proceeding from the premise that people 'are' a certain way and that they will always be that way, even when it comes to leading organizations.

We should look at people's behaviour – what they 'do'. People 'do' things – they behave – depending on the context they are in and on their past experiences of similar situations. We adapt our behaviour to the situation in order for it to serve us in the best possible way.

Here I want to provide an illustration of how the context of a behaviour really explains a lot. Sitting and turning our head from right to left and then back to the right again every other second sounds like a daft thing to do. But if the person is seated in the stands watching a tennis match, it would instead be daft of them not to turn their head. The situation and the context are crucial. So is being precise.

The behaviour analyst advocates observing and measuring what he can measure as this is also possible to manage. It is difficult to measure emotions and thoughts. So, let us instead look at what people actually do. How do we behave in our organization? Do we smile at one another? Do we greet one another? Are we punctual? Do we praise each other? Do we give honest feedback – both positive and corrective? Do we prioritize the right customers? Do we deliver by our deadlines? Do the employees behave in accordance with the safety instructions?

Organizations want to see clear results. Going by our 'gut feeling' in strategizing is not enough. What we say we do, what we feel and what we believe – all of that is irrelevant if we do not behave in the way that is expected. The organizations that perform better than their competitors have employees who behave more effectively.

In many organizations, employees ask – sometimes literally scream – for clear instructions. Nonetheless, in management contexts we talk about things like mindset, values, attitudes, outlook, drive, customer focus, and not about how to reinforce employees to do the right things in a timely manner. We need to know what we are supposed to do with more precision if we want to become a successful organization. We need to understand what behaviours are expected.

Understanding behaviour

To understand behaviour, we need to understand that it is part of a context. Behaviour is dependent on something that starts it and on something that

FIGURE 7.1 The context of behaviour

A (activator) leads to...	...B (behaviour) being performed...	...resulting in C (consequences)
Activators are phenomena in the environment that cause a person to choose behaviour based on prior experience. For example, activators include education, goals, job descriptions, demands, reminders or perceived peer pressure.	Behaviour is what someone does, says, thinks or feels, such as saying hello, talking, smiling, writing, submitting a report, etc.	The consequence is something that follows behaviour and 'lets you know' whether the behaviour was meaningful or not. There can be various kinds of consequences: attention, praise, happiness, complaints, acknowledgement, a feeling of being able, satisfaction, etc. These can be conscious and/or unconscious.

SOURCE Original model

ensures that it is sustained. Behaviour is contextual. In this regard, we refer to the thing that starts the behaviour as an activator, while what sustains it is referred to as consequences. This relation between the behaviour and its context is generally referred to as the three-term contingency, or the ABC contingency, and is illustrated in Figure 7.1.

We often distinguish between three types of behaviour: *motor, autonomous* and *cognitive*. Motor behaviour is bodily behaviour. Examples include when our arms move or when we speak. Autonomous behaviour is controlled by the spinal cord and the central nervous system, and includes the beating of our heart and our lungs' breathing. The third category is cognitive behaviour: this has to do with thinking, analysing, making decisions and contemplating. Motor and cognitive behaviour are controlled in the same way – they can be controlled at will and are *learned*. This is referred to as *operant behaviour*. Autonomous behaviour is *innate* and cannot be controlled by the individual. This is referred to as *respondent behaviour*.

Another way to classify behaviour is to use the terms *behavioural deficit* and *behavioural excess*. A behavioural deficit means that there is behaviour that we would like to see more of. This is behaviour that we want to reinforce. This is behaviour that we consider to be positive if we are to achieve the results we have set for our business. A behavioural excess means that there is behaviour we want to see less of or not at all. This is behaviour that we want to weaken or to eliminate entirely. To provide you with some examples, stealing from the organization where you work is obviously something we want less of, but how about explaining or nodding your head? I think we can all can agree that explaining or nodding can be good, but also that it can be over-used. This allows us to understand that behaviours' excess and deficiency is related to a behaviour's appropriateness in a certain context.

When analysing behaviour, we speak of it as having a *frequency*. This is an explanation of how many times the behaviour was performed during a certain period of time and thus provides us with a way of measuring behaviour. Another way of measuring behaviour is to describe its *topography*. This is a description of what the behaviour looks like – its characteristics. 'He always submits his reports on time' is topographically and frequency-wise a more precise description than saying 'He works hard.' 'She comes up with concrete ideas for cost savings' is clearer than saying 'She thinks about the costs.' A clear topography and concrete description of frequency provides a good explanation of a given behaviour, enabling another person to perform what is being described.

Results, performance and behaviour

One way to describe what something is, is to describe what it is *not*. In order to better learn what behaviour is and why it is important, we also need to learn what behaviour is not. We often confuse behaviour with other things. Many people believe that 'social' is a behaviour. Even more people believe that 'helping' is a behaviour. Helping is closer to behaviour, but we need to get even more specific in order to have a defined or *pinpointed* behaviour.

One difficulty in many organizations is the ability to distinguish between a result or an achievement on the one hand and a behaviour on the other. It is important to make a clear distinction if we are to influence the ways in which we work and achieve our goals. Throwing darts is behaviour. Hitting the bull's-eye is a result. Making a strong argument in a negotiation is behaviour. Winning the deal and leaving all parties satisfied due to a certain argument is the result.

How do results and behaviour relate to each other? The behaviour relates to performance and results in about the same way as KPIs relate to KRIs.

I need to learn how to play darts and you need to teach me how to get better. I throw the dart and get a bull's-eye by sheer accident. 'I throw' is the behaviour. 'Getting a bull's-eye' is the result. This means that I get to write 50 on the chalkboard next to the dartboard. My performance is having thrown a dart and got a bull's-eye.

If you want to influence the result I am supposed to achieve, what should you try to influence? Can you influence me to throw the darts accurately by saying: 'Score a hit dead centre'? No, you have to get me to change the way I throw the dart – my behaviour. Calling on me to score a hit dead centre may encourage me to practise, but it has no instructional value in terms of my improvement. You need to explain how I should throw the darts, how I should set my feet for balance, whether I should close one eye for better aim, and so on. You have to change the behaviour in order to change the result.

The reasoning can be described as follows:

Behaviour + Result = Performance

No wonder that we confuse the terms sometimes, as results are easily confused with performance. I would like to assign names that make it easier to distinguish between the concepts. For the sake of clarity, I use the term *key behaviour indicator* (KBI) – a key figure for behaviour.

A key result indicator (KRI) would be the result, and a key performance indicator (KPI) would be the sum of the KBI and the KRI.

Behaviour (KBI)   + Result (KRI)   = Performance (KPI)
Throws darts (KBI) + Number of bull's-eyes (KRI) = Throws and hits (KPI)

Why is it so important to distinguish between these concepts if we want to become a high-performing organization? This is critical. If we want to influence people to move in the same direction and achieve our goals, it is important to know what we can influence directly and what we cannot. We can influence behaviour and we want to influence the result. We cannot influence the result without influencing the behaviour. This is the main point. The behaviour also provides an early indication of what the result may be, which helps us make a correction if we are heading in the wrong direction before the consequences have grown too serious.

Behaviours and goals

I used to play hockey in my hometown for a club called Linköping HC for about 15 years. I had a coach back then who understood the difference between results and behaviour. As goals are what count in ice hockey, it is common for the focus to be on scoring goals. He who scores no goals wins no matches.

What my coach did was to set behaviour as goals: 'You need to have at least 10 shots on goal during each period' (KBI). Scoring goals was of course the result, but he didn't tell us to take to the ice and 'score goals' (KRI). He realized that his advice to go out and shoot on goal had a higher instructional value than if he were to say: 'Get out there and score goals.' He said: 'Go in and shoot as soon as you are in a good position.'

He was convinced that the number of shots from a good position – the KBI – would most likely lead to a goal (KRI). For him, the most important behaviour for scoring goals was to always shoot whenever you were in a good position. In sales we sometimes say, jokingly, 100 knocks, 10 talks, 1 closed sale. The more doors you knock on (KBI), the more sales you close (KRI). Behaviour that is crucial for achieving a certain result is usually called a key behaviour. And, as I have urged earlier, I think that a measure of that behaviour should be called the KBI.

Organizations govern their business based on key figures, and these are often of a financial nature, such as sales, profitability and returns. Controlling by financial metrics means trying to control something that can only be influenced indirectly – the result. In this case we are not controlling the behaviour (KBI) that creates the results (KRI). When we determine that profitability, quality or customer satisfaction are too low, in many cases it is already too late to do anything. Using financial metrics to control a company is often likened to driving a car by looking in the rear-view mirror.

Forecasts are indications or guesses about future performance. By looking at what creates financial results, we can correct for both risks and opportunities before the consequences. Anyone who is interested in realizing strategy wants to have indications as early as possible. To get that, we need to focus on what creates the results – behaviour. That provides a more certain 'forecast' than traditional forecasts do.

Extensive (mis)use of financial key figures causes many companies to fixate on short-term financial results. Managers who are under pressure to produce good quarterly reports are not on the lookout for big investments that need to be made for the future.

Xerox is an example of the consequences that focusing on financial results can have. Xerox basically had a monopoly on copiers in the 1970s. They made money, but customers were dissatisfied. The customers were annoyed at costs that were too high and at machine downtime. Xerox did not realize that customers were dissatisfied, but focused on and celebrated their profitability, which was very high. Their idea was just to let the customers buy the copiers. When they didn't work, they started selling service and backup machines at a juicy profit. Sales and profits showed that this was a highly successful strategy. But the customers didn't want service or backup machines. They wanted to use the copiers they had paid for, not spend more money. The competition heard about the customers' dissatisfaction and immediately started selling machines that were smaller in size and less technically advanced – *almost* as good – but which were easier to handle and more reliable as a result. The result was that Xerox lost significant market share. Over a four-year period, they went from having a relative market share of almost 100 per cent in the United States to under 14 per cent.[5] Because of increasing challenges by Japanese copiers, a consent decree that made Xerox give up part of its patents, what one can assume was a focus on the incredibly strong financial results that they could not influence directly, and possibly too little focus on delivering what they could influence, they were on the verge of bankruptcy. They then regained their dominance by beginning to lease copiers. Thus, understanding leading and lagging indicators makes a difference.

All organizations have some type of goal. Consequently, all organizations have key behaviours for achieving these goals, but they have often failed to specify what those behaviours are. In order to get better at realizing strategy, organizations must identify their most important goals, find the key behaviours that make it possible to achieve these, and then work systematically on influencing, preferably reinforcing, these particular behaviours. This is behavioural strategizing in a nutshell.

The fewer the goals and the clearer the instructions on which key behaviours (KBIs) lead to which goals (KRIs), the easier it is to influence the right behaviour and thus to achieve the goals. Too many goals and too much ambiguity about which behaviour leads to which goal make it much more difficult to achieve them.

Labels and attributes

Just as it is easy to confuse results with behaviour, it is easy to confuse behaviour with labels and attributes.

A label is something used in an everyday setting to assign some kind of general name to something in a way that helps us form an understanding of that thing. He is kind, she is nice, he is good at what he does, she is a bully, and so on. This helps us describe people in a simple way in our everyday lives.

A label is usually described or defined as an attribute, something a person is. Behaviour is usually defined as something a person does.

For the uninitiated, it may seem natural to talk about a motivating person and to see this as behaviour. The same goes for being enthusiastic, results-oriented or solution-focused. But if we want to work with behaviour, this is not clear enough.

Common expressions in organizational communication, business plans and strategies include 'focusing on the customer,' 'helping each other,' 'having the right commitment,' 'being safety-conscious' and 'delivering with quality'. These are crucial if we are to run a good business and become profitable or successful in any size or shape. The question is what these expressions really stand for, and what behaviour is needed in order to achieve them. In strategy documents, organizations' ambitions are rarely expressed in the form of behaviour. This is a weakness.

What is more important in order for a business to achieve its goals? Employees who are unmotivated but who behave the right way, or employees who are motivated but do not behave the right way? Motivated, driven and businesslike are just labels that say very little about the employee's behaviour. What we need to do is to define a number of behaviours that indicate the quality of being business-like, or whether someone is driven and motivated, and then work with these.

Some time ago, I worked with a public sector organization with a little over 10,000 employees. They wanted to become more behaviour-oriented and through that get better at realizing strategy. A little before I arrived, they had drawn up the following leadership profile to serve as a support in future executive recruitments. One of the goals was that the guidelines needed to help quality-assure the various elements of the recruitment process and thus optimize the conditions for 'hiring the right senior manager in the right place'. These descriptions are as follows and help us understand the importance of being precise:

- *Personal maturity:* Is emotionally stable, has self-understanding and is self-confident. Has the right perspective on relationships and distinguishes between the personal and the professional. Acts in a way that is adapted to the situation.

- *Teamwork skills:* Works well with others. Relates to others in a responsive and smooth manner. Listens, communicates and resolves conflicts in a constructive manner.

- *Commitment and trust:* Brings enthusiasm, energy and an appetite to the work. Is able to create a sense of participation and consensus around the business. Helps employees grow by being responsive to the ideas of others, by allowing failure, showing trust and relying on and utilizing employee skills.

- *Creative and change-oriented:* Is driven by a desire to identify opportunities to improve the business, themselves and improvements for the sake of the customer/user. Has the ability to quickly adapt to new or changed requirements and conditions. Has a high tolerance for uncertainty.

- *Goal-and results-oriented:* Is driven by a desire to work in a goal-oriented way and to achieve results. Sets clear goals for the business and communicates these to the employees. Sticks to the timetable, lives up to commitments and follows up on results.

- *Diversity-aware:* Ability to see and take advantage of differences. Understands how background, culture and group affiliation affect one's self and others. Has the ability to factor this into the calculation when making decisions and choosing a course of action.

- *Problem-solving and strategic analytic ability:* Sees contexts and prioritizes the right questions. Analyses complex problems, breaks them down into their constituent parts and solves them. Looks at long-term significance and second-order consequences, and adapts actions accordingly. Has the ability to see the business from a holistic perspective, is able to link the whole to the constituent parts, the future to the present.

The labels/attributes described here are indeed important in order to be thought of as a good manager, but what do they mean in behavioural terms? What does it mean to have 'the right perspective on relationships'? What does it mean to 'show trust'? What behaviour does that entail?

To be able to take advantage of this, it needs to be fleshed out and translated into behaviour. This means that the questions to answer are these: What behaviours should the person who is to be perceived in a certain way exhibit? What does a leader who 'has the right perspective on relationships' do? What makes for a person who 'shows trust'?

Practice makes perfect

A Swedish researcher, K Anders Ericsson, who lived in the United States since the 1980s, and who tragically passed away in 2020, spent time researching why and how people become extremely skilful in a certain discipline. He studied prominent classical violinists, gymnasts, chess players, mathematicians and physicists. His line of reasoning has also been applied to business executives and other specialists.

He came to the conclusion that a lot of practice is needed if we are to constantly improve. The figure he mentions is roughly 10,000 hours, which is approximately equivalent to 10 years of focused work – *deliberate practice* in order to become *masterful*.[6] Another factor is to learn what works, and then to repeat and refine the successful behaviour time after time. A kind of 'constant improvement' at the behaviour level. Learning theorists would refer to this as *shaping*.

To be able to practise something and become an expert, in other words, we need to know what to practise. We need to specify the behaviour we wish to develop in order to ensure that we are making progress. It is hard to know how to practise being driven, showing confidence or having the right perspective on relationships, which makes it hard to get better at these things. In order to develop leaders into even better leaders, we need to pinpoint the behaviour that being a better leader involves.

The same argument can be applied with regard to strategy. One common phenomenon in organizations is that strategy is something reserved for the very top of the organization. Strategy is linked to a specific level in the organization. It is therefore assumed that all managers at a certain senior level are skilled strategists. Of course, this is not always the case. Many managers have been promoted because they delivered, rolled up their sleeves and worked hard in purely operational terms. They have not had the opportunity to put 10,000 hours into behaviours that could be sorted under the umbrella 'strategic thinking'. In other words, they cannot be masterful in this domain. Unfortunately, this can have devastating consequences for the organization.

Many of those who practise learning to distinguish between results, labels and behaviour report having difficulties at first. It requires practice. Probably 10,000 hours to get really good. But once we have started to understand and have embraced looking at the world from a behavioural perspective, it is a really useful tool for understanding organizations and we find it hard to go back to the old way of looking at the world, just as it feels strange to go back to watching a black-and-white television. A former colleague of mine could barely say that this fellow 'is' this way or that woman 'is' the other way for a period of time. She had adopted a behavioural focus. She noted that it was much more clear to talk about what someone 'does' than what someone 'is'. She no longer wanted to describe how people 'were,' but what they 'did'. In some senses it is like reading: once you have learned it, it is difficult to unlearn. Just try for yourselves not to read the combined letters in front of you right now.

Once we have learned this, it becomes easier both for us and for others to understand what we mean. That's why it is so important to learn to identify behaviour. People who 'do' can improve their behaviour. People who 'are' may not know what and how to change.

Pinpointing behaviour

Behaviour is something clearly defined. When learning theorists attempt to describe behaviour in specific terms, they usually talk about *pinpointing* behaviour. To know how well we are performing, we need to be clear about what behaviour is and is not, and what performance is and is not. We need a clear definition to be able to measure the behaviour. If we cannot measure it, nor can we see how and whether we are influencing it.

There are several ways to pinpoint a behaviour with sufficient precision that we are able to work with it. One way is to use the acronym AMOR. A well-defined behaviour should be:

- *Active.* Behaviour is about activity. The psychologist Ogden Lindsley coined the concept of a 'dead man test' as a litmus test to show whether behaviour was active.[7] Everything that a dead person can do is not active enough to be behaviour.

- *Measurable.* It should be possible to measure the behaviour that is performed, either by counting the number of times (frequency) or by in some way measuring the quality (topography).

- *Observable.* It should be possible to observe the behaviour. As a rule of thumb, we can say that it should be possible to capture the behaviour on film.
- *Reliable.* Two or more people observing the behaviour should agree on which specific behaviour it is, on whether they can observe it, how many times it is performed, that it is active, and arrive at the same result.

Organizations rarely measure behaviour, precisely because it is difficult to pinpoint. Without a framework and practice, we may not know how to translate, for example, the label 'driven' into pinpointed AMOR behaviours. A first step to take to learn how to translate labels into behaviour is to list specific things that a person does that show that they are driven. Two behaviours that could serve as proof that someone is driven could be as follows:

- Takes independent initiatives to solve existing problems when there is time to spare.
- Always delivers high-quality reports at least 24 hours before the deadline.

Some organizations are suspicious of measurement. This could be due, among other reasons, to people's learning history and to past experiences with control and punitive cultures. It is sometimes considered to be both superficial and ugly. But when we do not measure, we miss out on the opportunities to naturally reinforce good behaviour that become clear when we do measure. Measurement and a focus on behaviour open up opportunities to create a high-performance culture that is not based on control of and follow-up on details, but instead on celebrating victories and spreading best practices based on learning. Reinforcing feedback can build commitment and help build a culture of adaptation and innovation.

Another common difficulty I encounter when people start working with behaviour is that they identify so-called 'non-behaviour'. 'Not arriving at meetings on time' is a common non-behaviour. 'Not contributing enough new suggestions' is another. Non-behaviour results in an incorrect and negative focus. It is better to reformulate it into something positive – arriving at meetings on time. The vast majority of people find it more enjoyable to celebrate victories than to force themselves above a minimum threshold – even if gaining those victories requires more personal effort.

But arriving on time is not sufficiently specific. We need to be clearer and more concrete. Arriving at meetings on time could be broken down to the next level as follows: 'Showing up to management team meetings on Monday mornings at least two minutes before the scheduled start'. That is more precise, and it has a higher instructional value. The more precise we are, the easier it is to influence and measure.

Behaviour that is correctly pinpointed should be active, measurable, observable and reliable. The less scope there is for interpretation as to what the behaviour looks like, the easier it is for the person who is to perform the behaviour to understand, and the easier it is to determine when it has been done, so that we can celebrate the victory.

Notes

1 E F Schumacher, *The Radical Humanist*, 1973, 37 (5), 22
2 B F Skinner (1969) *Contingencies of Reinforcement*, Meredith Corporation, Des Moines
3 B F Skinner (1969) *Contingencies of Reinforcement*, Meredith Corporation, Des Moines
4 M Sundel and S Sundel (1999) *Behavior Change in the Human Services: An introduction to principles and applications*, 4th edn, SAGE, Thousand Oaks
5 See, eg, A Bianco and P Moore, Xerox: The downfall, Bloomberg, 5 March 2001, www.bloomberg.com/news/articles/2001-03-04/xerox-the-downfall (archived at https://perma.cc/6Q3R-DJTT); R M Habib and R Yazdanifard. The underlying reasons behind Xerox's strategic management failures and possible remedies that could have been implemented, *International Journal of Management, Accounting and Economics*, 2017, 4 (8), 796–810
6 K Anders Ericsson, R Krampe and C Tesch-Romer. The role of deliberate practice in the acquisition of expert performance, *Psychological Review*, 1993, 100, 363–406; A Ericsson, M Prietula and E Cokely, The making of an expert, *Harvard Business Review*, 2007, https://hbr.org/2007/07/the-making-of-an-expert (archived at https://perma.cc/MDZ3-WFZZ)
7 See, e.g., O R Lindsley. From technical jargon to plain English for application, *Journal of Applied Behavior Analysis*, 1991, 24, 449–58

08

Activators

The igniting spark

Behaviour is the answer to the question: What does someone do? The *activator* is the answer to the question: What happened before the behaviour, what ignited the behaviour? The activator is the second component in the context in which the behaviour occurs.

How many times have you thought: 'I thought we agreed that this had to be done – why is nothing happening?' The reason that nothing is being done is easy to understand when we apply the principles that govern behaviour.

As mentioned, human behaviour is affected to a large extent by 'here and now' situations. No behaviour occurs in a vacuum. Behaviour is always a reaction, a response to something. Learning theorists use a number of different terms for this 'something'. It can be called a stimulus, a signal, an activator, a precursor or an antecedent. In this book I will use the term *activators*, as this is most commonly used when learning theory is applied to organizations.

Different types of activators

There are different types of activators. Behaviour can be activated by instructions, external events, someone asking something, someone saying hello to you, the telephone ringing, the clock striking 12, the boss walking into the room or having a targets document sent to you. These could be called external activators. Activators can also be internal, for instance things like anxiety, hunger, thirst and anger, or thoughts, a willingness to learn, ideas, and fancies.

There are new and different activators in each situation. Common intentional activators in organizations are strategies, goals, job descriptions and process descriptions. In addition, there are also laws and regulations whose purpose is to control behaviour. Direct prompts and orders are also activators.

Activators are around us at all times. We are aware of many of them and unaware of many others. The email that pops up in the lower right-hand corner of our computer screen can be an activator to make us open it. Someone smiling can be an activator to say hello in the corridor or out on the street. A project launch can be an activator for the organization to focus attention on a specific issue. The thought of the deadline approaching can activate someone to work a few hours extra that night. A goal that is set and communicated in an organization regarding customer satisfaction, number of realized change projects, etc, can also have the purpose of activating different behaviours.

Activators that are intentionally created are supposed to help employees prioritize their working day. The more clearly we are able to identify and use these activators, the better our chances, of course, of influencing our employees' behaviour and ensuring smooth business operations. If we want to achieve certain goals, we need to deliver activators that are clear and unambiguous, have a high instructional value and target the specific behaviour we want to influence.

Goals as activators

One of the most common activators in an organization is different types of goals. The purpose of the goals is largely to direct the organization's behaviour. *Management by objectives* or corporate performance management, in its widest sense, is commonly used in strategy realization. Realizing strategy is ultimately about achieving the goals we have set, no matter what types of goals they are.

It is important to have a picture of what goals are, the different types of goals that exist, and how we differentiate between different types of goals in order to get better at achieving them.

Goals can be defined in many different ways. A simple definition is this:

The result we wish to achieve.

There are proven positive correlations between management by objectives and actual performance. The purpose of goals is to try to influence people to perform. The conviction that goals make employees perform better by making them more motivated to do a good job is widespread in strategic and organizational research circles.

Almost all organizations have goals of some type. Goals can be a powerful tool for helping the members of the organization set priorities. By setting goals, we want to convey what needs to be prioritized – activate certain behaviour. And yet many organizations' goal formulation is often done as a formal annual exercise that has little to do with daily operations. In that sense, the formulated goals typically disregard important employee behaviour and therefore their usefulness in helping employees set priorities by pointing in a clear direction is reduced.

What we call goal and strategy formulation too often involves a management team revising last year's target levels and making minor adjustments because this is required and expected of them 'from above'. The purpose of goal and strategy formulation is to set a direction and to create the conditions for success. Unfortunately, this perspective is lacking in many organizations. Adopting this perspective, we can say in a somewhat caustic manner that strategizing is, too often, rarely particularly strategic.

Setting, evaluating and updating goals should be ongoing activities, so that the goals are adapted to prevailing circumstances in terms of content, the number of goals, target levels and time horizon. If an organization is to avoid having too short-term an orientation in its actions, long-term goals must also be set.

Goals should be clearly formulated in order to be effective and efficient as activators. Just like behaviour, goals should be measurable, observable and reliable to have an impact. For the person who is to achieve the goal, it is also important to understand the timeliness of when something should be achieved. Research can tell us a lot about how to set goals with high instructional value that helps employees perform better. Some common advice includes the following:

- *Measurable.* When we set a goal, we want to be sure that we have the opportunity to achieve it. To be able to evaluate whether a goal is achieved or not, it is important for the goal to be measurable.

- *Observable.* If we are to be in agreement and be precise, it is important to be able to determine objectively whether a goal has been achieved or not. We need to be able to see whether a goal has been achieved.

- *Reliable.* Two or more people should be able to agree whether the goal has been achieved. Goals that are unclear are difficult to understand, scatter people's focus and make it hard to see the purpose. Goals with an unclear endpoint make members of the organization unsure and less motivated to work towards the goals.

- *Timely.* In organizations there are often deadlines. Some tasks and thus behaviours must be done before a certain point in time or there will be consequences. A timeframe for goals makes them clearer as the effort that is needed to achieve them is easier to comprehend. In addition, goals that are changed too often create confusion about what is most important.

> The higher the instructional value of a goal – the more clearly it is described – the better the chances that an employee's energy will be directed towards the goal.

Goals at different levels

Max Weber, one of the pioneers of organizational research and known for his work on bureaucracy, talks about the *objective–means hierarchy*. The core idea of objective hierarchies is that a goal at a given level is able, in itself, to contribute to the achievement of a goal at a higher level (see Figure 8.1). Goals at various levels should be interconnected, all the way from the vision down to individuals' behaviours. In that way, individuals see their contribution to an overarching purpose.

There should be a clear and unambiguous connection between goals at different levels. Different situations and contexts require different types of goals. Goals at different levels must be interconnected in one way or another. This is sometimes referred to as goal congruence or alignment. These connections, however, need not be mathematically correct. There is not always a numerical logic between goals on different levels. For instance, if a main objective for a given year is to increase sales by 13 per cent, an example of a goal might be for employees in the sales department to spend a certain amount of their time getting in touch with new customers. Behavioural goals in support of that goal could include calling and talking to at least five new customers a week. There is a clear logical connection and drive in the 'correct' direction, without distributing the 13 per cent of increased sales on the different sales teams. This, of course, relates to the KBI and KRI discussion.

FIGURE 8.1   Objective–means hierarchies

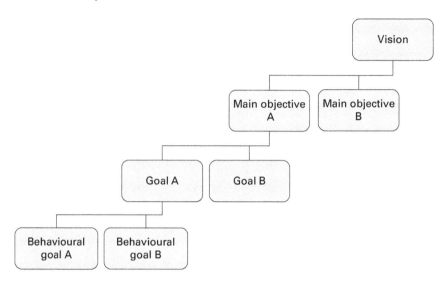

The latter, focusing on our share of the 13 per cent, would be to focus on a lagging indicator (KRI) which we can only influence indirectly, instead of focusing on a leading indicator: behaviour.

Let's have a look at a company that is investing in work environment and safety that I supported a few years back. The vision was to have accident-free workplaces and the idea was that employees should take the responsibility for it. One main objective therefore was to reduce the number of workplace accidents from 6.5 per million hours worked to 1.2. This change was to be enabled over a period of three years. This main objective needed to be made concrete and tied into daily operations, and that meant breaking it down into goals. In this case fewer actual accidents per month in the workplace was one example of a goal. Then it came down to behaviour. The question we asked was, what workplace behaviour should be reinforced and/or weakened, respectively, in order for the company to hit the goal of 1.2 in three years? What active, measurable, observable and reliable behaviour leads to a reduced number of accidents?

A significant portion of the accidents in this case were eye injuries that could be avoided if employees wore protective goggles. Putting on protective goggles as soon as you walked into the workplace was therefore an initial behavioural goal that was active, measurable, observable and reliable. For the managers, behaviours included asking all of their employees to share their ideas on how to improve safety management, do safety rounds and provide feedback and show appreciation when safety regulations were followed, and safety goals were met. To make sure that this and other safety-related behaviour managed over time was performed, we used rewards to reinforce the right behaviours.

One key success factor in this case was an alignment of goals. It was clear for everyone how goals on different levels connected, how each and every employee contributed to one part of the organization's vision.

Unfortunately, it is uncommon for organizations to actually formulate behavioural goals that are broken from a vision, and so on. Far too often, goals on one level conflict with goals on another level – below or above. This relates to the previous statement that measuring the same 'thing', or factor, on different levels is important if we want to perform and succeed over time.

The Swedish poet Nils Ferlin describes the difficulties with goals and hierarchical levels well in his 1933 poem *Infall (notion)*. In his poem he elegantly points to the problem of goal hierarchies and misalignment using the analogy of a multi-storey building. While the person on the first floor wants to sleep, he realizes that his ceiling is another person's floor. And this person on the second floor wants to dance.

Having conflicting goals within an organization, in Ferlin's case sleeping and dancing, makes it difficult to achieve them. Behavioural psychology makes use of the term *incompatible behaviour*. Different actions that are impossible to perform simultaneously. We cannot do a handstand and clap our hands at the same time. The same reasoning applies to goals in an organization. Many organizations have goals that are incompatible with each other, as they require incompatible behaviours.

But we don't need to turn to poetry to find striking examples. One of the most common goals seen in publicly listed companies is 'profitable growth'. This goal is not really one goal but two goals in one, namely increased profitability and increased growth. They also require incompatible behaviours – at least to some extent. The easiest way to increase our profitability is to only sell what is most profitable. The most common way to grow is to sell things that are not profitable as well, to 'buy market share'. In somewhat exaggerated terms, and from a behavioural perspective, profitability is about saying no to orders while growth is about saying yes, which are of course diametrically opposed behaviours.

The purpose of goals is to focus efforts in an organization. Goals in organizations, used properly, function as activators for different work-related behaviour.

Although we sometimes speak as if organizations have goals, we need to remember that the organization 'does nothing'. It is the employees in the organization who perform behaviour. It is the behaviour that causes organizations to achieve their goals. Every goal that is set, no matter on what level, should therefore be pinpointed by specifying the behaviour needed to achieve the goals, and which individuals are responsible for which goals. From this perspective, goals can be seen as a 'contract' between a person at a certain organizational level and someone at the level below. To establish a contract, all parties need to agree on what terms and conditions apply. Here again, we can see that participation in formulating goals is an important factor.

Participation in goal formulation

Researchers, myself included, suggest that an organization stands a better chance of creating a shared feeling for the goals, and thus a better chance of achieving them, if members of the organization are involved in formulating the goals. If so, strategic planning and strategic execution should be more closely linked than is generally the case. Business icon Jan Carlzon said this during his time at SAS: 'Anyone who does not have access to information cannot take responsibility. Anyone who does have access to information cannot help but take responsibility.'[1] In order for everyone to feel that they own a goal and to be prepared to work for it, the people responsible for delivering should have been participating in setting the goals.

In many organizations, those who set the goals assume that all employees are aware of goals, strategies, visions and policies, and of what is needed to get there. Yet most organizations have so many different kinds of goals, strategies, visions and policies, which in many cases are contradictory and decoupled from the individual employee's daily work, that this is rarely the case. Two-way communication about goals and means increases our chances of getting to where we want to go.

Individual goals that are related to the organization's overall goals are often perceived as being more reinforcing. In other words, the employee who performs the behaviour aimed at achieving a goal should be involved in the goal formulation process. Generally speaking, employees want to know how their work is related to the overall strategy. Achieving goals and having a sense that we are performing has a positive effect on our nervous system. If organizations know what behaviour leads to what results, the organization and the individual employee can form a shared picture of where they are headed, and of how to behave in order to get there.

Humans are herd animals. It is built into our brains. We want to know that we are doing a good job. We get information about our performance through what learning theorists refer to as *consequences*. We discuss this further in the following chapter.

Note

1 J Carlzon (1985) *Riv pyramiderna*, Bonnier Pocket, Stockholm

09

Consequences

No feedback is also feedback

Consequences are the third component in the behavioural context. The consequences that behaviour leads to are crucial with regard to the perpetuation of the behaviour. Understanding the impact of consequences is therefore key if we are to create a high-performing and successful organization. As used in behavioural psychology, consequences mean something a little different from how we use the term in everyday speech.

Whatever occurs as a result of certain behaviour and influences the likelihood that the behaviour will be used in the future is a consequence in the sense in which the term is used in behavioural psychology. In other words, not all 'consequences' are consequences according to behavioural psychology.

Imagine walking into an ordinary classroom or meeting room at a conference or training centre. You see a senior executive standing at the whiteboard – the vice president of a listed company – in shirt, tie and dark trousers, doing a drawing on the board. He looks a bit uncertain. At the same time that you walk in, you see that he has just finished drawing a flower on the board. Once he finishes the flower, everyone else in the room, also senior executives, starts to applaud and laugh.

This is a description of the final scene in a 'clicker exercise'. I like to use clicker exercises when I work with leaders to help them understand what a consequence is and why it is crucial to understand how consequences work in order to influence behaviour and thus to realize strategy.

A clicker exercise works as follows: One participant leaves the room. The task of the others in the room is to agree on what the person should do. In the example above, it was to draw a flower on the board. When the person walks in, the group has decided what that person is to do. Nobody is allowed to say anything. The only means of control is a little clicker that the 'control person' uses. A clicker in this case was a little plastic item that makes a loud clicking sound when you press it; this device is sometimes used in a dog training setting. The test subject is told that a 'click' means 'correct' or 'good'. When the test subject's behaviour is perceived to be moving in 'the right direction', the control person uses the clicker. The more actively the test subject is moving in the right direction, the more clicks he gets. The exercise shows that the consequences of a behaviour are crucial if we wish to have the behaviour repeated and for there to be a motivation.

So, what is actually going on when the click sounds? The click is a way of providing feedback on performance. It is a consequence delivered for 'correctly' performed behaviour. But what does this entail and what is the actual purpose of such a consequence?

The click teaches the person who has performed the behaviour that it was the 'right' behaviour. We teach the person that what he/she just did, i.e. walk to the board, pick up a pen and draw a flower, was correct. One definition of learning is that it is a relatively permanent change in behaviour arising as a result of a person's interaction with the environment. The interaction with the environment in this case was the click that the test subject received.

This simple experiment shows that the person performing the behaviour does not need to understand or be aware of any emotion. The consequences – the clicking – still makes him behave correctly. The clicking is a simple type of feedback that *nudges* the test subject toward the right behaviour. A nod of the head, a pat on the shoulder, praise, etc, are the equivalent of clicks in day-to-day work.

When behaviour has been learned, its consequences are critical to whether it will continue to be engaged in or if it will be extinguished. Behaviour is controlled in two ways. It is either controlled by external factors, which can include, for example, predetermined rules, laws and prompts. This is called *rule-governed behaviour*. Behaviour that is only controlled by these predetermined instructions will still be opted out of by the individual if it does not rapidly lead to positive consequences. It is common to rely on rule governance in traditional organizations (cf. machines) where carefully crafted work descriptions and action plans are used to govern the business.

Behaviour that is to have a chance of enduring in the long run needs to give the individual positive and expected consequences – 'clicks'. Behaviour that is controlled by conscious or unconscious 'clicks' is, as noted earlier, called *contingency-shaped behaviour*. Drawing a flower on the board was an example of contingency-shaped behaviour. On the other hand, if the person had simply been told to draw a flower on the board and had done so, this would have been an example of rule-governed behaviour. Rule govern-ance does work, but only once or twice, unless the behaviour is rapidly given reinforcing consequences. Rule governance is a gateway to new behaviour, but it is not enough to make the behaviour sustained.

> If behaviour does persist over the long run, this is due to its consequences. Behaviour is sifted out by its consequences by a process of natural selection. If the behaviour I performed had the desired effect, this increases the likelihood that I will use the behaviour the next time I am in a similar situation.

What drives behaviour?

If an organization is to achieve its goals, employees need to behave in a way that is conducive to goal achievement – in line with the strategy. This is what leadership, management and governance are about: getting everyone to contribute to the overall goal, getting all employees to do 'the right thing' and to want to do 'the right thing'.

Briefly put, management is about influencing what people do. It's about influencing behaviour. So, what is it that affects people's behaviour? Why do we behave the way we do?

I usually ask employees in the organizations or management teams I work with why people perform certain behaviours. Common conceptions are that something that occurs before a certain behaviour is what triggers it, that the personality controls what behaviour we perform, or that a person's values determine the behaviour they use. There is something to these answers, but the most correct answer is that we choose our behaviour based on what happened just after we behaved similarly in a similar situation. If we want to understand why someone acts the way they do, we need to look at what happens after the behaviour. If the headache tablet helps, this increases the likelihood that I will take one next time I have a headache too. Behaviour that leads to outcomes I like, relate to or anticipate, becomes last-ing. We sometimes describe this as the *function* of a behaviour.

A common belief is that values and emotions govern behaviour. There is much to indicate that the opposite is the case. In other words, behaviour controls emotions and values. American scientist Paul Ekman (on whose findings the TV series *Lie To Me* is built) and other modern psychologists such Amy Cuddy argue that we create our values and experience emotions based on the behaviour we perform. This is contrary to what is generally believed. The behaviour we perform can affect both the values and emotions we have and experience. To exemplify, you can start feeling a bit happy just by smiling. By gritting your teeth and making a fist, you can feel your heart rate increase and feel yourself getting a little angry. Behaving in a certain way can have physiological effects. What we do, our behaviour, impacts on the different hormones and neurotransmitters, such as adrenaline and dopamine, that our body produces. And therefore, to behave a certain way makes us feel a certain way.

Consequences and natural selection

Charles Darwin formulated his theory of natural selection more than 150 years ago. He claimed that the species that best adapts to its environment is the species that survives. The species that adapts and fills a role in its surroundings, such as the ecosystem, has a greater chance of survival. This process is constantly ongoing, and this is the way nature evolves. Evolution does not require awareness. Whether we like it or not, nature evolves. In a similar vein, people also adjust their behaviour to the changed situation they find themselves in. And, just like evolution, awareness is not a prerequisite. Sometimes we are aware of why we change behaviours, sometimes we are not.

We choose the products and services that are good, while the products that don't serve a purpose, or whose quality is too low, disappear. What we get is a new environment, a new market. The person who best adapts to their environment, to the market, to the outside world, will survive. The keyword here is adaptation. From a learning perspective, adaptation is no more than the ability to learn and relearn; a relatively permanent change of a person's behaviour repertoire; new behaviours that better fit the changed environment.

People's behaviour is governed by the consequences thereof. The same argument that Darwin had about the survival of the species applies to behaviour in an organization, and to an open market as well. We only know after launching a product on the market whether it worked or not. That which does not work is accorded lower priority by customers and is taken off the market. We humans opt out of the types of behaviour that do not work – sometimes consciously and sometimes unconsciously. Our whole nature is designed to use what works and to reject what doesn't work.

I mentioned earlier I would return to the saying 'What gets measured gets done', as this is not entirely true. If the result of the measurement is not provided to the person who performed the behaviour as feedback – consequence – then the likelihood of it being performed in the future will not go up. To be more scientifically sound, the expression should be 'what gets fed back gets done'. Feedback with information that helps us learn and develop presupposes some type of measurement or recording of something, which could account for the saying.

> In learning theory, we talk about behaviour being maintained or extinguished. Maintaining means that a behaviour is given enough reinforcement – and has a function – and therefore endures. Extinguishing means that the behaviour is not reinforced, that it does not serve any function, and that it therefore diminishes and eventually ceases to be used.

If we want to influence people to behave in such a way that the organization's strategy can be realized, the right behaviours need to become functional among the employees. They need to be reinforced. In theory this is simple, but in practice things are more difficult.

Consequences from a behavioural standpoint

Because consequences are what determine whether a behaviour will be used in the future, it is important to know how different types of consequences influence behaviour. There are four different types of consequences that a behaviour may have:

- *Positive reinforcement* is when we get something we want. This could be praise, winning the lottery, recognition, access to information, a feeling of having done something good, a pat on the back, a glance, attention, a smile or something else that inclines us to perform the behaviour in the future.

- *Negative reinforcement* is when we escape or evade something unpleasant. The unpleasantness may involve getting yelled at, bad publicity, headaches, not having to feel ashamed, not having to participate in an organizational change we do not want to see happen, fear, or something else that makes us behave in a certain way in the future in order to 'escape'.

- *Extinction* is when we do not get something we were expecting – both consciously and unconsciously. We don't get a pay raise or praise for our good ideas. We don't get the appreciation we expected for the effort we are putting in – no one cares, no one asks, no one shows interest or no one 'sees you'.

- *Punishment* is when we are subjected to something that we do not like – something aversive. This could be having to part with something we do not want to part with, e.g. money in the form of a fine, or getting something we did not want, such as a sneer or even a beating, as a result of our behaviour. Punishment makes us less inclined to perform a certain behaviour in the future.

Positive reinforcement and negative reinforcement increase the likelihood that a behaviour will be repeated in the future. Extinction and punishment weaken the behaviour and reduce the likelihood that the behaviour will be repeated. If we want to increase a certain behaviour (a deficit behaviour) in an employee or group in our organization, we need to reinforce that behaviour. We need to ensure that the behaviour pays off. There are no other ways to increase the behaviour.

If we want to get our employees to come up with new ideas, we need to reinforce the 'come up with new ideas' behaviour. Positive reinforcement in this case could take the form of encouragement, official recognition, a link between the number of new ideas contributed and some type of bonus or perk, or something else perceived as positive.

If we want to reduce a behaviour (an excess behaviour), the tools at our disposal are to either extinguish the behaviour basically by ignoring it, or to punish it. By ensuring that employees either lose something they want, get something they don't want or do not receive some type of reinforcement for their behaviour they want or expect, we can reduce the likelihood that the behaviour will be repeated.

In the long term, punishment is highly ineffective if we are to reduce a given behaviour. Research shows that punishment only works if it is immediate, severely *aversive* and happens every time the behaviour is performed. In practice, very few punishments have these attributes. Because a punishment must be immediate, this means the person who is to be punished needs to be caught in the act. Indeed, when the cat's away, the mice will play. What usually happens is that the person redoubles their efforts not to be caught in the act, rather than change their behaviour.

Organizations that are successful at achieving their goals reinforce behaviours that yield financial, quality-related and other positive results. They devote time to increasing positive behaviour such as keeping promises, coming up with new ideas, performing tasks thoroughly, supporting colleagues and generally behaving as is expected in a professional manner. An efficient way to drive behaviour and organizational results is to reinforce behaviour we want to see more of, not punish behaviour we want to less of.

Consequences and feedback

Feedback, from a behavioural perspective, is the collective name for positive reinforcement, negative reinforcement and punishment delivered as a consequence of the behaviour, that is to say, every kind of feedback a person gets. Extinction can be regarded as a lack of expected feedback.

In most organizations, employees would definitely like to make proposals regarding improvements, cost cutting or a new innovative business concept, but the research shows that employees who come up with new ideas rarely receive any kind of response/reinforcement. No consequence is also a 'consequence'. No feedback is thus also feedback.

People want to know whether they are doing a good job or not. We want to know how others perceive our performance. Feedback, even hard, corrective feedback, can be perceived as reinforcing if it is given correctly. Feedback does not have to take the form of either praise or blame – it can be much more implicit than that. Looking at things, being interested, asking questions, making suggestions for how to do something differently, showing numbers, looking at graphs or charts – all this can also be reinforcing.

By giving positive feedback 'openly' we can affect the behaviour of an entire group. This can be referred to as *vicarious reinforcement*. Someone else receives positive feedback, and that reinforces behaviour among those who witness the feedback. If others see that someone is given reinforcement for a certain of behaviour, this increases the likelihood that they will 'mimic' and perform the same behaviour. Similarly, there is *vicarious punishment*. The idea behind putting a punishment on display is to discourage others from engaging in the same behaviour. Behaviour that people refrain from performing due to possible punishments is usually said to be negatively reinforced. As noted, however, punishment is an ineffective form of feedback, and to avoid creating a culture built on terror, corrective feedback should as often as possible be given individually.

Let's say that a salesman takes the initiative to present his sales figures for last week to the sales manager and is then praised for his initiative. The other salespeople see the interest shown by the manager, and are reinforced, resulting in the behaviour of showing their sales figures to the manager due to the salesman's initiative.

When giving feedback, it is important to ensure that the recipient understands why you're giving a certain type of feedback and what behaviour and which result you are referring to. As noted earlier, performance is defined as the behaviour and its impact on an organizational result. Performance feedback thus needs to include both a behaviour and a result or long-term organizational consequence – both a key behaviour indicator (KBI) and a key result indicator (KBI). For instance, 'When you submit your reports well before the deadline, this helps Carl's group by giving them time both to do a little extra work with the client and deliver the next day.' Differentiating between behaviour and results, and describing the change we want to see, as well as what results we want to achieve, is a powerful way of communicating feedback.

Positive and corrective feedback

Another piece of advice is not to give mixed positive and corrective feedback at the same time. That reduces the instructional value of the feedback and makes it hard for the recipient to understand what behaviour we are referring to and how they can improve.

I had a manager who always said: 'I think this is good, but...' when she gave feedback. It didn't matter what it was about. There was always a 'but' and then something negative coupled with the positive. Every time she praised me, I waited for the 'but' and immediately started wondering what I had done wrong this time. The negative feedback overshadowed the positive feedback because of that little word – 'but' – and what came after. Because the feedback was seasoned with a 'but', all feedback from that manager ended up being a kind of punishment.

Unfortunately, this phenomenon is so common that there is a name for it: 'the sandwich method'. Something good, something bad, then something good again. It is important for feedback to be, and to be perceived as, sincere. When mixing good and bad feedback, it becomes more difficult for the individual receiving it to sense the sincerity.

To be sincere, a good tip is to stick to the facts. If our feedback is not supported by facts of some kind, if it does not tally with some type of measurement or evidence, and if there is room for interpretation, it should be handled with care. That is why active, measurable, observable and reliable behaviour is a truly good starting point.

We need to know our business, our colleagues and our organization if we are to give sincere feedback that refers to a specific behaviour, and thereby influence performance. Data can be an aid in this regard. 'Management by walking around' is an expression for another way to create opportunities to provide reinforcement. The expression originated at Hewlett-Packard in the 1970s and the idea was for managers to walk around aimlessly, talk to their employees and see how the company was doing in general, and that way get to know their business. The concept was then popularized in 1982 by the then McKinsey consultants Tom Peters and Robert Waterman in their book *In Search of Excellence*.[1] In the book, they emphasize that a management team that is out in the business and showing their interest is a success factor for organizations. Behavioural psychology would account for this success factor by noting that management reinforces the employees' work-related behaviour by showing interest.

A business leader I work with came to me with a will to improve and a story that illustrates the importance of knowing your employees if you want to influence behaviour and realize strategy. In his endeavour to do what was best, he completely failed because he did not understand his employees properly. The company he led had just landed one of its biggest deals ever. It was such a huge deal that it was impossible to say no, even though they actually didn't have the time to deliver. The manager asked everyone to help out. All the employees worked furiously for two weeks and just barely managed to pull off the delivery. The manager felt that the employees had worked so hard that they deserved a reward for their efforts. So, he served cake to all the employees and gave each of them a t-shirt with the company logo. In his mind, this was an intended reward. However, it did not work as a reinforcement – instead, it was perceived as a slap in the face after the two weeks of very hard work. Since we addressed it, we can all laugh at the situation today.

Everyday events can serve as positive reinforcement or negative reinforcement, or can serve as extinction or punishment, even though no one set out to deliberately modify behaviour in this way. Securing a good price at the negotiating table on the strength of a winning argument can probably act as positive reinforcement, so that the behaviour of using 'the winning argument' will be used again.

When a suggestion for improvement is submitted to a management team that does not believe it has the time to evaluate it, the person making the suggestion will not get a response. In the long run, not getting what we are expecting leads to a behaviour being *extinguished*. As mentioned, no feedback is also a form of feedback.

The same consequence may have a different function when experienced by different people. Being sneered at by someone after praising the manager's suggestion to hold a meeting can have a variety of reinforcing effects. It can serve both as *positive reinforcement* and as a *punishment*. Which one it ends up being depends on how I perceive the sneer. If it comes from someone I respect and like, it probably works as a punishment, and I will be less inclined to praise the manager at the next meeting. If the sneer was made by someone who frequently sneers and who I do not think is particularly good at their job, it can serve as reinforcement and motivate me to repeat my behaviour of praising the manager in the future. Different circumstances can determine if something is perceived as being reinforcing or weakening.

Reinforcement and punishment: Carrot and stick?

Reinforcement and punishment are easily associated with reward and punishment – as symbolized in the popular analogy of the carrot and the stick. This is not entirely correct.

It is the function and influence on behaviour of a phenomenon that determines whether the consequence of it should be called a reinforcement, a punishment or something else. A reward is not the same thing as positive reinforcement if it does not influence the behaviour in a positive way or increase the likelihood for the behaviour – or at least maintain it. Punishment as used in everyday language is not punishment from a learning perspective unless it causes the behaviour to cease at once – at least temporarily.

Rewards and punishment in everyday language are also based on the perspective of the person who administers the reward or punishment – what the leader or manager in the organization believes is a reward or punishment. What serves as punishment, what extinguishes behaviour, and what serves as positive reinforcement and negative reinforcement can only be determined by recording the effect it had on the behaviour. This is determined by the recipient's behaviour – nothing else.

Many leaders who have learned a smattering of behaviour analysis say that they are practising giving positive reinforcement. The problem is that as a manager we cannot determine what is positive reinforcement before we have seen whether the behaviour we want to increase is actually increasing. We can give a reward or positive feedback and hope that we have delivered a consequence that will positively reinforce the behaviour, but we cannot be sure until we see whether the behaviour has increased in frequency or improved in topography.

The effect of 'being tough'

We sometimes read about 'tough' managers, who are presented as saviours when they come into an organization and produce results quickly. A manager who is tough mainly reduces behaviours that are not considered to be good for the business in one way or another – excess behaviour. When building a business for the long haul, it is important to reinforce deficit behaviour. In other words, just being 'tough' is far from enough if we want to develop a business over the long term. Sometimes a person who minimizes problems and solves crises is needed, but someone who has done that for a long time will find it difficult to replace their negatively reinforcing and punishing behaviour with reinforcing behaviour.

The reason that being 'tough' is relatively common in spite of the fact that it does not create businesses that are successful in the long term is that vigorous action brings about quick results. These quick results provide positive reinforcement to those who recruited the tough manager. They see the progress made due to the toughness of the manager, which diminishes any anxiety they may have had regarding employing the manager in question. They avoid having to deal with something unpleasant (their worries about the business) and their behaviour (recruiting a 'hardball manager') is therefore negatively reinforced. This means that the behaviour will endure. The rapid progress also serves as positive reinforcement for the manager himself, who sees the results of his tough approach.

The more remote consequences, i.e. the fact that employees generally become 'too' cautious because of a hardline leader, are easy to ignore here and now. Lehman Brothers had a notorious boss by the name of Dick Fuld. He was known on Wall Street as a really tough manager who you did not want to go toe to toe with. We will never know, but it is interesting to speculate about what would have happened at Lehman Brothers if they had had a manager who encouraged employees to question the state of affairs and the level of risk taken in the business. In other words, a leader's 'tough approach behaviour' can be destructive to the business in the long run.

As we will see later on in this book, immediate consequences are stronger than remote ones, which makes it common to employ a more short-term focus. If we want to build a business, a tough approach, no matter how positive the short-term results, is not the answer. Instead, working with positive reinforcement to increase the behaviour we want to see more of is good advice.

Another negative effect of the manager who uses a 'tough approach' is that the person who deals out punishment is a bad 'model'. People learn new behaviour by imitating others. What this leads to is that leaders who use a tough approach train other leaders to use a tough approach as well. This has the practical consequence that employees who have been subjected to punitive behaviour mimic this when they end up in similar situations. This, along with vicarious punishment, can create widespread passivity in the organization. Most people agree that it is important to have an organization in which we can speak freely, just as most managers want employees who take independent initiatives. A punitive climate with too many hardline managers clearly inhibits this.

To really get to grips with 'problem behaviour', it is not enough to simply weaken or punish the things that are bad. The things that reinforce undesirable behaviour need to be eliminated in order for the behaviour to cease. If there is a reinforcer of a problem behaviour present, the behaviour will continue. A constructive way of working with problem behaviour is therefore to identify substitute behaviour that makes it impossible to continue engaging in the problem behaviour. The substitute behaviour is then *incompatible* with the problem behaviour. By giving an employee a time-consuming and challenging task and then following up and providing feedback continuously, we make it harder for the employee to spend time 'hanging out by the coffee machine', or whatever excess behaviour we want to address.

Different types of reinforcers

By grouping reinforcers into a number of categories, we can form an understanding of what possible alternatives there are for working to influence a given behaviour. Six categories of reinforcers are usually mentioned:

1 *Social reinforcers:* Praise, a smile, a glance, a question that shows interest, raising the brow in surprise, a laugh or a pat on the back.

2 *Monetary reinforcers:* Salary, bonus, option programmes, gratuities or an extra week of holiday.

3 *Symbolic reinforcers:* Awards, certificates or diplomas for the innovator of the month, salesperson of the week, etc.

4 *Work-related reinforcers:* Promotions, new and exciting duties, being appointed to the management team or being given increased responsibility.

5 *Emotional reinforcers:* A feeling of being knowledgeable, of belonging to a group or organization, the feeling of a job well done, or pride, or 'creating' or building something together.

6 *Cognitive reinforcers:* An understanding of something, the knowledge or insight needed to do something in a certain way, to solve a difficult task, or to have an insight into a complicated relationship, to learn something.

We often use monetary means to reinforce behaviour in organizations. To some extent, symbolic reinforcers are also used systematically. The other types of reinforcers are often forgotten and, in many cases, underutilized. More and more research indicates that salary is only seen as a *hygiene factor*. If the salary is too low, employees get annoyed at it, but being paid a little bit more rarely motivates them to perform a little bit better. Often, the social, emotional, work-related and cognitive reinforcers are more strongly correlated with actual performance. Getting on well with our colleagues, having fun, feeling that we are good at what we do and that we are developing is what has the greatest effect on whether we 'go the extra mile' or not. These reinforcers are all characterized by the fact that they occur right after the performed behaviour and are rarely 'externally imposed'. They come from within the individual. It has little to do with a bit more in the bank at the end of the month.

The token economy is a way of systematizing reinforcers that are not monetary in nature. Reinforcers in the token economy are tokens or symbols that are handed out immediately following desirable behaviour. They are not reinforcers in themselves. The tokens can be exchanged for actual reinforcers at a later stage. In practice I have used a wide variety of tokens in a wide variety of projects: coins, dots, tennis balls, styrofoam balls in tubes, a plastic aeroplane hanging on a clothesline, a to-do list to tick off and pictures indicating progress on a board. In sales organizations, lines on a board to symbolize orders are a common way of working with tokens. Once a salesperson has notched a certain number of lines, these can be traded in for something that has greater value for that person. Of course, what one person values is individual.

One demographic study after the other shows that coming generations are typically even more driven by individual development, freedom and values than previous generations. Those who learn how to appeal to these values are likely to have a good opportunity to attract tomorrow's top-flight employees. In practice, this means that many large, traditional organizations that were able to offer a 'secure' position need to consider how they plan to attract and retain the employees of tomorrow, who value something that is harder to offer than a high salary, e.g., personal development and freedom, an organization that behaves in accordance with its values.

A common work-related reinforcer is Premack's principle, later also known as 'grandma's rule'.[2] David Premack was an American researcher and psychologist who demonstrated that behaviour considered enjoyable to perform can be used as a reinforcer for behaviour that is considered less enjoyable to perform. What this means is that we allow a less desirable task to be followed by one that is more desirable. What happens is that the first task, which is less desirable, becomes more desirable over time because it leads to other, more desirable tasks. What we are doing here is letting a subsequent behaviour be reinforced by a preceding one, for example by first doing homework and then playing computer games.

Making sure that figures tally, for example those in a budget, can be a tough job in terms of administrative effort. However, this is important for everyone who has a financial responsibility. Some managers I have worked with over the years have found budgeting, forecasting and financial administration boring and therefore delegate it to an assistant, or similar. In many cases the assistant may not enjoy the work either. However, both the manager and the assistant generally consider it fun to analyse the financials and to think about improvements. By having a person perform a less desirable task and letting that task lead to a desirable one, we are using the desirable task as a work-related positive reinforcer. One way to spark more interest in working with figures, in other words, could be to link the administrative effort involved in running the numbers for the budget with the opportunity to analyse the figures after they have been 'lined up'. Ask any accountant or business data analyst. It's rare that putting the numbers in the right place was the part of accountancy or data management that attracted them to the profession – it was probably the ability to understand the business when all the numbers are in the right place. Comprehension and the feeling of doing something meaningful can be cognitive reinforcers.

Reinforcing individually and collectively

It is beneficial to use reinforcement to influence entire groups. Group reinforcement is a way to make sure that several people are given reinforcement at the same time. An example of work-related group reinforcement is to let a group or unit take a field trip to a customer, supplier or other business to learn from them.

Such reinforcements are unfortunately rare. In contrast, a common phenomenon seen in organizations today is 'worker of the month', 'salesperson of the week', etc. This can be devastating. Creating one single winner means that everyone else is actually a loser. And sometimes the rules determining who the winner is are arbitrary, which creates dissatisfaction, unnecessary envy within the organization and lower performance. Organizations strive not to hire losers. So why work in a way that creates losers? There are various ways to make sure that more people can become winners.

An IT consultancy I worked with many years ago developed a digital 'praise board'. The board offered a systematic way for employees to show appreciation for their colleagues' achievements. The employees could acknowledge one another as being proficient in one or more areas of expertise. The goal was to create an incentive system that was centred around the employees' specific competences and not around finances, and to make it clear that several employees (preferably all of them) should be recognized as proficient in the domains where they were proficient. It also helped the engagement managers, working closest to the customers, to design the projects with the proper competence, with sometimes scarce niche competencies. The board also enabled greater cooperation across different teams in the organization, and new types of businesses built around horizontal teams, across departments. This had not been seen in the organization before. In fact, they had been struggling to break open different silos for a fairly long period of time.

This praising phenomenon is now also seen in social media platforms like LinkedIn that offer an opportunity to endorse the people in our network. The desired effect is for more people to feel that they are good at what they do and to want to continue developing.

Going back to the negative consequences of 'worker of the month' programmes, what we do when setting up such a programme is create a climate where it is not necessary to do our best in order to get attention or to be a winner. The winner may not even have to try very hard. Remember the sales office located next to the Swedish Tax Agency? It may simply be enough to just be better than everyone else in the organization, and if everyone else is far below my level of performance, what do I do?

Let's play around with the idea of lending footballer Leo Messi or basketballer LeBron James to a lower-division club. Do we want Messi and LeBron to be chosen as the man of the match, or do we want them to perform to the best of their ability? For me the answer is simple, as it probably is for most people. But if we are not aware of the principles that govern human behaviour and set up systems that build on them, it's easy to go astray even though we want to do the right thing.

Behaviour that is only reinforced by 'artificial' and external consequences, such as official appointments, diplomas, annual recognition and MVP awards, is more rarely reinforced than the behaviours that are reinforced internally, spontaneously and randomly (intermittently) by way of what are called *natural reinforcers*. Natural reinforcers, such as a sense of pride or that we learn, the manager's interest, a wink, a friendly word, or the feeling that we made a nice pass, are just as important if an organization is to perform. The more a behaviour is reinforced, the greater its chance of being repeated in the future. Relying on monetary reinforcers that are both less effective and more expensive than social, cognitive and work-related reinforcers, in my opinion, seems downright stupid.

> By using several different types of reinforcers and finding many ways to reinforce behaviour, we can identify better and more effective ways to achieve our goals and to create an organization in which the opportunity to achieve goals in itself acts as a reinforcer.

Analysing the impact of consequences

To understand how strong a certain consequence is, regardless of the type, we can perform what is called a *consequence analysis*, or sometimes a PICNIC analysis. When performing an impact assessment, we look at the consequences that are associated with a specific behaviour in order to judge which ones have an actual influence on the behaviour.

Consequences are perceived in different ways. By categorizing how they are perceived, we can understand which ones have the greatest impact. All consequences are perceived as either being *positive* or *negative*. They are also perceived as being *immediate* or *distant*. Finally, they are also perceived as being *certain* or *uncertain*. This suggests that consequences can be positive, immediate and certain (abbreviated PIC), negative, future and uncertain (NFU), positive, future and certain (PFC), and a number of other combinations.

The consequences that have the greatest impact on behaviour are those that are positive, immediate and certain (PIC) and those that are negative, immediate and certain (NIC).

Consequences are combined in various ways in daily life and we are controlled by them on a daily basis – both consciously and unconsciously. By looking at the example of 'driving fast', we can learn something about the effects of various consequences. Getting there faster is perceived as a positive consequence of driving fast. The feeling of getting there faster if I drive faster is *immediate*. Not only that, I also perceive it as being *certain* that I will arrive more quickly if I drive faster than if I drive slowly. This means that there is a cognitive reinforcement that is positive, immediate and certain (PIC). But driving fast can have several different consequences, such as being pulled over by the police for speeding. This is not the worst thing that can happen, but for most people the consequence is nonetheless negative. It's no fun paying a fine. Yet the risk of getting caught is relatively low and it's not something that happens right now, meaning that the consequences, although negative, are distant and uncertain (NFU).

People who are not used to reading through comprehensive decision-support documents have a hard time getting started on a thick report, even though they realize that there is a long-term benefit to doing so. A skilled reader, on the other hand, has an easier time of it. For a seasoned reader, the consequence of reading the report is positive, immediate and certain. Right away (immediate) when I start reading the report, I gain an understanding (positive) of the decision I'm facing and how I need to tackle the issue. I know (certain) that most times I've read a decision-support document in the past, I have come away with a better understanding of the issue.

For the unaccustomed reader, the positive consequences are more remote. I may not understand until I have read the report completely, maybe a few times (distant). The negative consequences, on the other hand, are both certain and immediate. I know for sure (certain) that it will be a pain (negative) to read all this. I am uncertain whether I will understand it all, and I will probably feel a bit stupid (negative). It's a pain just thinking about the report (immediate).

The temporal aspect has a decisive bearing on the effect of consequences. Feedback should be provided immediately after behaviour is performed. Let's go back to the executive who was going to draw a flower on the whiteboard.

If the click had only come after a five-second delay, he would have already gone on to test new behaviours. The brain will argue: 'I pick up the marker. I get no response. I put the marker down. No response. I start moving away from the board. Response!' The delayed click in this description means that the behaviour that contradicts the goal is reinforced. In other words, immediacy, or timing, is crucial if we are to be sure that we are reinforcing the right behaviour. This is the power of instant feedback.

The temporal aspect also plays in on the use of positive and corrective feedback. If we wish to reinforce innovation, for example, every new idea, whether good, bad or even terrible, should be given attention through praise or a pat on the back right when it is shared – the praise can also be given when talking to the innovator about his/her idea. The assessment of the idea's quality can always wait until later. As noted, mixing positive and corrective feedback at that time weakens the instructional value and diminishes the power of influence on the particular behaviour.

Influence behaviour using consequences

Indeed, there are some common attempts at influencing employee behaviour using consequences. For instance, bonuses are common in many organizations. The 'to be or not to be' of bonuses is a hotly contested issue in many organizations and industries. Bonuses have a reputation of being behaviour-enhancing, but, as we now understand, this is far from definite. So, how do bonuses work from a behavioural psychology perspective?

An incentive system where employees receive bonus pay (positive) long after work performed, for instance in June for last year's work (distant), based on variables they cannot really influence (uncertain) has little impact on any specific performance-related behaviour. There may be other positive effects, such as creating a sense of belonging to the organization, which can be seen as cognitive behaviour we would want to reinforce. However, it is too blunt a tool to serve as a means of impacting the specific behaviours we want to influence that drive the results.

In addition, it may also have a number of negative effects. If the bonus is awarded in connection with a period during which an employee was disgruntled and left work before 2 pm every day, yelled at his colleagues, 'sold off' the company's property, refrained from making important long-term investments or overinvested in order to grow profits or the asset base in the short term (and thus his own bonus), then those behaviours are also reinforced. Once again, timing is crucial if we are to influence the right behaviour.

At one time, Shell gave its senior executives an opportunity to purchase options. They wanted to link the executives' bonus to performance – in this case performance was defined as the company's market capitalization. They also wanted the senior executives to show their loyalty to the company in symbolic terms. The executives were to invest in the company they led. This makes perfect sense. However, from a behavioural perspective on bonuses such programmes can backfire. In the case of Shell it is reasonable to assume that it was in the interests of the executives to keep the share price elevated; specific behaviour causing the share price to stay up or go up was reinforced. This can be one explanation why management consistently overestimated the company's oil reserves. Each time they estimated reserves, the consequence of a greater oil reserve made them more money and, as such, the increasing value of the reserves and of their individual net worth could be seen as a positive, immediate and certain consequence. Whether negligent or not, the case illustrates the difficulties of driving the right behaviour without understanding the mechanisms fully. When this was discovered, the chairman, group CFO and head of exploration resigned from their posts.[3] This unexpected negative, future and uncertain consequence did not have as strong an effect on their behaviour when estimating reserves as the positive, certain and immediate ones had.

Now let's take a look at a behaviour we have addressed before: securing a good price at the negotiating table using a specific argument. The consequence is positive, as you know that you got a good price. It is immediate and certain, as the counter-party's acceptance came right after the 'winning' argument. This means that the consequence is positive, immediate and certain. It has a strong impact on whether the negotiator will use that behaviour in similar future situations.

Praise is often considered a common way to encourage, motivate and hopefully reinforce behaviour. But depending on the situation, praise by a manager in front of others can function as a punishment and be completely self-defeating. Not everyone likes publicity. Some may not want to appear to be the boss's favourite for a variety of reasons, as this may entail several negative consequences later on. I have said so before, but I cannot stress it enough: it is the recipient who determines the effect, so if we want to influence someone, we need to learn what that person appreciates and does not appreciate.

The rationale for what an effective and 'instructive' consequence should be like does not only apply between people. Let's look at someone who works with a drill as a simplified example. The behaviour is to bring down the drill in order to make a hole in a metal sheet. When you have brought it down just as far as you should according to the 3D drawing you are using, a light flashes green. The consequence – the green light, the 'click' – is positive, immediate and certain. It lets you know that you have now performed the task correctly.

If we can learn how to work using consequences that are linked to different behaviours in this way in an organization, we will get significantly better at influencing behaviour and thus also performance. Realizing strategy is about managing behaviour and performance – influencing towards performance, influencing in order to achieve goals.

That which makes human beings so responsive to consequences is the same thing that made us so adaptable as we evolved. What put us at the top of the food chain in spite of the fact that we are weak, slow and small compared to other predators is that we are able to shift a future consequence in our minds in such a way that it appears immediate. Thanks to our abstract cognitive ability we are able to set targets, make promises to ourselves, create agreements, make use of the token economy, daydream about the future or form expectations regarding how things will turn out. We are able – regardless of whether it is a reinforcement or a punishment – to imagine the future consequence of a given behaviour in such a way that it is perceived as being immediate. In other words, we can make use of abstract, analytical thinking to make consequences immediate. This is the reason that more future and uncertain consequences work in the first place.

> In practice, only immediate consequences influence our behaviour. If a future consequence has an influence, we have shifted it 'this way' in time using abstract thinking.

Randomness as a reinforcer: Intermittent reinforcement

Reinforcements can be few and far between and still keep behaviour alive. We do not need to win every contract for which we submit a tender – we will still submit a tender next time. We do not need the phone to be picked up every time we try to call someone. We can handle it if the line is busy several times, or if no one answers. A term that is sometimes used to account for this phenomenon is *reinforcement schedules.*

Reinforcements of behaviour can either be *continuous*, i.e. those that occur each time the behaviour is performed, or *intermittent*, i.e. those that occur now and then. For example, we get our cup of coffee (reinforcement) every time we put money in the coffee machine or press the button. If no coffee were to be served at the first attempt, we would wonder what was going on and probably not insert any more coins. The vending machine, if functioning properly, reinforces our behaviour of inserting money continuously (every time).

If we shift our attention to the behaviour of inserting money into a different type of machine – a slot machine – here we do not get reinforcement (a win) every time. The slot machine reinforces the player intermittently. The player may only win one time in 100 on average, but still continues to play.

Reinforcements that are sparse or intermittent create a higher frequency of behaviour. Let's say that I'm a telemarketer and I manage to make a sale on my first attempt (reinforcement); in this case success will seem to be a matter of simply picking up the phone. If I do not succeed in making a sale on my first attempt, then I will place more calls. Thus, sparse reinforcement results in more behaviour. I pick up the handset more times if I do not succeed in making a sale every time I place a call.

At the beginning, before the behaviour has been properly learned, it is important to get continuous reinforcement. That way I will find it enjoyable and will continue to behave in this new and certain way. After that, the behaviour will increase if the reinforcements occur more sporadically (i.e. *thinning*).

This means that when we want to learn something new at work, we need frequent, continuous reinforcement at the beginning. Every time we practise balancing the budget, operating a new machine or doing our strategic analysis, we need to feel that we are learning something (cognitive reinforcement), that we receive praise or encouragement (social reinforcement), or that it is enjoyable (emotional reinforcement). As we get better at it, it is enough for the reinforcements to be more sporadic. Organizations that want to develop need to create an environment in which it is natural for reinforcement to be frequent in the beginning and then taper off after that. At the same time, the behaviour can be refined and made better and better thanks to reinforcement of the 'right' behaviour (the topography). If the reinforcements become too sparse, motivation disappears, and the behaviour is extinguished. No behaviour can survive a complete lack of reinforcement.

Once the behaviour is established and the person is able to perform it without having to think about it, the most powerful reinforcements are those that occur at random. This is sometimes referred to as *natural reinforcement*. This is well understood by the gambling industry. Few behaviours are as addictive as playing 'one-armed bandits'. Wins are random – that is to say, slot machine pay-outs are irregular – but as a player you can be absolutely sure that you will score a win sooner or later if you simply continue to play. In a PICNIC wording, a slot machine pay-out is a positive, distant (intermittent) and certain consequence.

The power of positive reinforcement: 'The extra mile'

We sometimes say, for simplicity's sake, that organizations have punitive or reinforcing cultures. Organizations that have a reinforcing culture – that is, those that are more characterized by positive reinforcement – perform better.

In organizations that are positively reinforcing, employees behave in a certain way because they want to. They find that this gives them something; they get something out of it. The employees in an organization that is negatively reinforcing, on the other hand, feel that they need to behave in a certain way in order to avoid something unpleasant. Unfortunately, a culture of negative reinforcement is common in many organizations. 'Everything's all right if no one says anything' is a common expression that reflects this fact.

Many companies are low-feedback organizations where general feedback on employee performance is unusual. People generally want to know how they are performing. Feedback drives behaviour. If we want to create a high-performing organization that is constantly developing, proceeding from the premise that 'everything's all right if no one says anything' is not the right method. In practice this would mean that you will almost exclusively get corrective feedback. How developing and encouraging is that?

There is research to indicate that, on average, 40 per cent of a company's strategic potential profit disappears the moment the strategy 'leaves the table'.[4] Other studies show that 70–90 per cent of all strategic change initiatives fail to achieve their goals.[5] Yet others say that nine out of ten strategies are not properly realized.[6] Although strategy is in fact under the control of management it is undeniable that accomplishing real change and succeeding in realizing strategy is demanding. One reason may be that few organizations are truly good at pinpointing result-driving behaviours to positively reinforce. By focusing on the positive rather than forcing some stat up to a minimum level, we can accomplish more. It is in fact useful for an organization to positively reinforce the behaviours that create good results for the business.

This all sounds good and simple, but how do we do it in practice? Some advice in this regard is to get to know our business, be sure to understand the business logic and the people whose behaviour creates the results. Get to know our organization, get to know the employees and get to know what serves as positive reinforcement for different employees, departments, units or organizations. There are positive reinforcers to use for an organization. These can open up an opportunity for employees to start thinking that it's fun to perform, instead of feeling compelled. Begin by considering which social, work-related, cognitive, symbolic and emotional reinforcers you do not use systematically today.

A rule of thumb for creating a culture of positive reinforcement is to give positive feedback eight times as often as corrective feedback. This can be a way to create an organization in which the employees perform because they want to, not because they have to.

When do we work best? When we have to, or when we want to? There is a term known as *flow*. Flow is a mental state. It's the feeling we get when everything is working, when we get a lot done and are able to handle the challenges we face, and often time flies. Imagine if we could design workplaces that create such an environment. Who wouldn't want to work there? Someone who finds work enjoyable performs better than someone who works so as not to 'lose' salary. The difference in performance between two employees where one is driven by positive reinforcement and the other by negative reinforcement can be absolutely crucial to a company's success.

In organizations characterized by punishment and negative reinforcement, we can see that there is a low frequency of a given behaviour before a deadline. The closer we get to the deadline, the more behaviour in terms of frequency or diligence in terms of topography. Just after reaching the minimum level required to avoid the negative consequence, we typically stop performing the behaviour. This means that we will deliver exactly what is required just before the deadline, neither more nor earlier. In this case, our focus is on the result that has to be achieved for the sake of avoidance, not on performing the behaviour in the best possible way. This means that we are driven by negative reinforcement, i.e. by the avoidance of something unpleasant. This is not how to get an organization to perform as well as possible and outperform its rivals. Obvious signs that negative reinforcement is in place include: seeing a delay in performance until the deadline is approaching, with performance decrease as soon as targets are met or requirements are removed; and negative talk about the workplace or company. In such cases, there most often are no structure, plan, method or tools for positive reinforcement. If we want to become higher performing, these need to be developed.

If we look instead at an organization that is positively reinforcing – where there is a structure, a plan, a model and tools – we see that it shows a more stable and higher frequency of the behaviour. The behaviour is not performed in order to deliver a certain result of a certain quality at a certain time, but rather because we personally feel that we get something out of it. We feel that we contribute, that we learn, that we are a part of something, that we want to help our colleagues, which lead us to want to perform. The behaviour is positively reinforced. As a result, we do not stop performing the behaviour simply because a certain minimum level has been reached; rather, we continue, in spite of having achieved the goal, to do even better.

Magnus Böcker, one of the founders of OMX Nasdaq and former CEO of the Singapore Exchange, among many things, had this to say in an interview about this behaviour challenge, in a way that I find telling: 'It is always easier to manage people who want to do the right thing than people who do not want to make mistakes. If it's just about not making mistakes, you don't take the same responsibility'.[7] Magnus also expressed an opinion that too many employees focus on trying to please their bosses; this quote illustrates this standpoint.

Unfortunately, Magnus passed away due to cancer far too early.

The difference between the minimum level achieved in a negatively reinforced organization and what we can achieve in an organization that is positively reinforcing is sometimes called *discretionary effort* – in other words, 'going the extra mile'. The impact that a focus on pinpointing behaviours that drive a particular result has had on the organizational results of my clients has been between 5 and 45 per cent on a variety of different goals, ranging from across a wide field of organizational results such as sales, profitability, safety, leadership, customer satisfaction and quality. Without having subjected these experiences to academic scrutiny, I feel it is safe to say that the effort to achieve this focus on positive reinforcement is well worth it.

It is more efficient to reinforce positive behaviour than it is to punish negative behaviour if we wish to create long-term success. We foster better performance by reinforcing things that are positive – the things that drive results – not by spending time on weakening behaviour that does not create value.

Establishing operations

Do you always find a freshly baked cinnamon bun just as tasty? Is it always just as fun to lead the monthly meeting with the management team? Of course not. Our hunger, craving or a stomach bug will affect how tasty we think the bun is. In the same way, agenda items, the colleagues in the group, the mood of the management team, etc, will affect how fun the meeting is. Factors, conditions that affect the impact of consequences – of reinforcements and punishments – such as hunger, a stomach bug, the mood of the group, personal preferences or values, are called *establishing operations*.[8]

If I tell you that you need to talk about significant future downsizing at the management team meeting on Monday, you may look forward to the meeting with less relish. If I tell you that the customer you are going to meet told me how interesting she thought our company and our products are at our first meeting, this increases the reinforcement for behaviours that relate to being well-prepared at the next meeting you are having with that customer.

Persuasion means trying to change the establishing operations, the conditions that determine the effectiveness of a consequence. This is the 'weapon' we use to change behaviour when we cannot remove or add a reinforcer. A common example of a very clear and powerful establishing condition is when alcoholics turn to faith instead of the bottle. The sense of community found in the church, mosque or otherwise, which is positive, immediate and certain, becomes a more important and potent form of positive reinforcement than the temporary reduction in anxiety provided by alcohol as negative reinforcement.

Establishing operations can reduce the value of the reinforcement by so much that it goes from being a reinforcement, to being a punishment. Almost everyone enjoys praise and appreciation. But appreciation needs to come from the right person. Praise from someone we don't like, or even fear, is rarely reinforcing. The dislike is an establishing operation that lowers the value of the reinforcement and almost turns it into a punishment.

In other words, and from a leadership standpoint, being well-liked means that you have access to an establishing operation, or condition that makes you a potential provider of reinforcement. This gives you the opportunity to influence your surroundings. It is easier to influence people if we are well-liked. If we are well-liked, it is easy to get people to follow. It's simple: would you rather follow (really follow, in a voluntary sense, not coerced) someone you like or someone you are afraid of? It doesn't take long to answer.

There is much research to indicate that people do more for someone they like. This discretionary effort we've been talking about is especially true of managers. Managers who are well-liked by their subordinates almost always have better performing businesses in the long run. Any seasoned successful senior executive knows that without the support of your team, your organization, it impossible to build something. In addition to employees being willing to go the extra mile for someone they like, well-liked managers are able to retain their staff. This is of course an advantage when specialized human resources are scarce. Studies show that between 65 and 75 per cent of everyone who changes jobs does so because of their manager.

This quality of being well-liked is often referred to as *likability*. Likability is not about being nice for the sake of being nice, but about behaving in such a way that others perceive us as being fair, thereby earning their respect and fondness. Reinforcements given by a well-liked manager are more powerful than those given by one that is not well-liked.

There is a classic tale of two bricklayers. One believes that he is laying bricks and the other believes that he is building a cathedral. Building a cathedral is probably more reinforcing. If we are more clear about linking the employee's individual achievements and work-related behaviour to overall goals, it becomes easier for the employee to see the part he or she plays in the big picture – this is cognitive and emotional reinforcement. This is yet another reason why it is important to let employees participate in formulating the goals they are to achieve, where possible. 'Seeing' the future cathedral increases the amplitude of the reinforcement to go on laying bricks, and thus acts as an establishing operation.

> Organizations have values and norms – these are sometimes described as culture. Values and norms often act as establishing operations. Visions, challenges, education and role descriptions also have an effect on how the reinforcement is perceived, and these are therefore also conditions that establish how we value certain consequences.

The strength of behaviour analysis

What makes people behave the way they actually do, and how does the brain learn new things? *Behaviour analysis* is an umbrella term for a set of principles that explain the origin and perpetuation of behaviour. Behaviour analysis is based on behavioural psychology principles developed through experimental scientific methods over the course of more than a century. The ideas behind it are based on Darwin's idea of natural selection – that the behaviour that fills a role is perpetuated. Researchers like Watson, Pavlov, Thorndike and Skinner made contributions by testing, strengthening and developing the science. Applied behaviour analysis is not *one* theory but is made up of the collective results of many different researchers and research streams. Findings borne out by the research are added to the domain, while other hypotheses have been discarded. What every part of this domain has in common is that behaviour is always in focus. We might say that behaviour analysis is an instrument used to understand the world and people.

Behaviour analysis explains why people behave the way they do and makes it possible to help them behave in new ways, or to stop behaving in old ones. Behaviourism is the basis of behaviour analysis. *Cognitive behavioural therapy*, which gained increased currency in the later decades, is ultimately based on behaviour analysis. Applying these techniques to organizations and leadership is usually called *organizational behaviour management*.

The law of human behaviour says that people behave the way they do due to what happens when they behave the way they do. Times change. Markets change. People's behaviour changes in every new context. But the laws that govern human behaviour remain constant. Understanding the impact of the consequence on certain behaviour provides an opportunity to influence behaviour, increase performance, achieve goals, create real change and realize strategy.

In nearly all organizations I have worked for, and with, it was more common to hold planning meetings than follow-up and feedback meetings. The information that was communicated widely in these organizations was generally about what was to be done going forward, not what had been done, what results it led to, and what learning and opportunities for development they could derive from them. This is a sign that organizations focus too much on activating (sending out signals) instead of on delivering consequences (following up and providing feedback). This relation is illustrated in Figure 9.1.

FIGURE 9.1   Organizations' balance between activator and consequence efforts

A $\longrightarrow$	B $\longleftrightarrow$	C
Activator	Behaviour	Consequence
80%	Employed	20%
20%	Effect	80%
Planning	$\longleftarrow\longrightarrow$	Learning

SOURCE Adapted from L Braksick (2007) *Unlock Behavior, Unleash Profit*, McGraw Hill, New York

In somewhat simplified terms, we can apply the Pareto principle (the 80/20 rule) to make a point and say that organizations generally spend about 80 per cent of their resources on activators. That is, on goal formulation, planning, developing processes, work descriptions, etc – work that involves sending out signals to the business about what is to be done. Only the remaining 20 per cent is spent on what could be seen as consequences – such as follow-up, reflection and feedback. It is the consequences of certain behaviour that determine whether the behaviour will persist.

Further, we can also apply the Pareto principle to the factors that affect behaviour. The opposite ratio holds for how behaviour is influenced. Twenty per cent of a behaviour is influenced by the activator, and the remaining 80 per cent is influenced by the consequence. This means that organizations generally spend 80 per cent of their resources on managing and controlling factors that account for just 20 per cent of the impact on behaviour. On the one hand, this can be regarded as a waste of resources, but it can be seen as a huge untapped potential on the other. Indeed, there is enormous underexplored potential when it comes to new ways of strategizing, leading and managing organizations that are based on behaviour analysis. The aim of this reasoning is not to give exact figures, but to indicate a phenomenon. That is, too many organizations fail to achieve their full potential for lack of knowledge about what actually impacts human behaviour and thus drives the organization's performance and results.

What positive effects would it have if we just managed to shift the focus a little bit – why not 50/50 as a first step? How would it affect your organizational results – e.g. growth, customer satisfaction, time to market – if you invested 50 per cent of your resources on what actually drives business behaviour instead of the 20 per cent being spent today? How much better could your organization get by focusing on the factors that influence behaviour and that actually have a serious impact on your results?

Organizations that want to get better at achieving their goals should spend more time setting and delivering consequences, and less on sending out activators that get drowned out in the noise. They should invest more in highlighting good examples, spreading best practices, communicating achievements and how they were achieved, and less in communicating directives, orders and formal approaches.

In the more than 200 organizations I have worked with in my years, I have yet to hear an employee in any organization say that there are too few 'decrees' coming from the top (unclear, yes; but too few, no). In contrast, I have heard many employees in many organizations wonder if the copious amounts of information being reported are actually being followed up on or reflected upon, and whether any learning is drawn on the basis of the information. I have also heard, far too many times, employees wondering how in the world they are to manage all the central initiatives that are being 'pushed down' on them, and simultaneously deliver to the customers. And this, basically regardless of size and shape of the organizations. How much better could organizations get if they shifted the focus of their strategizing from the activator side to the consequence side?

Behaviour analysis and realization of strategy

The purpose of behaviour analysis is to understand and to improve behaviour. Behavioural strategizing's purpose is to understand the business, identify the organization's potential for development, and continuously change and adapt it for the better by focusing on behaviour.

When we identify potential for development and find opportunities for improvement in an organization, we often proceed on the basis of a market situation that has changed, the organization's ability to build competitiveness, a business plan or a strategy with goals entailing that we need to do something new or different. In behaviour analysis, we look for the key behaviours that are critical if the organization is to achieve the specific goal, e.g. market fit. The purpose is to identify and influence key behaviour that creates the results we seek.

In order to build competitiveness, realize strategy and succeed, we need to find out which behaviour (KBI) contributes to which results or goals (KRIs) and do whatever we can to positively reinforce that behaviour.

If an organization has posted weak sales figures for a time and wishes to expand its customer base, we need to identify what specific behaviour leads to an expanded customer base. If we want to ensure that we are handling investments professionally, or that our managers coach their employees, we need to understand which behaviours serve as proof that we are doing this. If we want to build a creative and innovative culture, we need to identify the behaviour that makes for a creative and innovative culture, and try to influence it.

Once we have understood which behaviours lead to which results and have analysed what influences the behaviour – the activators and consequences associated with it – we can try to add new reinforcements and to remove existing punishers. This way, we can make it more or less likely that the behaviour will occur again. When we change a behaviour's contingencies, we change the premises that determine whether the behaviour will be maintained or not.

Unless the 'right' behaviours are reinforced, it does not matter how many goals or targets management sets or how much information is communicated about rules, guidelines, policies, and so on. An organization with a genuine ambition to change its business to constantly adapt to the market needs to break overall goals down into key behaviour and behavioural goals, and these need to be followed up on. That's what we call realizing strategy in a behavioural way.

Performing behaviour analysis

There is a company with cutting-edge expertise in eye-tracking technology that develops products and solutions that are able to track where people are looking. Retail chains buy the company's products to track where in the store customers look the most: at red price tags, at items positioned at shoulder height, and so on. This way they can plan how to design a store in order to boost sales. The organization is research-intensive and needs to stay at the cutting edge of the technology in order to be competitive, so having an innovative culture is crucial. One of their overall goals is to strengthen their innovative culture. The organization launched a project for this purpose. How would they go about doing that from a behavioural perspective?

Performing a behaviour analysis is reminiscent of grammar and of how we identify the various parts of speech in a sentence. We want answers to three general questions:

1 What is the behaviour?

2 What 'leads to' the person performing the behaviour?

3 Why does the person perform the behaviour?

What is the behaviour? Who does something? Which behaviour is the foundation of an 'innovative culture'? What key behaviour is proof of an 'innovative culture'? Is that behaviour measurable, observable and active? If we were to film an 'innovative culture', what behaviour could be captured on film?

In order to make progress in its effort to focus on behaviour, the organization drew up a list of excess and deficit behaviours that affect the building of an innovative culture. The list was long at first: thinking new thoughts, reading the latest research findings, trying out new ideas, being in touch with universities, researchers and institutes, clinging to established ideas, questioning conventions too rarely, etc.

Based on the list, however, the organization identified a deficit behaviour that they thought was more important than the others in order to promote an innovative culture, and that they thought would lead to the result increased sales in 'new business'. The pinpointed key behaviour, of which they wanted to increase the frequency, was for employees to 'contribute concrete suggestions and ideas for improvement'. Because this was a deficit behaviour, the goal was to increase its frequency, and to accomplish this they needed to find a way to reinforce it.

Once the key behaviour is pinpointed, it's time to look at the activator. The activator is the answer to the question of what leads to employees contributing suggestions for improvement. In what situations do they usually contribute? Have they contributed in the past? When did it happen for the first time? Do the employees often do this? What might the employees' contributions be in response to? Are there circumstances in which they never contribute? As I mentioned earlier, every behaviour is a reaction to something in its context.

A clear activator in this example was the management team's expressed ambition to become a more innovative organization. The organization also had the long-term goal of making it onto a particular magazine's list of the most creative companies, which they hoped would help them attract new cutting-edge talent. In addition to the 'artificial' and externally imposed activators, there was also the employees' opinion (internal activators) that their work could be more efficient, and perceptions among employees that they had not shared enough knowledge with each other.

Behaviour with reinforcement endures

When we know what started the behaviour – 'contribute concrete suggestions and ideas for improvement' – we can try to understand why the employees perform the behaviour, or why not. This means finding the reinforcements. What do they get out of contributing ideas? What function does the behaviour 'contributing' have? What happens after they have contributed new ideas? What are the social, monetary, symbolic, emotional and/or work-related reinforcers that influence this behaviour? Are the consequences positive or negative? Are they immediate or more distant? Are they certain or uncertain?

In this case, a traditional organization would have settled for the employees wanting to contribute ideas on their own initiative because the company had a goal, and for managers and colleagues to give feedback on whether the ideas were good and valuable. However, there is research showing that in many cases those who contribute new ideas do not get any feedback at all. No feedback means no reinforcement, which leads to the employee behaviour of coming up with new ideas being extinguished.

We know that behaviour with reinforcement endures. The organization was convinced that this was a strategic success factor and needed to find many different ways of reinforcing the behaviour of 'contributing'. In order to reinforce this behaviour, they created a reinforcement system and a visualization board to be able to measure, evaluate and provide feedback on how development was going.

The organization felt that it was primarily the managers' responsibility to encourage employees. All managers to whom new, concrete ideas for improvement were presented were supposed to make a mark on a shared digital whiteboard. The idea was that this would give the employee positive, immediate and certain reinforcement (as a token) of his or her behaviour of contributing new ideas. The managers had one column each in which the number of ideas per employee each week were tabulated. The weekly results were then summarized in a cumulative presentation. Next to the first board there was another board that was used to write down brief descriptions of all the ideas. If there was an idea that someone had thought about or considered to be good, they were free to make a mark next to that idea. This way the organization learned which ideas many employees thought were good, with the effect that new ideas generated more ideas. It also gave employees an opportunity to positively reinforce each other's behaviour of coming up with more ideas (intermittent reinforcement).

To ensure that the feedback given really was positive, the managers asked their employees what kind of work-related reinforcement they would like to have after reaching a certain number of marks on the board. Some employees went on a field trip to a nearby supplier to take a look at their business, share experiences and discuss ways of working together going forward. Some visited a nearby university where they were able to hold a meeting with a prominent team of researchers in their field of interest.

The organization also introduced a follow-up and brainstorming coffee/after work hour at 3:30 pm every other Friday. At these meetings, the development director and CEO looked at the board and how many suggestions per employee each workgroup had come up with. The groups that wanted to were able to comment on their results. The group with the most ideas that week got to select their three best ideas and briefly present them. The group whose number of suggestions had increased the most was given a chance to let those in attendance know what they had done to bring about the increase. After that, one or more employees would be called on to present the actual improvements that their ideas had given rise to.

The organization increased its average number of ideas from 5 to 25 per year per employee. Over time, the ideas gave rise to three new business areas/products and services. Four years after project launch, these account for around 30 per cent of the organization's turnover. Turnover itself has increased by 20 per cent.

Whirlpool had similar experiences. In 1999, they kicked off an innovation programme to develop new and better products to combat a period of poor business performance.[9] At the end of 2011 they estimated that the products and services that had come out of the innovation programme accounted for $3.6 billion, or close to 20 per cent of total revenue.[10]

By focusing on reinforcing a pinpointed key behaviour, the initiative at the eye-tracking company was able to have an effect. Most organizations know that focus leads to results, but don't have the courage needed, and/or fail to make the prioritization and de-prioritization of the behaviour needed in order to establish a clear focus.

The strength of behaviour analysis lies in the fact that the analysis itself can apply to any behaviour, irrespective of complexity or scope – anything from wearing safety goggles when you step up to the lathe to making 'impossible' strategic decisions. The limitation is that you can only focus on one behaviour at a time. Understanding the business and the individuals 'doing' the work in the business is thus absolutely critical in order to identify and influence the right key behaviour.

Lack of motivation or lack of knowledge

There are always reasons why employees fail to wrap up the consolidated financial statements, or why their review of the sales material is careless, or why they ship concrete panels without grinding them, or why they delay making the adjustments needed in a new system.

When a key behaviour is a deficit behaviour and someone is not performing the desired behaviour, this is due to at least one of two things. One is that the person does not know how to perform the behaviour. In this case, this is a *lack of knowledge, skill or competence*. The second reason is that the person is not getting reinforcement for the behaviour. In this case, we are looking at a *lack of reinforcement*. Whether consciously or not, the person makes a decision to perform a certain behaviour or not. In addition, some basic conditions need to be in place, such as time to perform the work or access to the right tools.

If lack of knowledge is the reason that the person is not performing a certain behaviour, the person needs to learn new behaviour. In this case, no behaviour analysis or reinforcement will avail. It is then the responsibility of the organization and the manager to help their employees learn this behaviour if it is part of the job description, or to eliminate the tasks that the employee cannot perform.

A rough and ready litmus test to determine whether a deficit of a certain behaviour is due to a lack of knowledge or skill is to ask ourselves this: 'If the person was given a million dollars to perform the behaviour here and now, would he or she be able to do it?' If the answer is yes, we are probably looking at a lack of motivation, or rather a lack of reinforcement. If the answer is no, we are probably looking at a lack of knowledge or skill. I couldn't speak Chinese fluently even if someone were to promise me €100 million as a reinforcement. Nor could I prepare a correct set of consolidated financial statements for a global multi-business corporation. The money has no effect. However, I do hope that I would be able to learn Chinese and prepare consolidated financial statements – at least to some extent – if I were given the opportunity to practise so that I could acquire the right knowledge and behaviour.

I once had a colleague who worked at a concrete factory. He asked two employees to use something called a 'helicopter' to grind the surface of the concrete panels produced at the factory to make them smoother. They answered that they would see to it that day. But it didn't get done. The next day he asked why it wasn't done. He got no answer to his question but was told that it would be done the same day. The day after that it still wasn't done. Then he asked again why it hadn't been done when they had promised to do it. He was then told that they didn't know how to operate the machine and that they weren't certified to operate it. In this case no matter how much my colleague had used different reinforcers, it would not have made a difference.

When we want to increase deficit behaviour, we need to find out why there is a deficit. A model that that helps us in these situations is the EKOR model. Each letter stands for something that needs to be in place in order for certain behaviour to be performed: expectation, knowledge, opportunity and reinforcement. If one of these is lacking, change will most probably fail (see Figure 9.2).

FIGURE 9.2   Four prerequisites for behavioural change

SOURCE Adapted from L Braksick (2007) *Unlock Behavior, Unleash Profit*, McGraw Hill, New York; and J Hiatt (2006) *ADKAR: A model for change in business, government, and our community*, Prosci, Loveland

In order for change to appear, the individuals who are supposed to change their behaviour need to understand the set expectations; they need to have the competence to behave in a different way; they need the opportunity, physically, resource-wise or other; and they need to be reinforced in their new behaviour.

Expectations mean that the person needs to understand what specific behaviour is expected. If the instruction or activator has low instructional value, it is not easy to perform the behaviour requested. The person may not even understand that it is requested of him or her. If the result to be achieved is unclear, it is difficult to know what behaviour is required in order to get to the result. Asking 'Can you fix this sales material?' has a lower instructional value – and thus results in a lower understanding of the relevant expectations – than asking 'Can you go through the spelling errors, punctuation and sentence structure in this sales quotation to make sure that the language is grammatically correct?'

Knowledge means that the person has the skills needed to perform the behaviour – in other words, that he or she is able to handle the topography. It is not uncommon for people to not have the competency needed to do what is expected of them. This is especially common in complex occupational roles involving extensive leadership or strategic challenges where responsibilities are in fact unclear, where the tasks span a variety of domains, and where the decisions made will have consequences that are impossible to foresee. The Peter principle, coined by the Canadian author and educator Laurence J Peter, says (somewhat tongue-in-cheek) that people will be promoted until they hold a position that exceeds their competency. If this is true, lack of competence is a common cause of a lot of deficit behaviour in organizations. This makes learning even more important to succeed in working life – especially for work in leadership positions and in high-level strategic roles. There is a body of research suggesting that organizations would gain by taking those with the highest learning capacity and making them managers, instead of those who perform best in their existing roles. This opens up a new perspective on succession planning for many companies and possibly helps remedy some behaviour deficits organizations have today.

Opportunity means ensuring that the person is able to perform the behaviour in purely practical terms. The person who is to perform the behaviour needs to have the physical or mental capacity of the kind required. Not everyone is able to handle everything. To carry a heavy workload, you need physical strength. Opportunity can also involve practical issues like having tools, a method description or the key to a cabinet where information or material is stored. A system developer who does not have access to the systems being developed cannot perform the right behaviour even though the expectations, skills and motivation to perform the behaviour are all in place.

Reinforcement means motivation to behave in a certain way. We know that all behaviour that does not fill a role will be extinguished. What reinforcement is there for the person to perform the behaviour? What does the person get out of performing the behaviour? No reinforcement, no behaviour.

In the concrete grinding example, we can say that the employees knew what the task was, so the expectations were fairly clear. Yet the skills were not there. The people did not know how to use the machine. Nor was there an opportunity. They were unable to perform the behaviour on a practical level because they did not know how to start up the machine. So, in the case described, it was both a matter of skill and a matter of opportunity. Not everything is a matter of motivation.

When we are dealing with expectations, skills or opportunities, we cannot use the consequences of behaviour as a management tool. In this situation we need to take other actions. These can range from a clarifying talk to sort out expectations, through training or drills to teach new skills, to eliminating other work tasks so that the employees actually have concrete opportunities to perform the task. When it comes to motivation, however, we can get a clear answer as to how to use reinforcers as management tools by performing a behaviour analysis.

Sometimes, and in similar models, these prerequisites of behavioural change are seen as sequential and related to each other. For instance, in order to be motivated (reinforcement) you need to know the direction (expectations). This is not entirely correct. We may be perfectly able (opportunities) and willing (reinforcement) without knowing the exact expectations. We might also not be reinforced simply because we know the expectations, have competence and the opportunity. In many organizations I have supported over the years, the expectations from the top management on future changes are clear, the individuals are more than competent to perform the expected behaviours and they have the opportunity. What is lacking is their motivation. They believe the change is not the right one. And this is, of course, perfectly fine. It is OK to disagree, but since management is responsible, as an employee further down in the hierarchy, you've got three choices: 1. Accept and change yourself; 2. Voice your opinion to try and change management; and 3. Exit. Everyone benefits from having employees or being an employee in an organization that builds on a mutual will to do something together.

Notes

1   T Peters and R Waterman (2004) *In Search of Excellence: Lessons from America's best run companies*, 2nd edn, Profile Books Limited, London

2   D Premack. Toward empirical behavior laws: I. Positive reinforcement, *Psychological Review*, 1959, 66 (4), 219–33

3   See, e.g., NBC News. Shell says it overstated profit by $432 million, NBC News, 3 July 2004, www.nbcnews.com/id/wbna5353713 (archived at https://perma.cc/7JTM-SNR4); US Securities and Exchange Committee. Royal Dutch Petroleum Company and the "Shell" Transport and Trading Company, PLC pay $120 million to settle SEC fraud case involving massive overstatement of proved hydrocarbon reserves, 24 August 2004, www.sec.gov/news/press/2004-116.htm (archived at https://perma.cc/8S93-SV68)

4   M Mankins and R Steele. Turning great strategy into great performance, *Harvard Business Review*, July 2005, https://hbr.org/2005/07/turning-great-strategy-into-great-performance (archived at https://perma.cc/66LC-2KEU)

5   M Beer and N Nohria (2000) *Breaking the Code of Change*, Harvard Business School Press, Cambridge, MA; A Pettigrew and R Whipp (1991) *Managing Change for Competitive Success*, Blackwell Business, Hoboken; J Kotter (1996) *Leading Change*, Harvard Business School Press, Cambridge, MA

6   D C Hambrick and A A Cannella, Jr. Strategy implementation as substance and selling, *The Academy of Management Executive*, 1989, 3 (4), 278–85; H Mintzberg (1994) *The Rise and Fall of Strategic Planning*, The Free Press, New York; D Miller. Successful change leaders: what makes them? What do they do that is different? *Journal of Change Management*, 2002, 2 (4), 359–68; C Zook and J Allen (2001) *Profit From the Core*, Harvard Business School Press, Cambridge, MA

7   K Hugo. Börs-vdn: som vill göra nytta för många. Svenska Dagbladet, 2 January 2014, www.svd.se/bors-vdn-som-vill-gora-nytta-for-manga (archived at https://perma.cc/HZ9Y-R37C)

8   M McDevitt and E Fantino. Establishing operations and the discriminative stimulus, *The Behavior Analyst/MABA*, 1993, 16 (2), 225–27

9   J D Rapp. Inside Whirlpool's innovation machine, 23 January 2013, www.managementexchange.com/story/inside-whirlpools-innovation-machine (archived at https://perma.cc/DVS5-BYVW)

10 M Morena. Whirlpool's innovation journey: An on-going quest for a rock-solid and inescapable innovation capability, 23 January 2013, www.managementexchange.com/story/whirlpools-innovation-journey (archived at https://perma.cc/A7KF-7HWR)

KEY POINTS
Part Three: Unexpected simplicity

What is behaviour?

Behaviour is what someone does, says, thinks or feels. Behaviour is active, measurable, observable and reliable. Behaviour can be motor (moving, talking, laughing), it can be autonomous (breathing, the heart beating) or it can be cognitive (thinking, analysing, feeling).

What affects behaviour?

The basic thesis is that, in any given situation, people behave in the way they believe or think is most beneficial to them. Behaviour is influenced by the knowledge that people have and the consequences that similar behaviour had in previous situations.

Behaviour is affected by two factors. Activators start the behaviour. External activators may include strategies, training or laws. Internal activators may include wanting to perform, uncertainty or perceived peer pressure. Consequences determine whether behaviour will endure. Positive and negative reinforcement reinforces behaviour. Extinction and punishment weaken behaviour.

Why are consequences crucial for performance?

All results come from behaviour. Consequences determine whether behaviour will endure. By analysing what consequences certain behaviour has, we can understand why behaviour arises, endures or disappears. Positive, immediate and certain consequences are the most powerful.

Common ways of delivering consequences as reinforcers are monetary (pay, bonus), social (praise, recognition), symbolic (diplomas, certificates), work-related reinforcers (new tasks, increased responsibility), cognitive (insight, learning) and emotional (joy, sense of belonging).

How can behaviour analysis help create higher-performing organizations?

Organizations generally allocate 80 per cent of their resources to managing and controlling factors that account for just 20 per cent of the impact on behaviour – activators – and only 20 per cent of their resources to what has 80 per cent of the impact on behaviour – consequences. By identifying what activators and what consequences are present in an organization and placing more focus on consequences, they can more easily achieve their results.

If we want to achieve other results tomorrow than those we have today, we need to develop or improve our business. All development involves a change of behaviour. Using behaviour analysis, we can find out which behaviours lead to the results we want to achieve tomorrow.

What does 'unexpected simplicity' have to do with behaviour?

The logic, theory and working methods behind behaviour analysis are simple. Species that fail to adapt to their surroundings, as well as products or services that no one is asking for, disappear. This also applies to behaviour. The behaviour that does not serve a function does not receive any reinforcement and ceases to be performed.

PART FOUR

Strategy is behavioural change

Do not repeat tactics which have gained you one victory, but let your methods be regulated by the infinite variety of circumstances.

SUN TZU, *THE ART OF WAR*, 5TH CENTURY BC

Traditionally, strategy has been about planning and optimization. In today's market, these two are becoming less relevant and are giving way to innovation and change. By considering strategy from a behavioural psychology perspective, we can explain the way in which strategy, change and learning are tightly coupled and how new ways of strategizing can create lasting competitive advantages.

IN THIS PART

This part will shed light on the following questions:

- What is strategy?
- What does a behavioural view of strategy look like?
- Why is behaviour important if we want to realize strategy?
- How are change and learning related to the realization of strategy?
- What is meant by 'strategy is behavioural change'?

10

A behavioural view of strategy

What strategy is, and is not

The word strategy derives from the Greek word *strategos*, a title coined in conjunction with the democratic reforms in Athens circa 508 BC. Strategos can be seen as political and military tribal sub-divisions, and collectively there were 10 strategoi that formed the Athenian war council during this time. Strategos was compound of *stratos*, an army spread over ground, that someone needed to lead (*agein*, Ancient Greek for 'to lead').

Given the military origins of the term, we usually say that strategy is about winning a war, while tactics are about winning a battle, although in practice this division rather seems to create discussion of what is what, rather than to help clarify the way forward. Much of the traditional literature on strategy makes use of military metaphors. One strategy classic is Sun Tzu's *The Art of War*, written over 2,000 years ago. It's an amazing little book that says a lot about the world we live in today in terms of the strategy challenges that organizations face. However, in a philosophic sense, much of our perception and understanding of strategy and management is based on older literature from a relatively limited field of inquiry, often originating in economics. The result is that traditional views predominate in this area, despite the fact that strategy is actually a relatively new area of research.

Few knowledge domains are as fraught with as many words and terms as strategy and management. There is a reason why the term 'corporate bullshit' is sometimes used to disparage business language. And no wonder. Strategy, or strategic, is often added as a prefix to anything that we believe is important.

To quote Lars G Nordström, a truly senior CEO and board director in Scandinavia I admire a lot, and whom I have had the pleasure to get to know:

> Too often, 'strategic' seems to be added when organizations don't know what they are doing but need to put some weight behind it. A strategic acquisition: an acquisition where we have little idea if we'll get a return on our investment, but we want to do it. A strategic project: a project we believe is important but have no business case for. A strategic change: a change we think is important, but we don't bother exploring its consequences more properly. Thus, I advocate less 'strategy' and more tactics; less focus on what to do and more on how to do it, when to do it and, not least important, who is going to do it.

This illustration of how 'strategy' is used, as sad and provocative as it is, is also accurate in far too many cases. 'Strategy' and 'strategic' are often merely empty words, or prefixes, used to shortcut a proper job to understand how to get better as an organization. Indeed, in many cases, the practical strategizing in organizations – how, when and who – can be improved significantly.

Oxford strategy professor Richard Whittington, one of world's leading strategy researchers, also 'nails it': 'strategy work is serious business'.[1] I could not agree more. Unfortunately, this is far too seldom the case as many organizations are without knowledge of what strategy is and is not.

Strategy is not something that is important in a general sense. It is more precise; it has to do with how limited resources of all kinds are employed to ensure the organization achieves its objectives. I thought I would try to sort out a number of concepts used in strategy and put them in their proper context before developing an alternative view. To set the stage for the coming section, we can say that strategy can be explained in concrete terms as described by dimensions and levels. These will be elaborated next.

Strategy dimensions

Strategy is multidimensional. This simply means that several different perspectives, or dimensions if you will, need to be addressed if we want to approach or do it properly. The dimensions I believe are the building blocks of strategy are: accountabilities, arenas, affairs, actions and aims.

These five dimensions can be presented in a way that brings them together and discusses ideas from the field of strategy research that are normally dealt with separately. Although I believe that all dimensions are constantly present, and interplay, we also need to understand one by one, even if they emerge clearly different in different contexts. The main point is that it is not possible to understand strategy just by understanding how the arena works or what the issue of accountabilities is about. We need five As to understand strategy, and they together form an overall picture (see Figure 10.1).

Accountabilities is tightly linked to the organizational purpose. Organizational purpose is the organization's motive for existing. The French term *raison d'être* is sometimes used as well, meaning the reason for something existing, and it is a good way of describing what this is all about. Accountabilities and purpose are also related to another key concept: *stakeholders*. All organizations have several different stakeholders towards which they are accountable in some way. Customers is one group. Another is the shareholders and the organization's responsibility to maximize their profits. Yet another group is the employees of the organization. In public organizations, the citizens are an important stakeholder. Society and the environment are also stakeholders, which shows that stakeholder is a wide concept that needs to be addressed in strategizing.

Arenas, or context, refers to the arena in which the strategy applies. The external arenas include the outside world, and the particular branch of industry. The internal arena also includes the organization itself: its structure, processes, people and culture. Strategy needs to consider the internal arena, the

FIGURE 10.1   The five As of strategy

Strategy dimension	Strategy issue
Accountabilities	How can we live up to the reason for our existence?
Arenas	In what contexts are we operating?
Affairs	What are we going to do and not do?
Actions	How are we going to work with strategy?
Aims	How are we going to meet the future?

SOURCE Adapted from P Wadström, S Schriber, R Teigland and M Kaullio (2017) *Strategi: arenan, affären, arbetssätten, ansvaret, avsikten*, Liber, Stockholm organization where it is supposed to have an impact. In that sense, strategy needs to try to manage the organization's structures, processes, culture, resources in a way that harnesses the common forces of the entire organization. And, lastly, in a strategy we would want to know whether there is a proper fit between the internal and the external arenas. These are matters of arenas.

Affairs is a question of strategy content; it is manifested in what is described in an organization's strategies, business plans, goals, objectives, etc. These contain descriptions of how the organization will be successful. Typically, it relates to what businesses to be in, what products should be offered in what markets, which competencies are needed in order to deliver, which suppliers and partners are important, and which processes do what. The manifestation of strategy affairs is what is most similar to a classical strategy or business plan: the strategy 'document'.

Actions refers to the processes and activities of strategizing, the way in which the organization works with strategy formulation and strategy realization. Is strategy integrated into all parts of the organization, or is it something that is only done in some parts? Is it an annual occurrence, or are strategy talks held everywhere all the time? How does the organization push through strategic change options? Where do the initiatives come from? How does the organization measure and follow up to ensure that it is realizing its strategy? These are the types of questions strategizing regarding actions should answer.

Aims has to do with what we want our organization to become in the long run – how to balance future and existing. A vision is sometimes used to depict such a future state and is naturally related to the goals of an organization. These goals are typically a matter of affairs, which means that there is a strong relation between the aims and the affairs in terms of goals, targets and objectives. But besides describing a desired future state of the organization, aims should also make distinctions about how to manage the organization to create its own future.

In my experience, many organizations are fairly good at working with affairs, the strategy content. They are good at explaining where they operate and what to do. Sometimes they are also good at differentiating themselves. They run their megatrend, industry and organizational analyses, and the result is often described in an instructive way in various plans. This is also quite natural, because strategy in the corporate world is a relatively new area, and this is the perspective from which it emerged: economics.

One area that has potential for improvement is actions, the process of working with strategy to ensure that it will actually be realized: strategizing. Strategizing behaviours today need to be more dynamic, more focused on learning and adapting if we are to work with strategy efficiently.

Another area with potential for development is accountability. Organizations often have some type of vision that could serve as the organizational purpose, but it is rarely acute to the point that it steers or leads the rest of the business. The more clearly we are able to answer the why, the easier it is to solve the questions of when, what, where and how. If we have a clear purpose for why we have a strategy, this will have consequences in terms of what is to be done and how. If the purpose of the strategy is to ensure that the organization continues to develop in both the short term and the long term, the answers to the questions of what, where and how will be affected by this. If the purpose is to produce a budget and an annual plan, ideally one linked to the budget, this will have consequences for how the work is carried out.

At one point I was responsible for a portfolio of projects whose task was to improve governance in an organization. The first thing I did was to develop a management philosophy together with the top management team that made the decisions. I wanted to sort out why we needed to have governance and control at all. Answering the question 'Why do we need to have governance?' made it simpler for those of us in the projects to prioritize our resources going forward. We got a clear picture of the purpose of the governance, and thus also a good picture of the characteristics of strategizing processes and the objectives of the project.

If I had instead asked what the governance should look like, I would have got a number of different wishes that may not have brought about the effect of governance that we were looking for at all. If we answer the why first, it is easier to stick to it. We can ask ourselves why we exist as an organization and why we have a strategy. Working through 'why questions' can sometimes feel like time poorly spent because there is a perception that it does not produce any concrete results. Yet the result may be consensus regarding the purpose of the organization and the strategy. Although it is not concrete per se, this is a good result that will make the rest of our strategizing easier and more efficient. The time it costs will fairly quickly pay off.

Strategy levels

It is relatively common for organizations to strategize in a fairly traditional manner, fairly firmly based in a view of the organization as machine. This is naturally the case in large organizations that have existed for a long time; there is a legacy and they 'grew up' when conditions were stable. But this approach is also common in smaller and younger organizations, even start-ups. I will address why I think this is the case later. Now I will settle with describing what I mean by traditional. One characteristic is that these organizations see strategy as what the upper echelon engages in. This has two problems: first, it excludes issues that are highly strategic from their 'strategic agenda' just because they are farther down in the organization; and second, it excludes important input from competent individuals.

I once worked with the vice president and head of a business unit in a publicly listed company with around 20,000 employees. When we talked about participation he said, 'They don't do strategy' of his middle managers. If he meant long-term, higher-level planning and the setting of corporate goals, then what he said was true. In this case, the long-term planning was performed at the highest level. However, if we appreciate that strategy includes ensuring that the strategy is realized and contributing to long-term competitiveness, then middle managers definitely 'do strategy'. They most certainly behave in a way that contributes to the direction, the performance and the success of the organization. After a discussion we managed to clear out what he meant and I got chance to advocate my view with benefits of a greater openness in strategizing. His view, though, is unfortunately not uncommon at all.

Sometimes challenges are perceived as being 'strategic' when they end up at a certain hierarchical level in an organization, often at the top. This is a common and serious misconception. It is not the levels in a hierarchy that determine whether a challenge is strategic or not. Strategy challenges exist at all levels. Different organizations, and different parts and different levels of organizations need strategies to address different challenges. Strategy issues have to do with the organization's long-term ability to perform and different behaviours are needed to meet up to different strategy challenges. Different strategy challenges are typically managed by answering questions that mirror the levels of strategy.

To get a sense of these strategy levels, the literature generally mentions four levels of strategy that are typically not well understood and applied in organizations: corporate strategy, business strategy, operations strategy and

FIGURE 10.2 Strategy levels and related challenges

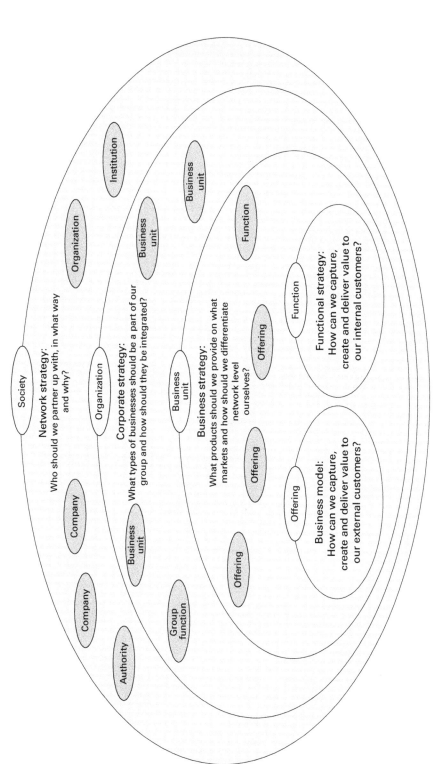

SOURCE Adapted from B De Wit and R Meyer (2004) Strategy: Process, content, context: an international perspective, Thomson Learning, London; and P Wadström, S Schriber, R Teigland and M Kaullio (2017) Strategi: arenan, affären, arbetssätten, ansvaret, avsikten, Liber, Stockholm network strategy (see Figure 10.2). Although these are theoretical levels, they are often applied in practice, with various degrees of success, as well.

Network-level strategy has to do with how organizations collaborate with other partners, industry colleagues, suppliers, in, e.g., alliances and partnerships. In most industries, organizations are dependent on suppliers and partners if they are to be able to supply a qualitative service or product to their customers. Property owners are dependent on contractors in many cases. The contractors are dependent on the companies that supply windows. The window manufacturers are dependent on machine suppliers, the suppliers of wood, glass, etc. We previously touched on the fact that organizations are open systems, meaning that they are affected by the outside world. This is particularly pertinent regarding the organizations that are a part of 'your supply chain' and on which you are dependent to be able to deliver. The aim of a network strategy is to get the most out of our collaborations with suppliers and partners. This means that in some relations pressuring price is good strategy, and in other cases building partnerships, alliances or joint ventures is a more appropriate strategy.

Corporate-level strategy is about managing a set of businesses. It is about deciding which types of business should be a part of the group (i.e. setting corporate scope) and finding ways to support synergy across organizational boundaries, such as businesses, departments, divisions or units (i.e. corporate management). Each level in an organizational hierarchy should add value, otherwise it should not exist. At the most overarching level in an organization this is about identifying synergies within resource utilization, sharing skills, tapping into increased negotiating power in respect of external parties, making use of common support functions, drumming up business together, coordinating strategic initiatives, etc. Unfortunately, it is common to see corporate management teams where the respective unit or company manager reports on 'his/her' area rather than looking at the big picture, which is the responsibility of a corporate management team.

I worked with an organization that wanted to increase its cross-unit synergies. The goal was to make better use of internal resources. The group was purchasing material from competitors in an amount of around €50 million annually. The material they were buying was already present internally in the form of spare capacity, but they did not have a good way to control and realize this synergy. So, we decided to set goals to more properly monitor synergy realization. The measure we set was that the share of what could be purchased from a sister company in another unit should be purchased from that sister company instead of a competitor. This was our key result indicator (KRI) that we followed up and provided quarterly feedback on. The ambition was good, but the result was already in at the end of each quarter, and €12 million had gone to the competition. By focusing on something that was a leading indicator (KBI) and more frequent follow-ups (e.g. monthly), it would have been possible to take actions to influence the result at an earlier stage. It would have been smarter to use a behavioural metric instead of a result metric. Later in the process, we changed this metric into how many times employees actively made contact 'across organizational boundaries' to create synergies between business units. Although this demanded some manual labour to get data, the benefits gained undoubtedly covered that increased cost several times.

Business-level strategy has to do with prioritizing which products and services could become successful in which markets, which competitors are present in these markets, and how to differentiate ourselves from or get better than the competition. This is probably what many people associate strategy with, but as understood it is not the whole picture. In business strategy, focus is on the strategy for a division, business unit or similar. Such units typically have a portfolio of products and/or services for intended markets. These markets may be defined geographically (e.g. the US, China, the EU) or by the branch of industry (e.g. aviation or oil). Central business strategy questions to address include: How do we compete? By size and scale? Standing out as the exclusive alternative? Would we be more prosperous if we address only a certain niche?

Functional-level strategy focuses on how a particular offer, service or product should be optimized in order to fit the prevailing business environment and customer demands. All organizations have some type of offer – products or services. These products and services typically have explicit or implicit target customer group(s) that can be classified and prioritized in different ways, for instance as A, B and C customers. In order to reach the customers and to be able to sell to them, some type of customer relationship is required, as are distribution channels. In order to be able to supply the offer to the selected customers, the organization needs to have processes to work with and employees who possess the right competency and who perform the work in a good way. These are typical issues dealt with within this functional strategy. They include how to ensure that we can supply what the customer needs, which resources we have access to in the form of staff, tools and materials, and how these need to be employed to deliver on our promise to customers.

Traditionally, strategy focuses on business strategy and the other levels are often neglected or considered less important. In order to strategize properly, different behaviour is required at different levels. Network behaviour has to do with 'harnessing the strength of weak ties', talking to people in the market, entering into cooperation agreements and finding organizations around the world that constitute a good complement to our own business. Corporate strategic behaviour has to do with identifying plausible synergies, and to realize them, collaborating, identifying opportunities with other departments, and acting in the best interests of the entire company are important behaviours. Business strategy behaviour focuses on finding ways to decide on a product–market mix and how to differentiate from others. Functional strategy behaviour is related to packaging our offer, performing customer analysis and understanding which partners and competencies are important to be able to supply that offer to our target customers. Strategizing needs to include all of these components in order for the organization to become successful.

A strategy that does not define organizations as open systems in which the outside world both influences and is influenced by one's own organization, is a strategy that does not take into account suppliers, partners or customers (network strategy). That is hardly a strategy worthy of the name. For someone who sees that there are lessons and resource utilization opportunities present between different organizational units, a strategy lacking in synergistic thinking (corporate strategy) does not rise to the level of a strategy. In other words, addressing one level – e.g. focusing on the offering, customers, products, internal processes and competencies – is not enough if we are to strategize in a way that makes us successful.

Different views on strategy

Just as there are different levels of strategy, there are different views. The view of the world influences our view of strategy and how we work in an organization. It can be useful to discuss various *strategy schools of thought*.[2] Which strategy school of thought is applied in different organizations often depends on a few 'leading' people's views of the outside world and of their own organization; we sometimes talk about *personified strategy*.[3]

People perceive the outside world in different ways. If we take two extremes, we can perceive the world as being completely unpredictable and confusing, or as entirely possible to predict and control. Most of us, however, probably see it as somewhere in the middle. The same reasoning applies to one's own organization. It can be perceived as being an irrational chaos, a rationally bounded entity that can be controlled down to the smallest detail, or as falling somewhere between these two extremes. Our way of looking at the outside world and organizations has consequences in terms of how we view strategy and how we strategize.

If the outside world is perceived as being graspable and controllable, we end up far down on a vertical axis; if we believe that the outside world is unpredictable and confusing, we end up far up on the same axis. If our view is that organizations are rational and logical, we end up on the far left of a horizontal axis. On the other hand, if we perceive organizations as being irrational and difficult to control, we end up on the far right of the axis.

Based on this, we get a matrix reflecting the various approaches to our outside world and different strategy schools of thought, the location of which is based on the respective position or perception. The point of this model is to indicate how different ideas about our way of looking at the world can have consequences in terms of what our strategizing looks like. And strategizing is of course nothing less than the behaviour individuals in an organization perform to develop and realize strategy.

Planning orientation and learning orientation in strategizing

Following the argumentation above, and in simplified terms, there are two partly opposing ways of looking at strategy. In one, the world is relatively controllable – the lower left quadrant of the matrix; in the other, we believe in a greater measure of uncertainty – the upper right quadrant.

The first view of strategy means that the strategy process and strategizing is viewed as being rational, logical, easy to understand and sequential. The aim is to plan and control things so that employees 'do as they are told'. This view is based in what we academics refer to as an industrial–organization economics perspective (IO), which was developed mainly during the 1950s and 1960s.[4] For the sake of clarity, I henceforth refer to this as *planning-oriented strategizing*.

The second approach, henceforth called *learning-oriented strategizing*, sees that the strategy process and strategizing need to reinforce creative thinking and spawn new ideas and innovative solutions, rather than promote uniformity and conservative results. This view has a stronger foundation in the organization and behavioural sciences literatures.[5]

When I carry out an assignment involving the development of strategizing in an organization, I often ask people on the board and/or in the management team to indicate where on the graph their perceptions fall by making an X. Interestingly, almost no one places their X down in the lower left-hand corner, where the outside world is graspable and controllable. That is where organizations and their members are rational. The reasoning behind this view is that if only we analyse and plan thoroughly enough, nothing can go wrong. However, although most view the world as in the upper right-hand corner (or quadrant), their ways of strategizing are clearly dominated by rigorous analysis and planning. They strategize in a planning-oriented manner, i.e. they plan things in detail with a long time frame, do budgets on a nitty-gritty level for several years ahead, and they do it to an extent that one might wonder if they want to control the world. If they don't believe they can, to what purpose and why is this so, one might ask. One of my answers to why this is the case is that many individuals responsible for designing and performing the organization's strategizing don't know how to strategize in any other way.

Planning-oriented strategizing can be described on the basis of a number of sequential phases. First, we identify what we wish to achieve. After that we analyse key questions. Once the analysis is complete, various proposals are drawn up, and those that are considered best are selected. After that comes implementation. Planning and execution need to be detailed and seen as a series of logical activities. Planning is sequential: define, diagnose, design, decide and implement.

The basic attitude in all this is that a problem has one clear solution that is the best. Information gathering and analysis are supposed to lead to an optimal solution. This order is fine when a problem is clear, the information is reliable and the environment in which the problem occurs (i.e. market and/or organization) is clearly structured, and may be controllable. This is logic, easy to grasp and to communicate to different responsible managers in the businesses. Something is right, and something is wrong. Clear; no ambiguity.

However, the world and most organizations do not always meet these criteria, and few problems relating to strategy are quite so clearly defined. They are typically *wicked problems*, meaning that all real-world problems are related to all other real-world problems;[6] they are interconnected; they are built up by many factors that in themselves are difficult to define; they do not have a clear solution and require creativity; and they cannot be solved by thinking. We need to act then see what happens, to get input on how to solve, or manage, it. There is typically no answer key when it comes to strategy.

> There is no optimal solution; no 'one correct answer' in strategy. Everything is Pareto-optimal. Thinking first is good to help us know how to act in a forward-looking way and what behaviour is important, but sometimes it's not possible to think or plan ahead. In this case, doing needs to support thinking.

Doing first then thinking is truly odd when it comes to strategizing for a planning-oriented individual. Strategic planning is viewed to be based on the assumption that management formulates strategies. And then it's up to the organization to execute them.

In practice, planning-oriented strategizing often means that management and managers set goals and schedule activities to achieve the goals based on their competency and their circumstances. This is related to the vice president I mentioned earlier, who initially argued that middle managers don't strategize. But what if those who set the goals do not understand the business or market best? What goals do we get in that case? What if there is not *one* best solution? For that matter, if executives are able to do the operational work better than the employees who actually perform it, one might ask whether we have the right person in the right place. Those who have knowledge of the business or customers need to be involved.

Learning-oriented strategizing argues that an organization's long-term goals and activities – behaviour – need to adapt over time. This makes frequent and continuous evaluation and feedback of results important instruments for teaching the organization what kinds behaviour have the intended effect and should therefore be reinforced. It is the foundation for adaptation. Strategy then assumes a more 'emergent' character.

From learning-oriented strategizing, based in behavioural psychology, strategizing can be seen as an ongoing process that involves questioning, innovating, adapting and formulating and realizing strategies that will lead to the organization's most important goals being realized. This process is in progress all the time whether we want it to be or not, and it is important to take advantage of it.

If learning is important, strategy must have an emergent character. Basically, this means that strategies are created by employee behaviour across the organization. Strategy formulation and realization then become a more continuous process to follow up on and feed back insights to the organization, rather than a brief planning process performed once a year and that has a clear start and finish.

Basically, planning orientation argues that we should think first and act later, and learning orientation wants us to act first and think later – to behave in some way and then draw conclusions. How else would we learn?

The lure and difficulties of planning orientated strategizing

I once worked full-time on an extensive strategic change initiative for a little more than three years. Because it was a large and complex project with a lot of IT and external consultants included, planning was important. The planning was also extensive and therefore time-consuming. The consequences of the project were truly critical and so we needed to be thorough. However, the conditions kept changing continuously as we planned – as conditions do, things happen. In practice, this meant that as soon as we had finished planning, the conditions had changed so much that the planning was no longer consistent with reality. So, we basically had to start the planning over. Because the situation was uncertain and unclear, we planned the project a total of three times. Still, we, and the board that was the main stakeholder, never felt entirely confident about the plan, and wanted to keep tweaking it. In addition, the management team did not except the uncertainty we could not avoid. When the project started, the timetable called for a three-year project. The actual time it took was closer to six years. This planning also made for anxiety in the sub-projects, in total 46, whose work was governed by the decisions we made at the project management level. Further, this led to impatience and to many project participants not feeling well. This in turn meant that the project was further delayed, that it became more expensive, and that much of the budget was spent on planning instead of delivering.

In short, we had the wrong view of our project. As I have discussed above, we knew that the conditions were changing and that the scope was unclear with respect to many issues. We knew that it was hard to secure decisions and that it was a complex project. Although we knew this, we, and the senior stakeholders, couldn't handle the complexity that it entailed, and the only thing we seemed to be able to do was to plan and then plan again, instead of making decisions and acting. Planning has many consequences. For some individuals in our group the planning behaviour was positively reinforced by, for example, a sense of certainty that we would deliver something great or keep to our budget (somewhat illogical as more resources were spent on planning and less on action). These consequences are positive, immediate and certain (PIC). However, in practice it was of course nothing but a false sense of certainty, as our planning took us nowhere nearer our goals. For other individuals in our group the planning was negatively reinforced by the decreased risk of being dumbfounded by the board. Although negative, it was also immediate and certain (NIC). This shows that reinforcement is individual and related to the expected function and consequence of a behaviour. In a sense, we were heavily reinforced by a string of consequences that kept us performing planning-oriented strategizing, and initially we did not seem to be able to break free.

This is truly common behaviour, not only in major projects or programmes, but also in the course of everyday business. In contrast to planning, which is reinforced, taking strategic action has negative consequences (punishment) that are immediate and certain because it forces us to act without having the feeling that we have thought things through properly. The conclusion of this is that, in order to achieve the goals we set, we need to start acting in spite of uncertainty in the planning.

One of the most common themes in strategizing comes down to managers' need for control – control over decisions and strategies, over the present and the future, over thoughts and deeds, over workers and other managers, over markets and customers. Policies, rules, strategies, approaches, training sessions, codes of conduct, centralizing tendencies, a 'one-company approach' and so on are all intended to influence how we are supposed to behave. But, as we have seen before, these are only activators, and do not have the same actuating power as consequences. So, what all these efforts amount to in the end is actually unclear. And, last but not least, if strategy is aimed at carving out long-term competitive advantages, are these best created through control? As you have noticed, not much supports that.

Benjamin Disraeli, a 19th-century UK Prime Minister, once wrote something I say a lot: 'What we anticipate seldom occurs: but what we least expected generally happens.'[7] If that is true, which I believe it is, this means that we cannot possibly control the decisions and thoughts of every member in the organization, still less the outside world. All the same, many strive for this type of control. These efforts to gain control inhibit the creativity and innovation that form the foundation of long-term success.

Planning-oriented strategizing has several obvious drawbacks. It often leads to companies setting goals that are too short-term. If bonus payments are contingent on a given number of site visits with a focus on safety being carried out by year-end, you can be sure that the frequency of these visits will increase in November and December. The same goes for all goals that are linked to various externally imposed reinforcers, such as bonuses.

Another objection to planning-oriented strategizing is that those who only formulate a strategy – and do not need to realize it – often see organizations as impermeable entities that cannot be influenced by the outside world. But, as we know, organizations are not closed systems that live in their own world: *no business is an island*.[8] This means that no matter how much time and effort you put into analysis to be able to plan, there will always be uncertainty. When all factual issues are sorted out, there is still a great amount of *residual uncertainty*;[9] uncertain issues that no analysis could ever make certain.

Strategizing in uncertainty

Knowledge about uncertainty in the outside world has caused more agile and fleet-footed project methods to gain ground. Now, 'near zone planning' is common in many areas, as are shorter cycles and more frequent feedback loops, particularly in project management. However, this is still unusual when it comes to strategizing and what we could call strategic planning, which is odd, since an organization is often even more vulnerable to changes in the environment than a project.

The world is unpredictable and confusing. A financial crisis erupts in the course of what to many people feels like just a few hours. A pandemic breaks out, and in just a couple of months large parts of the world are paralysed, and continue to stay paralysed for a long time as we try to contain the virus. Companies that did not exist 15 years ago are now among the world's most highly valued enterprises and are the most sought-after workplaces for young talent. Organizations and their members make bizarre decisions and behave irrationally. Companies form cartels. Companies purchase 'stuff' for use in their own organization from direct competitors despite the fact that they have spare internal capacity. Companies play tricks with their accounting. Employees 'freeze' each other out. Seen from the outside, these can appear to be irrational behaviours. But this does not alter the fact that this behaviour exists, meaning that there is some type of reinforcement going on.

Real-world correlations are difficult to interpret and understand. Everything depends to a greater or lesser degree on everything else (cf. *wicked problems*). Fortunately, human beings are not static, controllable or even rational. Instead, they are dynamic and are often governed by reinforcements we do not always see, which means that they can sometimes be perceived as being irrational. Because the outside world and organizations are populated and controlled by people, this makes organizations irrational as well. Behaviour analysis is a way of understanding the reinforcements that behaviour has. It is a way of understanding this 'irrational' world.

David Orrell and Tomas Szedlacek are two researchers. One is a mathematician and the other an economist. In their book *Bescheidenhet* (German for modesty), they describe a world where – similarly to the claim made by Heraclitus over 2500 years ago – 'everything is in flux'.[10] They see a world where modern-day fortune tellers (economists and analysts) draw up decision-support documents with long-range forecasts that are far more uncertain than those made by meteorologists. Their thesis is that the world cannot be predicted using mathematics or logic, and that modesty would be an appropriate attitude when presenting forecasts for the future. Everything is in flux and we really do not know what will happen tomorrow. Those who see that world have a hard time justifying a five-year plan in the belief that if we simply analyse and plan well enough, we will achieve our goals.

Strategy, *a* strategy and behavioural strategizing

A person who views organizations as being controllable, bounded entities does not feel the need to answer the questions about how to realize the developed strategy. Coming up with a plan means that it will be realized. With this view, there is no significant difference between strategy and '*a* strategy'. But in reality, the difference is great. Strategy boils down to making a number of decisions whose purpose is to create competitiveness, and then sticking to or re-evaluating these decisions, following through. '*A* strategy' is where we describe these decisions – often in advance and in the form of a plan – and if we do it properly, we also describe how we are to realize it.

In short, there are two main reasons that organizations have a strategy:

1 To describe where the organization wants to go: a vision, goal, a description of the place we want to get to.

2 To describe how the organization will get there: behaviours, actions, timelines and so on.

Initially the strategy literature separated *strategy formulation*, or *strategy development*, from *strategy implementation*, or *strategy execution*, and saw these as two relatively separated elements. So, the formulation, or the planning, is what traditionally constitutes strategy. To then deliver according to plan from this perspective could be termed implementation, execution, operations or daily management, and should be supported by follow-up, or controlling. This is seen in planning-oriented strategizing.

However, as we now know, strategy is about more than just formulating goals and plans – it's also about getting there. If we consider that actions, the process for the way we strategize, are an important part of the strategy, we realize that the formulation process is not even 'halfway there' if all we have is an idea for how to draw up the plan. We need to have an idea for how to deliver on it. Strategizing cannot be boiled down to an annual review of goals for the next period (e.g. a year), a list of activities and a budget. It must also include evaluating and ensuring goal achievement and feedback to the business for course-correction purposes. It is easy to come up with a plan that is out of touch with reality if we do not simultaneously have to consider how the plan is to be realized. Because the goal can be nothing else than to realize our strategy. It can never be to produce the strategy itself. Therefore, we need to think about how it is to be realized during the planning stage. How the plan might be realized has a significant bearing on what actually will be realized and should therefore not be divorced from the planning.

> Strategizing is behavioural. It is a question of creating action. It is the behaviour that the employees in an organization perform based on the progress of an organization to achieve its goals – not a plan.

Emergent strategizing and adaptation

Changes in organizations' outside world and in their respective markets require them to adapt more quickly: they must change as the world changes. This means that the model where we separate formulation from realization is outdated. It's no longer feasible to have a five-, three- or even one-year plan formulated by senior management which it is then up to the rest of the organization to realize. The strategy formulation process needs to be a much more integrated part of daily business operations so that it can be adapted to the outside world. Employees that are closer to the customers, closer to the market and closer to the future need to be participating in the development of strategy for the entire organization. That enables adaption to surroundings and stronger solutions to strategy challenges.

An organization that wants to be successful needs to take into account and take advantage of what is happening in its surroundings. To do so, emergent strategy is an alternative. Emergent strategies are formulated and realized in alternation. For a planning-oriented individual it can be difficult to conceive of action without intention. But for a learning-oriented individual it is equally difficult to conceive of intention without action.

The notion of how emergent and planned strategy results in realized strategy was elegantly illustrated in 1985 by top-class strategy academics Henry Mintzberg and James Waters.[11] In short, *planned strategy* combined with *emergent strategy* is what forms a *realized strategy*. This means that parts of what was planned are realized, while other parts are not: *abandoned strategy*. Some things that were not planned surface and are also realized, i.e. *emergent strategy*. And thus only a limited part of the planned strategy is realized; this limited part could be referred to as *deliberate strategy*.

In extension, this means that strategizing is not about establishing detailed action plans. It is about influencing behaviour in the direction in which the organization wants to move. This means that creating a vision, formulating objectives, operationalizing them into measurable targets, evaluating outcomes frequently, reflecting on progress, learning from experience, experimenting to find more efficient ways and constantly changing our organization on this basis are all critical behaviours in the strategizing – not just performing analysis and long-range planning.

In the environment of naturally high growth that prevailed in the wake of the Second World War, strategy, structure and systems offered organizations much-needed discipline, focus and control. Yet today's economic environment is one of overcapacity and fierce competition. Discipline and control are not as crucial. However, innovation, adaptation and resilience become increasingly important when growth slows and the pace of change picks up. The boundaries that separate companies and industries from each other are blurred when new technologies and new markets meet in new ways.

AT&T, Vodaphone and Telefonica, which have been dominant telecom operators in the US, the UK and Spain respectively, are now beginning to dip their toes in (or even wade into) the IT industry. Google is an obvious future competitor. AstraZeneca spends considerably more money on marketing than on research and development.[12] It is starting more and more to resemble a product company like Procter & Gamble or Unilever than a traditional pharmaceutical company. This 'ambiguity' creates new growth opportunities in the borderland where traditional companies and branches of industries meet. Who is actually a competitor? The organizations that do the same thing we do or the organizations that any presumptive customer is partnering up with instead of us? Or is the term even wider? Is it organizations that we have to compete with in any discipline, for example regarding access to critical resources?

Today, a company's most scarce resource is rarely the financial means at the disposal of senior management, but rather the knowledge and expertise possessed by front-line employees – those who actually meet the customers or do the job, those who behave to realize the strategy.

Leaders who want to gain and sustain competitive advantage by how they strategize need to spend less time formulating a strategic plan and more time encouraging innovation, adaptation and change. They need to let everyone in the organization help each other tackle a tough question: How are we going to get even better in the future, again and again and again?

Successful organizations continuously learn about and from the outside world, and 'craft' strategies that are considered appropriate at that time. The key to becoming a successful organization is not to formulate the right strategy, but to create a clear link between strategy, behaviour and change throughout the organization. This requires a strategic understanding – the understanding and insight that the 'chaotic' environment in which we live and work is here to stay and that it is practically impossible to create a 'perfect' strategy. We can refer to this competency as *strategic IQ*.[13] And, like every other competency, it is made up of behaviour that can be trained.

Realizing strategy through behaviour

In many organizations, far too much of strategy is about developing plans and visions, and setting goals. And far too little is about how we actually realize the strategies. The strategy itself is not what gives us an enduring competitive or even comparative advantage. It is the realization that yields actual success.

Anyone can imitate IKEA's, Google's, Toyota's or FC Barcelona's strategy, but no one has managed to copy the realization thus far.

Being able to execute requires competency beyond analysis, planning and imitation. We need to be able to discuss how and what is to be done, to prioritize and de-prioritize activities, to allocate responsibility, to follow up on what is being done and the result thereof, and to provide feedback on the results to those performing the work, thus creating learning. We need to be able to evaluate the company's business environment and its risks and opportunities, to coordinate people and competencies, and to strengthen the behaviour that yields results. Basically, it's about making an effort to see the reality and then acting accordingly. Too many organizations bury their heads in the sand. This is one main reason why they don't become truly successful and outperform their rivals in the long run.

By spending more time on evaluation, feedback – consequences – and continuous changes, all organizations can increase the degree to which their strategies are executed. In behavioural psychology parlance, we might say that strategizing needs to shift its focus from being used as an activator to instead being used as consequences. No strategy can be realized without people acting and behaving in some way. Behaviour causing organizations to create a better fit with environment, better fulfilment of customers' demands and more efficient ways of working needs to be reinforced.

Through the process of evaluation and feedback, the organization is reinforced, learns and changes continuously in order to better meet the outside world's and the market's demands. In the 20th century, the debate about strategic change centred on something that needed to change in the organization, and if so *what*. But in the 21st century change is a matter of course in all organizations. Now the debate about change has more to do with how we are to manage to change enough, and fast enough.

In true Darwinian spirit, organizations need to change to adapt to a constantly changing environment if they are to survive. If the change happening outside is faster than that happening inside, we will soon be left behind. There is probably someone out there who is doing more than us to stay ahead of both us and the market.

Notes

1   R Whittington (2003) The work of strategizing and organizing: For a practice perspective, *Strategic Organization*, 1 (1), 117–25
2   H Mintzberg, B Ahlstrand and J Lampel (1998) *Strategy Safari: A guided tour through the wilds of strategic management*, The Free Press, New York

3 See, e.g., M Löwstedt. Exploring the concept of strategy using a practice lens: The case of a large construction company, Licenciate thesis, 2010, Chalmers Technological University, Gothenburg.

4 See, e.g., R Coase (1937) *The Nature of the Firm*, Oxford University Press, New York; M E Porter (1980) *Competitive Strategy*, The Free Press, New York; F M Scherer and D Ross (1990) *Industrial Market Structure and Economic Performance*, 3rd edn, Houghton Mifflin, Dallas; R Schmalensee and R Willig (1989) Government intervention in the marketplace, in *Handbook of Industrial Organization*, R Schmalensee and RWillig, Elsevier, Amsterdam

5 See, e.g., J B Barney. Strategic factor markets: Expectations, luck, and business strategy, *Management Science*, 1986, 32 (10), 1231–41; J L Bower (1970) *Managing the Resource Allocation Process*, Harvard University, Boston, MA; RA Burgelman. A process model of internal corporate venturing in the diversified major firm, *Administrative Science Quarterly*, 1983, 28 (2), 223–44; R M Grant. The resource-based theory of competitive advantage: Implications for strategy formulation, *Knowledge and Strategy*, 1991, 33 (3), 3–23; C Helfa and M Peteraf. Understanding dynamic capabilities: Progress along a developmental path, *Strategic Organization*, 2009, 7 (1), 91–102; C E Lindblom. The science of "muddling through"', *Public Administrative Review*, 1959, 19 (2), 78–88; H Mintzberg and J A Waters. Of strategy: Deliberate and emergent, *Strategic Management Journal*, 1985, 6 (3), 257–72; J B Quinn. Strategic change: Logical incrementalism, *Sloan Management Review*, 1978, 20 (Fall), 7–21

6 See, e.g., H W J Rittel and M M Webber. Dilemmas in a general theory of planning, *Policy Sciences*, 1973, 4, 166–69; R O Mason and I I Mitroff (1981) *Challenging Strategy Assumptions*, Wiley, New York

7 B Disraeli (1837) *Henrietta Temple*, Book 2, Chapter 4

8 H Håkansson and I Snehota. No business is an island: The network concept of business strategy, *Scandinavian Management Journal*, 1989, 22 (3), 187–200

9 H Courtney, J Kirkland and O Viguerie. Strategy under uncertainty, *Harvard Business Review*, 1997

10 D Orrell and T Szedlacek (2013) *Bescheidenheit – für eine neue Ökonomie*, Carl Hanser GmbH & Co, Munich

11 H Mintzberg and J Waters (1985) Of strategies, deliberate and emergent, *Strategic Management Journal*, 6 (3), 257–72

12 See, e.g., R Anderson. Pharmaceuticals industry gets high on fat profits, BBC News, 6 November 2014, www.bbc.com/news/business-28212223 (archived at https://perma.cc/TS7G-DJ3F)

13 See, e.g., J R Wells (2012) *Strategic IQ: Creating smarter corporations*, Jossey-Bass, San Francisco

11

To realize strategy is to change

This year's strategy is rarely identical to last year's. If a strategy does not contain exactly the same actions, results or goals as the previous strategy, the realization involves some type of change. And even if, God forbid, we as an organization decide to do exactly the same things, with the exact same resources, the outside world has changed; which means, if we want to survive, we have to adapt. We have to change anyhow.

All changes in organizations require members of the organization to learn to develop existing or new behaviour, or to stop engaging in old behaviour. This may involve a new way of managing costs, a new way to use a system, a new way of greeting customers entering our store, a new way of looking at a complex issue, or an improved way of casting the foundation of a house.

To realize strategy is to develop and change an organization and its members. And it is not possible to change an organization without changing the behaviour of its members. This is a fundamental assumption – an axiom. People do not develop unless they learn new things. If they do not learn to behave in new ways, and if they do not change or refine their working methods, the organization does not develop. Behaviour is indeed the lowest common denominator.

The majority of organizations claim that their employees are their most important resource, and that the employees' knowledge is becoming increasingly important. This is particularly true in knowledge-intensive and service-based companies. Yet many of them have only a vague notion of the laws of human behaviour or the principles of learning, and how these can contribute to enhanced organizational performance. Enhanced performance is achieved when employees learn new, more effective behaviour.

If we want results that are different from what we have today, this means that we cannot continue doing exactly the same thing. We need to change how we do things. We need to change behaviour. The behaviour of employees creates value for the organization that they are part of, and it is the task of the organization's leaders to bring out the best in each employee. This means that, from a management perspective, it is difficult, if not outright impossible, to separate strategy, and of course strategizing, from change and learning.

Revolutionary and evolutionary organizational change

It is sometimes assumed that change can be planned and controlled by a central person or group acting on the basis of a common idea. When more and more organizations are having difficulties realizing strategies that entail change in spite of increased planning efforts, there is reason to doubt whether planning and centralized change is the right method for changing the behaviour we want to change.

Another option is to let the change emerge unintentionally. Those who initiate and realize the change can be located at different levels and in different departments within the organization. Change initiatives can come from senior management, from middle managers or from the grassroots. Formal strategic change through planning accounts for a large part of the change management that goes on in organizations, but far from all of it. Additional methods need to be used to succeed in pushing through new ideas and change initiatives.

The literature in this area usually talks about two general ways of looking at change in organizations. Namely, *revolution* and *evolution*.[1] These are sometimes also referred to as *top-down* and *bottom-up*, respectively. A revolution is an abrupt and radical change that takes place over a short period of time and is driven through from above, or from the centre. Proponents of revolutionary change believe that people are generally reluctant to change and have a strong preference for stability. Instability leads to uncertainty, political power games and conflicts between different parts of the organization. Periods of instability should therefore be kept short. Revolutionary change is generally considered necessary when there is a deeply rooted organizational rigidity or inertia that needs to be overcome.

Proponents of evolutionary change argue that grandiose plans calling for total change over a short period of time do not bring about any lasting effect. After some time, individuals fall back into old patterns of behaviour, and no real change, i.e. behavioural change, has taken place. Revolutionary change can work as a quick-fix solution, with attractive results in the short term, but a thorough change is something that should be done gradually and accomplished with small successive steps. Evolution is thus a process where a number of continuous, small changes gradually develop into a larger, constant process of change, and where the majority of the employees have participated.

Many researchers, including sage Harvard professor Michael Tushman, argue that evolutionary and revolutionary change processes complement each other and that a combination of the two is the ultimate way to drive change. The most successful companies are marked by relatively long periods of adaptation and small adjustments, all of which support the basic strategy. Such a period of relative calm is called *convergence*.[2] However, these periods need to be interspersed with periods of revolutionary, dramatic and sweeping changes when these are necessary, usually when the outside world changes significantly. These periods are called *upheaval*.

People are in need of both experimentation and order. The same goes for organizations. Organizations cannot survive without adapting to new conditions. Nor can they live without the stability that allows them to make use of all the changes that have been made. The founder of IT giant Oracle, Larry Ellison, is said to have expressed this in a striking way: 'We gather around change'. Over the past two decades, Oracle has bought 100 or so companies, including large ones like Sun Microsystems and PeopleSoft. Over the same period, they grew their sales from just over $10 billion to nearly $40 billion.[3] In 2021, Oracle has approximately 136,000 employees; at the start of this century they had fewer than 40,000. This growth has probably involved both laborious and costly changes for Oracle. And yet this is a striking example of how organizations that manage to integrate change and strategy can become successful and carve out a unique position for themselves.

Disruptive events in history have had disruptive consequences for organizations. The dot-com crash at the shift of the millennium forced IT consulting companies to lower their hourly rates by up to 50–60 per cent. This tends to make an organization think about how it should lead its business. The banks are subject to a completely different capital adequacy regime under the Basel III regulations issued in the wake of the 2007–08 global financial crisis. British Airways, KLM and Lufthansa were still fighting for survival after the deregulation of the airline industry when the COVID-19 virus spread and forced several governments to invest to avoid bankruptcy. As a result, 'upstarts' like Ryanair and Norwegian Air, that had been quite successful over the last decade due to their continuing challenge of the incumbents, are also struggling badly.

Many changes cannot be foreseen, but by working continuously and systematically with strategizing, by having an extremely explicit change and adaptation take on it, organizations can manage to mitigate the worst effects and continue to perform even in difficult circumstances. Indeed, Bill Gates warned about the effects of a pandemic in 2015. He said, in relation to a pandemic, that 'there's no need to panic... but we need to get going'.[4] Since March 2020, panic has been obvious, and the countries and organizations with systems that to some extent were prepared so far have had better chances of tackling the virus. And, of course, this is just one example. To be slightly more philosophic, 'Chance favours only the prepared mind', as French 17th-century chemist and biologist Louis Pasteur allegedly put it.[5]

Companies with a planning orientation in strategizing will often tell themselves: 'We just need to get through this, and we'll be done.' But no matter how good things may be after a change, it doesn't solve all the problems. And, to say the least, radical changes are definitely risky. Companies with this approach will often suffer from what is sometimes referred to as *repetitive change syndrome*.[6] Changing and changing again, back and forth, focusing on 'details', e.g. 5 per cent reduction of the workforce every two years, without having a long-term idea of where they are going in terms of vision or strategy. To be cruel, much of this is not change, and it is definitely not strategy. It's crisis management. And, what is worse, constantly changing and not giving the organization a period of stability to settle down, convergence, is not good for the performance of the organization. So, organizations that suffer from this syndrome typically slowly deteriorate. In the end, both management and employees forget the purpose of all the changes that are underway and, worse, they become paralyzed waiting for the next wave.

The increased speed of change and organizational complexity mean that we need to view change as an ever-ongoing process and a part of strategizing. An organization is never 'finished'. This means that the work to change an organization to adapt to its environment is constant and always in progress. Change, settle down, change, settle down. Almost all large organizations go through a major change or reorganization every three to five years. Such major changes might very well be necessary as things evolve outside the organization. In addition, an organization's successes over a couple of years tends to preserve its way of functioning, which adds to the need to drive change. However, as noted, stability is also needed. It is, of course, impossible to say how long the intervals should be as this depends on how dynamic and competitive the environment is that the industry is in.

What is true, though, is that successful organizations create internal forces of stability. Organizational structures become entrenched and only changes that are compatible with existing beliefs are allowed. This creates a culture and a history around the company, which in many cases is a good thing. All organizations want to be able to point to a strong history – a good reputation. *Storytelling* is when a company describes its history to create a strong culture and hopefully successes in the future. This, however, has risks associated with it: and one major risk is spelled complacency.

Self-reinforcing behaviour poses a threat

Over time, *self-reinforcing* behavioural patterns are created. When behaviour is self-reinforcing, it does not require any external reinforcers. The behaviour persists simply because it is reinforcing in itself. This means that the behaviour can be perceived as being enjoyable, or interesting, or that the person performing it feels competent, or that it feels safe to avoid having to change something that has worked for half a century. A strong culture with a lot of self-reinforcing behaviour can blinker an organization. This may result in the organization avoiding threat detection due to its strong conviction.

> The longer the period of success, calm and stability, the more vulnerable the company is. Companies live under a kind of paradox that can be summed up as follows: 'The better things are going for us, the worse off we are.' Success can very well breed decline.

Many of the best ideas in organizations are never realized, precisely because new insights and initiatives often conflict with well-established patterns of thought and behaviour. One of AstraZeneca's greatest successes, Losec, is an example. The Losec project was stopped twice, the first time because it was not considered effective enough and the second time due to side-effects that were unwanted. Although stopping something may not be wrong, we must be certain that we are not stopping things because they contrast with our own assumptions. In this example, Losec became one of AstraZeneca's most successful products after a bit more work 'under the radar'.

There are also several examples of giants in their respective industries that were on the verge of bankruptcy because they believed that the structure or business model that brought success during the post-war period would also bring success in the information society, or will keep bring success in the knowledge society we compete in now. General Motors (GM) and IBM are two examples of companies that pulled through. Kodak did not.

The core of change is to break free from outmoded rules and assumptions. Long-term successful organizations realize the importance of constantly challenging prevailing principles and not allowing themselves to be guided by norms or culture. In principle, using the phraseology of behavioural psychology, it comes down to teaching our organization to be contingency-shaped rather than rule-governed. Major disruptive changes are necessary, but long-term success is created by reinforcing innovation and by questioning prevailing 'truths'.

In organizations that want to perform better, it should be easy to learn new behaviour and to improve existing behaviour. Organizations that are high-performing are organized so as to actively create and reinforce new, more efficient behaviour. Organizations that take a planning-oriented approach often reinforce a number of behaviours that themselves inhibit learning, innovation and adaptation:

- Employees focus on their own duties and lose sight of the 'big picture'.
- Employees blame others for their problems.
- Management acts without realizing that they are contributing to the problems they want to solve.
- Employees focus on isolated events and on short-termism.
- Employees underestimate slowly emerging threats.
- Employees never learn about the results of their decisions, so they don't have an opportunity to learn from experience.
- Employee disagreements are silenced instead of being reinforced.

To become a successful organization, member behaviour that leads to continuous improvements needs to be reinforced. *Kaizen* is a Japanese word that roughly translates as constant improvement.[7] Kaizen is an ongoing process of improvement that involves everyone in the organization, both employees and leaders. The starting point for improvement is recognizing a need. The need stems from a problem. If there are no problems, nor is there any need for improvement. Complacency is Kaizen's, and therefore improvement's, archenemy, which is why problem-awareness and problem identification are encouraged. Unfortunately, problem-oriented individuals often get punished with gibes, scorn and the like: 'Is there anything else you want to complain about?'

An organization becomes better by identifying as many problems as possible and by reinforcing problem identification and problem solving. Of course, simply identifying a problem is not enough, but if no problem is identified, no problem will be solved. And let us be forthright: all organizations have problems. By constantly striving to identify and bring problems up to the surface in order to improve and adapt the organization to the outside world, it is possible to avoid *organizational inertia*.[8]

Learning is crucial for achieving future goals

The employees' willingness to learn is an important aspect of becoming a high-performing and adapting organization. As we learn, we find new problems and new solutions. Knowledge and behaviour within an organization must be kept continuously up to date. Organizations have to bring in new information and acquire new knowledge, while also questioning and challenging the organization's prevailing truths. Learning is important, as is relearning. We sometimes use the terms *generative learning* and *adaptive learning*.[9] Generative learning is about creativity and questioning, while adaptive learning is about being able to manage something in a good way. Both are needed in order to achieve future goals.

Learning usually occurs by us first doing something and then consciously or unconsciously reflecting on our behaviour. It is an informal, often unexpected process of our brain and is part of the process of change, and therefore strategizing, in an organization. If we do not learn anything new, we cannot do anything new. No one knows when learning may occur. It can occur anywhere and can include something as narrow as learning how to say hello in Serbian or something as broad as understanding the way in which the organization's values actually mean something to me as a person and the person I want to be.

Many consider John Dewey to be the father of activity-based learning. He coined the concept *'learning by doing'*[10] at the end of the 19th century. He claims that learning must be seen as the continuous reconstruction of experience, and that the process and goals of learning are the same thing. Thus, learning and doing are tightly connected and reinforce each other: doing, reading, reflecting and so on. Learning is by itself a value that can also bring about other values, for instance in the organization.

Learning in strategizing

As we have discussed earlier, we humans sometimes need to think first to be able to do something thereafter. We must also do first to be able to think afterwards. Action is important if we are to be able to think. If we insist on always thinking first and acting later, we impede learning and creativity in the organization. Unfortunately, this is what organizations do when they strategize in a planning-oriented manner. Separating strategy formulation from strategy realization impedes learning, innovation and the ability to change the organization. For the sake of the company's long-term development and success (e.g. profitability), it is important to integrate strategic planning with the realization of the strategy. By integrating these two parts, we can take advantage of the entire organization's competency during the analytical phase, while at the same time better understanding the business and creating opportunities for the future. This way, learning becomes a natural part of strategizing.

Behaviour is learned in four different ways. These different ways of learning are often intertwined and are happening in parallel during the actual learning process.[11]

- *Insight learning* is when the person first thinks about how he/she should behave in order to attain a certain result, and then performs this behaviour. This is the most unusual and the most demanding way to learn new behaviours. Insight learning is needed when I am in a situation and know what I want to achieve but need to figure out what behaviour creates that result – for example, when I am faced with a unique strategic dilemma that requires a totally novel approach to solve it. Insight learning requires abstract thinking, the ability to try to solve the problem 'in your head'.

- *Instructional learning* is when rules or instructions describe how a behaviour is to be performed. The instruction is generally given in oral or written form. Based on a given instruction, the goal is to do exactly what the rule says. To manage that, both intelligence and a language in which we can use abstract terms to describe the behaviour are required. Operating instructions, rules, manuals, orders and strategies are examples of this.

- *Model-based learning*   is when I see, hear or perceive something that a role model does and mimic the behaviour based on that. We can also mimic the model with a temporal delay. We do not have to perform the behaviour right then and there but may remember what the model did and mimic it a number of days, weeks or even years later. Most social behaviour is learned in this way. This learning can be both unconscious and ill-considered. Model-based learning is often what keeps a culture – its deeply-rooted habits – alive.

- *Learning by shaping*   is when the behaviour is learned based on the reinforcing consequences it has. *Trial and error* is when the shaping process happens randomly. But it should really be called 'trial and success', as the successful behaviour is what gives us reinforcement so that we learn. Shaping is always involved in the learning of complex behaviour and behavioural patterns. Examples of this include walking, writing, reading or strategic reasoning.

Shaping behaviour frequency and topography

If strategizing entails adapting to changing environments, learning is crucial. What we need to learn is new behaviours that better fit the surrounding conditions and therefore help the organization to compete and succeed. There are two different ways of shaping behaviour. One way is to influence the *frequency* (number of behaviours within a certain time frame) and the other is to influence the *topography* (the appearance of the behaviour).

Shaping the frequency means influencing the quantity of a behaviour. This is something we do if we want to see more or less of the behaviour, as with excess and deficit behaviour. Continuous and frequent reinforcement is required early on in the learning of new behaviour. If I then want to continue increasing the frequency of the behaviour once the behaviour has been learned, I make sure that the frequency of reinforcement gradually tapers off. Remember the slot machines and intermittent reinforcement mentioned earlier in the book. The more I am able to try out and refine the behaviour before I get reinforcement, the greater the training effect.

Shaping the topography means trying to influence behaviour to become more precise (or more functional) through gradual refinement. When we run our first investment calculation, we will probably make a few simple mistakes, lose sight of a few variables and forget a source or two. As we become more capable, we lose sight of fewer variables and sources. Shaping topography is about reinforcing the things that look best over and over again, while ignoring the mistakes. The result is that the good parts of the behaviour become enduring, while the bad parts are extinguished. This relates to the 10,000 hours of *deliberate practice* that makes a master.

When we are to learn something new and complex, it is important that we learn in the right order. Academic scholars sometimes talk about *hierarchical learning*.[12] An easy way to describe this is by saying that we first need to learn how to use a computer before we can send an email. To be able to work as an accountant, we need to be able to add and subtract. Once we are able to add and subtract, we can learn how a balance sheet or income statement is structured. Once we understand that, the opportunity to understand a business from a financial perspective opens up. Once we have learned how to analyse income statements and balance sheets, we can make proposals as to how a company can tweak its profitability. In order to create an adaptable organization, it is important to understand what employees know how to do, what they need to learn, and in what order they need to learn this in order to change their behaviour. Behaviours that consitiute the basis of the learning hierarchy generally create many possibilities to learn more things and find new reinforcements for such new behaviour. These are typically referred to as 'behavioral cusps'.

The acquisition and application of new knowledge is a key issue in any organization. One important set of behaviours in high-performing organizations is learning how to find information and how to transform it into new knowledge, knowledge that can then be applied to developing the business. Actively searching for and obtaining new information is such a behavioural cusp that it opens up the possibility of a number of new reinforcers – learning new things, understanding things and feeling competent.

> When we want to change our organization, for example by making the production process more efficient or by increasing product quality, it is important to identify the behaviours that employees need to learn, and the order in which these should be learned. For preventive purposes, it is also important to create an environment that makes it possible for employees to constantly learn new things and reinforces them in so doing.

Notes

1 See, e.g., M Beer and N Nohria (2000) *Breaking the Code of Change*, Harvard Business School Press, Cambridge, MA

2 M Tushman, W Newman and E Romanelli. Convergence and upheaval: Managing the unsteady pace of organizational evolution, *California Management Review*, 1986, 29 (1), 583–94

3 See, e.g., J P Pederson (2005) *International Directory of Company Histories*, vol 67, St James Press, Detroit; United States Securities and Exchange Commission. Oracle Corporation fiscal year 2020, 2021, https://d18rn0p25nwr6d.cloudfront.net/CIK-0001341439/8a227df9-679d-4dbc-ae1e-b62c435b22ee.pdf (archived at https://perma.cc/R6RU-GNRZ)

4 B Gates. The next outbreak? We're not ready, TED: Ideas worth spreading, YouTube, 3 April 2015, www.youtube.com/watch?v=6Af6b_wyiwI (archived at https://perma.cc/2W4R-DYEL)

5 L Pasteur. Lecture, University of Lille, 7 December 1854

6 E Abrahmasson. Avoiding repetitive change syndrome, *MIT Sloan Management Review*, 15 January 2004, https://sloanreview.mit.edu/article/avoiding-repetitive-change-syndrome/ (archived at https://perma.cc/WC2H-NHCE)

7 M Imai (1986) *Kaizen: (Ky'zen): The key to Japan's competitive success*, McGraw-Hill, New York; M Imai (1997) *Gemba Kaizen*, McGraw-Hill Professional, New York

8 See, e.g., D N Sull. The dynamics of standing still: Firestone tire and rubber and the radial revolution, *Business History Review*, 1999, 73 (3), 430–64; J Howard-Grenville. The persistence of flexible organizational routines: The role of agency and organizational context, *Organization Science*, 2005, 16 (6), 618–36; C Gilbert. Unbundling the structure of inertia: Resource versus routine rigidity, *Academy of Management Journal*, 2005, 48 (5), 741–63

9 See, e.g., P Senge (1990) *The Fifth Discipline: The art and practice of organizational learning*, Doubleday/Currency, New York

10 See, e.g., D T Hansen (2012) *John Dewey and our Educational Prospect: A Critical Engagement with Dewey's Democracy and Education*, State University of New York Press, New York

11 O Wadström (2007) *Att förstå och påverka beteendeproblem*, 4th edn, Psykologinsats, Linköping

12 See, e.g., J Rosales-Ruiz and D M Baer. Behavioral cusps: A developmental and pragmatic concept for behavior analysis, *Journal of Applied Behavior Analysis*, 1997, 30, 533–44; M D Hixson. Behavioural cusps, basic behaviour repertoire, and cumulative-hierarchical learning, *The Psychological Record*, 2004, 54 (3), 387–403

12

Exploiting competitive advantages

Big, best, fast and beautiful

Prioritization of strategy

One of the main purposes of strategy is to create *competitive advantage*. How do organizations gain lasting competitive advantage? In order to answer that question and to make an assessment, we need to take into account the outside world, the organization's own position, the organization's structure, history and customers, ways of working, etc. In essence, strategizing is about prioritizing and de-prioritizing. To be able to choose, we need to understand the consequences that the choices will lead to. Realizing strategy is having the courage to choose in spite of knowing that the choice also has negative consequences. Every strategic choice is actually a judgement call with both benefits and drawbacks. Choosing also means rejecting the options not chosen. Setting priorities is therefore a key issue. Strategy is really more about rejection than anything else. There are almost always more options for a goal and reaching the goal than there are opportunities to test them. For a company that fails to reject options, the strategy will only be the sum of all the deals they make.

One of the founders of NetOnNet, one of the early only-digital home electronics sales organizations, Anders Halvarsson, had this to say about the consumer electronics industry in the summer of 2011: 'Everyone wants to be everything to everyone, and everyone wants to do so everywhere.'[1]

If everyone does everything for everyone, who has a unique offer? What is the source of competitive edge? If we don't reject options, the strategy will be nothing more than something we can look back on after the fact and pat ourselves on the back or, worse, start blaming for lack of success. It definitely won't be a way to influence behaviour in our organization to increase efficiency. A strategy needs to be a policy instrument and an aid to help us set what can sometimes be tough priorities, not a document that explains why things turned out the way they did after the fact.

A question I sometimes ask management teams when we work on differentiation is: *Who would truly miss your organization if you were to disappear?* The answer I often get is that the customers would miss them. That is both an obvious and a natural answer. But I am not as sure as they are that it is true. If an organization goes bankrupt, there is almost always at least one alternative. If British Airways were to go bankrupt, I can just go to Lufthansa. If Samsung shuts down, I can go to Apple. If Audi shuts down, I can go to Volvo. And so on. Very few are irreplaceable. Would your customers really, I mean really, miss what you provide? No matter how much we would like to believe that, unfortunately it is not very often true. Which of the things that you own would you not be able to find a substitute for? Your K2 skis? Or would you be fine going with Dynamics? Your iPhone? The bank you use? All changes entail a disruption of habit. Habit, as noted above, is the same as negatively reinforced behaviours. Everything that is reinforced is difficult to change. But with regard to your iPhone, wouldn't you come to like a Samsung mobile phone almost as much fairly quickly? Every successful company is unique in some way, but we should be aware that we are replaceable, and that the competition is fierce.

If all companies within an industry are present in the same market with about the same products and about the same strategy for producing and delivering them, there is no differentiation. This means that organizations' profitability and survival will be threatened. In their book *Blue Ocean Strategy,* INSEAD professors Chan Kim and Renée Mauborgne coined the term 'red ocean' to describe a market with cut-throat competition.[2] The red symbolizes blood due to this cut-throat competition. Declining margins, bankruptcies and a lack of differentiation between different companies, their products and services are some of the hallmarks. The goal is to get to the blue water – to have what they call a 'blue ocean' strategy. We get there by strategizing in a way that helps us differentiate ourselves from our competition. And this is done by setting priorities, focusing on the things at which we can excel and get better than our competition.

The consumer electronics industry mentioned above is indeed a good example of a red ocean. Even when you're out shopping you hardly know what brand of store you are in. They sell the same products at the same prices – as retailers seldom have their 'own' products – run similar promotions, run almost the same adverts on TV and on the web, and have approximately the same geographical locations. Somewhat sardonically, we might say that customers choose the store that has parking available closest to the entrance. This, of course, has consequences. Since 2011, and the abovementioned interview with Anders Halvarsson, several large consumer electronic chains have filed for bankruptcy. But consumer electronics is merely one branch of industry. What does the situation look like in the banking world? What differentiates the big banks from each other? What about the construction industry? The network providers? The food chains? The insurance companies? Or, to get really close and take a good look at ourselves, how does it look in the industry in which you operate? How well differentiated is your organization from your competitors? What's your true uniqueness?

Generic sources of competitive advantage

So, how do we *differentiate* ourselves from our competitors? One of the world's most influential strategy researchers, Michael Porter, professor of strategy at Harvard Business School, talks about *three generic strategies*.[3] As we saw in the introduction, over time, changes in the outside world have forced organizations to develop different strategies to create competitive advantages. Just like our current situation, different periods have been characterized by different challenges, and have therefore given rise to new generic strategies. A generic strategy can be described as a basic idea about how to run a business in order to create competitive advantage. The three generic strategies can be symbolized by innovation, customization and economies of scale. In this book I call them *big*, *best* and *fast*. I have also added *beautiful*, which is primarily based on competitive advantage by brand recognition and strength. I will develop these later.

The research is fairly unanimous, and history has numerous examples showing that organizations gain and sustain competitive advantages by a focused strategy. It is important to excel in what we need to excel in and to eliminate the things we do not need to excel in. As noted earlier, this makes setting priorities an important issue. Focus and specialization are common words for a reason. A rule of thumb is that if an organization invests less than 50 per cent of its development resources in fostering competitiveness within one generic strategy, they will be relegated to a constant battle for survival, and get stuck in the middle. The more targeted the investment and attention, the greater the risk that we have backed the wrong horse, but the greater our chances of standing out as well. No organization can focus all its energy on leveraging economies of scale, tailor making, innovating or building brand at once. Every organization needs a reasonably efficient production operation, everyone needs to 'tailor' things somewhat for customers, everyone needs a bit of innovation and everyone needs a bit of 'sizzle'. So, strategy from this perspective is a continuous act of balancing and rebalancing focus.

Succeeding in strategy realization means getting an organization's employees to behave in a way that empowers and drives strategy, within that focus. This means that we have to pinpoint the key behaviour that builds a competitive advantage, and then find the right way to spur it by positive reinforcement. Some strategies are incompatible, as strategy is manifested in behaviours and some behaviours are incompatible. It is not possible to customize products down to the smallest detail while at the same time mass-producing. It is not possible to mass-produce while at the same time trying to sell the mass-produced products as luxury goods. Yet this is exactly what many organizations are attempting to do when they are not focusing their attention.

As a customer, we do not choose to buy a suit at H&M only to drop it off at a Savile Row tailor to have it tailored. H&M and the tailor do the same thing but in completely different ways, using a completely different business logic and different, and incompatible, generic strategies and thus behaviours. H&M's competitive advantage lies in their size being *big*, while the tailor's advantage lies in customizing the product for each unique customer – being the *best* at tailoring. Many companies have not thought through and defined a position on whether they want to be, for instance, H&M or the tailor.

This is particularly difficult for large organizations with many different business operations, because in this case we may have both an H&M and a tailor under the same corporate roof, or within the same conglomerate. This means that working out how different companies or business areas are to become successful is an important *business strategy* issue as well as an important *corporate strategy* issue. This in turn may mean that different behaviours need to be reinforced in different parts of the same organization. And this means that all reinforcers, such as an incentive model, need to be adapted to accord with the generic business strategy. Beyond that, it is also important to work out how these different businesses can function well together and benefit from each other. This is, as noted, a corporate strategy challenge that also requires bringing influence to bear on the right business strategy behaviour.

Big as a competitive advantage

The post-war period was marked by economic growth in industrialized societies – not least in Europe. Because nearly everything that was produced was also sold, companies had to produce as much as possible in order to be successful. The generic strategy for the majority of organizations was to get *big*. That was one of the most important things. It was important to become a market leader and to grow to the point where they could mass-produce, to learn from every serially produced unit, to learn how to manufacture even more cheaply, to utilize economies of scale, to lower prices and gain market share and competitive advantages as a result. Because mass production was a crucial part of the puzzle, there was a constraint on product portfolio variety. We cannot do everything uniquely for everyone and focus on doing what there is the most demand for.

Figure 12.1 clearly shows the traditional normal distribution of large volumes in a market. By analysing its industry or market and looking at where the bulk of the demand is, a big player can identify where it should focus. The possibility of repetition inheres in performing what there is the most demand for. Sticking to the middle – sofas that cost between €600 and €1,000, cars that cost between €25,000 and €40,000 or, related to services, management consultants that cost between €100 and €180 per hour.

FIGURE 12.1   The normal distribution of a market and the bulk of business

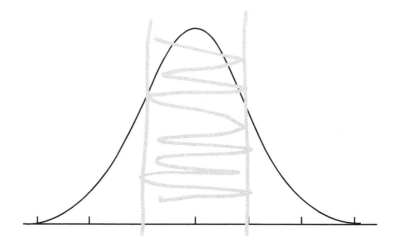

In this logic and in those days, planning was an important tool used to produce as many units as possible per spent financial unit per minute. Society experienced an economic upswing and companies were able to find an outlet for all of the products or services they produced. Demand outstripped supply. This made it natural for organizations to adopt a *market-based strategy* – an outside-in perspective on strategy. That is to say: what the market wants is what is produced or mass-produced.

Learning and behaviours are important if we are to become big. In order to be able to constantly produce things a bit better and a bit more cheaply, we must always have a standard – a baseline – against which we can measure and provide feedback on experience in an attempt to ensure continuous improvement, i.e. more efficient behaviours. Examples of companies where being big really has turned into a competitive advantage include IKEA and Toyota. Every single unit they produce needs to be cheaper and better than the previous one. Although the prices of lumber, logistics and other components that go into the total cost of the Ivar bookshelf are going up, IKEA manages to lower its costs overall, and thereby increases the profits. This logic can be visualized by what is called the experience curve (see Figure 12.2). The e-curve describes how each unit produced can be produced a bit more cheaply each time if we learn, improve our behaviours and get better each time. This is of course further accentuated in digital production, when the second, third and so on are even less costly as, in a simplified way, you merely press 'enter' to get one more unit.

FIGURE 12.2   The experience curve

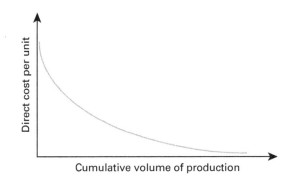

Honda is one of the world's largest motorcycle manufacturers. In the fiscal year 2020 the company had approximately 218,000 employees. According to their own figures, they produce more than 14 million combustion engines annually. In that sense, they are one of largest engine producers in the world. By producing that much, they are able to accumulate an enormous pool of experience. In this pool, they can identify which employees are the most competent, in terms of their behaviour, at each production element, disseminate the learning and develop their production methods to support behaviour in order to produce even higher-quality products at an even lower price. Because the numbers are so large, every little improvement has a significant impact on the bottom line.

Economies of scale and synergies are crucial if a company is to benefit from being big as a competitive advantage. The organization needs to identify the behaviour that leads to benefiting from the economies of scale. That is to say, key behaviour like developing, measuring and improving standards, to incite small improvements, to reinforce error identification in order to improve standards and reinforce compliance with best practices – what IKEA calls '*the concept*'. However, to ensure that the concept is developed and put to the test, it needs to be challenged. In the IKEA case the group encourages certain stores *not* to follow the concept. On the contrary, their task is instead to challenge the concept and see how the work can be done in even more efficient ways.

Best as a competitive advantage

As a result of the 1973 oil crisis, organizations came to see their dependence on the outside world in a different light. Growth was no longer a given. Organizations did not always get their hands on the resources they needed to produce at full capacity, and when they did, they did not always manage to sell everything they produced. As a way of reducing risk and lowering costs, many companies chose to become niche players. They wanted to become the *best* at what they did. What this meant was that they segmented their market and prioritized the customers that were most important, so that they could then provide exceptional service to these selected, priority customers. Many organizations then strove to become the very best at producing and supplying unique products and services to a small number of individual customers.

Taken to its logical conclusion, being the best means having total customer focus. The purpose is to tailor products or services to individuals or individual customers. In the long run, this entails significant variation in the portfolio of products and services offered by the organization. The focus is on working so close to the customer that we know exactly what the customer wants, preferably before even they do, customizing our product down to the smallest detail, and thereby exceeding the customer's expectations. Examples of organizations that use being the best as a competitive advantage are Savile Row tailors in London, joiners who build kitchens and bookshelves on-site, and the renowned architectural firms that offer a unique product for each individual occasion, e.g. in competitions.

To really be able to customize, power needs to reach far out in the organization, vested in the employee who works closest to the customer. The person who is close to the customers knows them best, knows what they want, and needs to be able to make the decisions required in order to satisfy the customer. Long decision paths, centralization and standardization stand in clear contrast to customization. While trying to employ big as a competitive advantage requires traits that resemble the organization as a machine, they are downright dangerous for the organizations focusing on being best. It is therefore rarely profitable to invest in being both big and best. They are incompatible; they demand incompatible employee behaviour, to a large extent. However, in spite of how different best is from big, exploiting best as source of competition is also a market-based strategy that is based on meeting existing needs in a (niche/-s) market, not the bulk.

Orange County Choppers has a handful of employees and is run out of a garage on the East Coast of the United States. For a couple of years they appeared in a TV documentary series. They only build choppers (a modified motorcycle), and they tailor them to the exact wishes of the customer. They buy screws, cylinders, engine blocks, mufflers and other parts from various suppliers and then assemble the chopper in their workshop. They make components that are not available for purchase in-house. They build a limited number of choppers every year – compare this to the hundreds of thousands of units built each year by Honda.

Being the best requires behaviour that leads to being able to tailor a product to the customer's needs. This can involve performing a thorough market analysis, segmenting the market in a clear way, setting priorities between different customers, always asking the customer if they got exactly what they wanted, always adjusting details to make the customer happy and trying out our new ideas and prototypes on customers at an early stage in order to finalize the products together, thereby ensuring that they get exactly what they want.

It goes without saying that learning is an important parameter if a company is to be able to customize. Every product is unique. Unique involves something new. And new means that we need to be learning new behaviours all the time.

Fast as a competitive advantage

The launch of the internet in the early 1990s dramatically increased the availability of information. There has been talk of an information revolution. It has long been thought that information is able to generate knowledge, which could be harnessed to create competitive advantages.

The main idea behind exploiting fast as a competitive advantage is strong innovation, research and development allowing a company to be the fastest to come out with 'something new'. A key concept for companies that want to use innovation as a competitive advantage is *core competencies*. The concept was made world-famous by two researchers, Gary Hamel and C K Prahalad in the early 1990s.[4] What this means in simplified terms is that the unique competency that an organization has puts the organization in a position to be the first to offer the market something unique. Organizations that want to be fast have an inside-out perspective on strategy rather than outside-in (the perspective of those that want to be big and best). This is sometimes referred to as *resource-based strategy*.[5] By focusing on one's own organization, or rather valuable, rare, imperfectly imitable and organizationally appropriable (VRIO) resources the firm possesses, controls and can employ, it is possible to create competitive advantage. With these resources it is possible to develop products and services that are so good that a need for them 'arises' in the market. We create demand by creating the supply.

The purpose of the organization in being fast is to create what is referred to as a *temporary monopoly*. Terms like 'time to market', 'patents' and 'version launches' are frequently used in connection with maintaining such temporary monopolies. This makes it important to manage product life cycles, and to get the timing of product launches right.

Companies whose generic strategy is to be fast often incur high research and development costs. The economic logic is that they will then be able to recoup these costs thanks to their temporary monopoly, which allows them to command a high price. Three concrete examples of first movers are Nokia, Comviq and Gore Associates. Nokia was one of the first mobile phone manufacturers to integrate a camera into the mobile phone. The 7650 model provided a number of advantages over the competition. It wasn't anything unique, but Nokia were the first to bring the idea of a camera in the phone to market, which gave them a temporary monopoly and allowed them to gain market share. Comviq, a Swedish challenger mobile network operator, is said to have been the first company in the Nordics to let subscribers make free calls to other Comviq subscribers. As a result, subscriptions spiked among young people who wanted to make free calls to each other. This was of course eagerly encouraged by the parents who needed to pay the phone bills, at a time where every ten minutes cost approximately one euro or pound. Jokingly, Comviq representatives state that the parent–teacher association meetings were Comviq's prime sales channel. Gore Associates is an innovative chemical company whose entire business concept is based on creating temporary monopolies. They manufacture guitar strings, synthetic blood vessels, brake cables for bicycles and of course Gore Tex.

Segway is a means of transport with zero climate impact. Based on the organization's expertise, they created a means of transport that no one had made before, giving the company a temporary monopoly. Because no one can offer the same product, GE – which now owns Segway – can hopefully make sure that its research investment will pay off. Another example where time to market combined with proper research is the race for a COVID-19 vaccine between Pfizer-BioNTech, Moderna and Oxford University/Astra Zeneca among others. The organization that first produced a viable vaccine with desired features had a tremendous *first mover advantage*.

In order to benefit from fast as a competitive advantage, organizations need to create structures that reinforce innovation, encourage interdepartmental collaboration, dare to try out new ideas, dare to fail, invest in research and development, identify critical behaviour that may help create unique products and services in the long term, and engage in active scenario planning and business intelligence in order to identify future business ideas.

Beautiful as a competitive advantage

No matter how good a product or service is, no matter the price, no matter whether it is custom-made or not, it represents the organization that produces and delivers it. Organizations, their employees and their products symbolize something. We can refer to this 'something' as a brand. Being *beautiful* means having a brand that is so good and strong that it becomes a competitive advantage unto itself, almost regardless of the products we put the label on. It is a resource that is valuable, rare, imperfectly imitable and organizationally appropriable (VRIO).

Roughly speaking, the knowledge society dates back to when the IT bubble burst around the turn of the millennium. The thing that makes it possible to 'predict', and to some extent defend us against, shocks in the outside world – information – is precisely what creates the rapid pace of development in the outside world and the pressure on organizations to change. In the past, access to information could pose a barrier to entry for companies that wanted to establish themselves in a new market. Today, companies that are not yet established have access to almost the same information as already established companies do. Access to information is no longer a competitive advantage in itself. The transformation of information into knowledge is what creates competitive advantages or puts up barriers to entry. This transformation is nothing less than learning.

In order to put up barriers to entry for new contenders, it is becoming increasingly important to create loyal customers. One way to do that is to have your customers co-create the brand. Organizations want to have customers who share the organization's values, and vice versa. This makes it important for companies to be associated with certain characteristics – for the experience of shopping for or owning something to feel important, exciting, or to confer status in itself. Beyond the function that a particular product has, organizations want more senses to be involved in the product or service.

I bought an iPod in 2005. I remember feeling a sense of community with the other people – relatively few at that time – who were wearing the iconic white earbuds on the subway in Stockholm. But when the iPhone was launched in 2007 it became common to see the white earbuds, and four or five years later many people bought new earbuds when they bought an iPhone. Now other manufacturers have white earbuds, and headphones in all sizes, colours and shapes exist. The white earbuds symbolize something else, or nothing, today.

Sticking to the iPhone, it is one of the most successful mobile phones, in spite of its performance being not much better than the alternatives. Apple's idea is for the customer to experience a value that includes design, aesthetics and a 'feeling' of owning something unique. The unwrapping experience – the 'fancy' white box – is a part in this.

If our brand is strong enough, we do not need a temporary monopoly. Nor is customization required. We do not need a super-efficient production system resulting in low prices to sell our products, goods or services. It is enough to have a strong brand. We can call this 'beautiful' as a competitive advantage.

Organizations that tap into exploiting beautiful as a competitive advantage have become more common the last decades. In an increasingly individualistic world, one where I want to 'realize myself' – and at the same time in a global world where everyone competes on the same terms – it becomes increasingly important to be associated with something unique. With this personal positioning, a number of products with strong brands can help me communicate exactly who I am. This means that the value of the product is something completely different from the cost of producing it or the functionality it offers. Therefore, many companies that are successful in pursuing a competitive advantage by being beautiful are often business-to-consumer and luxury brands where pure function is subordinated to other 'purposes', e.g. communicating something about me. Some examples include Louis Vuitton – a hair tie is rarely worth €180 in functional terms; Hermès – a handbag is rarely worth €8,000; Ferrari – a car is rarely worth €300,000; and Patek Phillipe – a watch is rarely worth €80,000. But, for the reasons discussed above, they are successful.

Another example that shows how younger generations (Generation Z born between 1995 and 2014) are approachable using a beautiful strategy is the 'idol cult'. Names of stars like Justin Bieber or Rihanna are put on a perfume, a clothing brand or a handbag. The idea is that the person's brand is strong enough to make the product both interesting and expensive, regardless of quality or value. Sometimes it works, sometimes it doesn't. The core of utilizing being beautiful as a competitive advantage is sometimes referred to as the enactment or co-creation of value, meaning that the buyers and users of the product are involved in creating its value. When the 'right' people use a certain product, others feel a sense of affirmation if they too are able to own it. From a learning perspective, this is referred to as *vicarious reinforcement*.

Harley Davidson is a motorcycle manufacturer that makes use of its strong brand. They successfully cultivate the myth of the modern cowboy, of human freedom, and the notion that Harley Davidson is the only motorcycle for real riders. This lets them charge almost twice, or three times as much as many other motorcycle manufacturers while providing the same quality. And they have developed merchandise and clothing associated with the brand so no one should 'miss' whether it is in fact a Harley that passes on the street, or not. Strategically, this is a clever move.

Being beautiful as a competitive advantage employs an inside-out perspective and can thus be regarded as a resource-based strategy. The idea is to provide the market with something that helps buyers fulfil themselves.

Being beautiful as a competitive advantage requires organizations to ensure that the 'right' people have and use the products, that the products are seen at the 'right' shows, that PR about the product is disseminated through the 'right' channels. This requires creating collaborations with established, large brands that are associated with what we want to be associated with. H&M's collaborations with different high-end and trendy designers (e.g. Versace, Lanvin, Moschino, Giambattista Valli) are a clever way to sprinkle a little bit of 'beautiful' over the organization and its products. And, in this area, *influencers* in social media have had an enormous impact on organizations' success in the last decade. But, have no doubt, H&M's generic strategy, what makes them competitive, is their ability to leverage on 'being big'.

In short, to exploit beautiful as a competitive advantage we need to provide our customer with something more than functionality; we need to 'boost' our brand with something else, related to a feeling, aesthetics, design and/or an experience so that customers co-create the value of our brand because it helps them fulfil themselves by using our products or services.

This relation between pure function and pure aesthetics can be illustrated as a continuum, with two extremes exemplified by mining and open casts representing pure function, and art for art's sake representing pure aesthetics (see Figure 12.3).

FIGURE 12.3   The pure function–pure aesthetics continuum

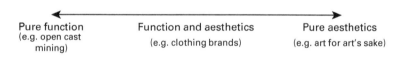

SOURCE Original model

Naturally, most organizations combine function and aesthetics in different combinations to position themselves as advantageously as possible. And in some cases (e.g. fashion) design is more important than in others (e.g. microprocessors). Despite this, Intel has really made a point of making computer manufacturers show that their computers have 'Intel inside' to provide guarantees of the quality of the product.

Notes

1 A Erlandsson. Mätt på priskriget, Svenska Dagbladet, 26 June 2011, www.svd. se/matt-pa-priskriget (archived at https://perma.cc/62KJ-BRUT)
2 W Kim and R Mauborgne (2005) *Blue Ocean Strategy*, Harvard Business School Press, Cambridge, MA
3 M E Porter (1980) *Competitive Strategy: Techniques for analyzing industries and competitors*, The Free Press, New York
4 See, e.g., C K Prahalad and G Hamel. The core competence of the corporation, *Harvard Business Review*, 1990, 68, 79–91; C K Prahalad and G Hamel (1996) *Competing for the Future*, Harvard Business School Press, Cambridge, MA
5 See, e.g., J B Barney. Strategic factor markets: Expectations, luck, and business strategy, *Management Science*, 1986, 32 (10), 1231–41; E T Penrose (1959) *The Theory of the Growth of the Firm*, John Wiley & Sons, New York; D J Teece, G Pisano and A Shuen. Dynamic capabilities and strategic management, *Strategic Management Journal*, 1997, 18 (7), 509–33; B Wernerfelt. A resource-based view of the firm, *Strategic Management Journal*, 1984, 5 (2), 171–80

KEY POINTS
Part Four: Strategy is behavioural change

What is strategy?

Strategy is behaviours in action. Strategizing is an organization's way of deciding where to go and navigating to this decided point.

Strategy consists of five dimensions: accountabilities (e.g. purpose, values, mission) arenas (e.g. the world, the industry and the organization), affairs (e.g. strategies, business plans, goals, objectives), actions (e.g. processes, behaviours, routines) and aims (e.g. long-term ambitions, today–tomorrow balances).

Success requires focusing on one of the four generic strategies: big, best, fast or beautiful. In order for a strategy to be realized in a business, overall goals and strategic ideas need to be broken down into behaviours.

What does a behavioural view of strategy look like?

Having a behavioural view of strategy means establishing a clearer connection between formulation and realization, which in practice means that more employees need to be involved in strategizing and goal setting.

In behavioural strategizing, learning and change are crucial parts of strategizing. Strategy development and strategy realization are impossible to separate from each other.

The focus of behavioural strategizing is on delivering impacts by engaging in more frequent follow-ups and providing more frequent feedback, rather than by using activators in the form of goals, information, rules and decrees that get lost in the noise.

Why is behaviour important if we want to realize strategy?

All realization of strategy – all results in a business – is created by employee behaviour. We can more effectively realize strategy by first understanding the principles of behaviour and breaking the strategy down into concrete behaviours.

Behavioural focus throughout strategizing, from external analysis, through goal setting and planning, to follow-up and feedback, makes for clarity about what is required and what the impacts will be in the organization (positive and negative) when the behaviour is engaged in or refrained from.

How are change and learning related to the realization of strategy?

The world is changing faster and faster. The organizations that are able to maintain a continuously high rate of change have a better chance of achieving lasting success as they are adapting to changing circumstances.

All realization comes down to getting an organization's members to behave in a new way. This requires that employees learn new behaviour. The more challenging the goals, the more sweeping the change and the more learning the organization will have to do.

What is meant by 'strategy is behavioural change'?

Too many organizations make a hash of strategy by just engaging in a few days' planning, or by revising the budget and an action list at an annual management meeting. This isn't strategy. Strategy is about creating the organization's future and ensuring long-term success, and this demands behavioural change. For an issue as important as the future, larger parts of the organization need to be involved and more diligence in the doing is critical.

PART FIVE

Smart as a competitive advantage

Through wisdom is an house builded; and by understanding it is established: And by knowledge shall the chambers be filled with all precious and pleasant riches.

PROVERBS 24:3–4

In a world where nothing is constant and where change is a must, we need to be quick on our feet to manage to adapt and become successful. Behavioural strategizing includes leading an entire organization so it monitors the outside world, looks for new information, transforms it into knowledge, employs new learning as sources of competitiveness and enables the organization to discover the opportunities of tomorrow. This is the essence of smart as a competitive advantage.

IN THIS PART

We will address the following issues in this part:

- How is behavioural strategizing related to the ability to compete?
- What is the focus of behavioural strategizing?
- Why is innovation an important part of behavioural strategizing?
- How do we create organizations that utilize smart as a competitive advantage?

13

From individual insight to competitive edge

The aim of being big, best, fast or beautiful is to create a competitive advantage by making choices having to do primarily with the accountabilities, arenas and affairs of strategy – the reason for doing something, where to do it, and what to do. While this helps in creating a successful organization, behavioural strategizing adds a dimension. Organizations can in fact explore how to work with strategy, i.e. actions, how to strategize and how such strategizing enables learning and adjustment to changing circumstances, as a source of competitive advantage.

Organizations cannot develop a 'perfect strategy', as we do not know what tomorrow will look like. We never will, regardless of sound promises from 'analysts'. However, we can train and educate ourselves, our colleagues and our organizations on how to strategize so as to learn and to adapt to a changing outside world. From a behavioural psychology perspective, learning becomes a critical aspect if we are to be able to adapt the organization to the market and the outside world. To harness constant learning and adaptability could be referred to as *smart as a competitive advantage.*

The world in 2021 is complex and difficult to grasp. This means that we need to find ways to interpret it and manage our organizations in a suitable way. For organizations that 'grew up' in the 20th century, the obvious solution has been increased structure, planning and control. But this can be a problem, because too much structure, too much planning and too much control can actually inhibit a company's creativity, innovation and adaptability. Learning and adaptation are largely based on spontaneity. Because they are crucial to tomorrow's success, many organizations are in the process of killing themselves with 'red tape'. What made General Motors, among others, so successful in the post-war period – their ability to create structure – is what is now in the process of stifling them.

During the second half of the 20th century, strategy, structure and systems offered much-needed discipline and control. 2021's economic environment is different, however. Overcapacity, fierce competition and an ever-changing market are the norm for the vast majority of organizations – large and small. Discipline and control are no longer the most important factors in order to create profitability. At some point towards the end of the 20th century, we underwent a paradigm shift. From a situation in which technology drove development, what we now see is that the brain is driving it. In the past, technology was the bottleneck. We dreamt up better things than we were able to build from a technical point of view, but now technology offers the possibility of building more advanced things than we can dream up. The brain is the bottleneck. And therefore it seems reasonable to develop our brains to try to learn more, better, faster.

If we believe that the pace of development, e.g. technological change, will continue to be rapid, if we believe that customers will continue to make tough demands, if we believe that there will be increased competition for the very best talent, then we need to be able to adapt, we need to be able to learn faster, and we need to be quicker to change ourselves. Realizing this and working actively to benefit from this insight by focusing on behaviour is part of exploring 'smart' as a competitive advantage.

Information, intelligence, knowledge and competence

For organizations to actually get an edge by being smarter than their competition, they need to gather information, transform it into knowledge and use it in order to develop, to compete. In that sense, *competence* is a hardcore word that suggests the ability to compete. When I lecture on adaptability, knowledge and competitive advantage, I usually ask if there is anyone who knows what a dodo is. Most do. But, for the sake of argument, the dodo was a turkey-like bird that lived in Mauritius until the 17th century. The dodo had a good life and feared no evil when seafarers stopped over at the island on their way between India and southern Africa. The dodo had never seen people and was therefore not afraid. It was a large and nutritious bird, and it was easy to catch. The bird had not learned that man was dangerous. The dodo did not have time to adapt to the new conditions and to develop a natural fear of people, which caused it to go extinct.

Knowledge and awareness of what was going on in the outside world was literally the difference between life and death for the dodo. New knowledge can mean the difference between life and death also for organizations. What would happen in an organization if the employees did not learn new things? The organization would probably be left behind by its competitors and lose customers; management would probably be replaced and eventually the company would go bankrupt. New knowledge and therefore learning is needed for survival. There is no doubt about that.

When I started school in the late 1980s, I was issued with an atlas. Everyone who started school back then got one. The reason they gave us an atlas was so that we could have it for the rest of our lives. Giving kids something lasting was a good idea, but the fact is that the world changes. The differences between my atlas and the world today are stark. The Soviet Union does not exist today. The fourth-largest economy in the world, Germany, is no longer divided into East and West Germany. The Balkans have been redrawn. Also, on a local level, maps are changed. Small municipalities break free and become separate municipalities with new municipal boards to avoid the legacy and 'shackles' of being part of a slow colossus. Other municipalities and counties have merged to avoid increasing cost and decreasing tax income due to an ageing population. Our geography is also our market, and it is changing. We need to understand how things are changing and how we can deal with that.

Uniqueness of information and competition

Where do you find information about what the outside world looks like today? And what it may look like in five years? What are the trends and tendencies, and what is actually 'true'? Where do Ericsson's strategy developers seek out information that can help them create the next big success around 5G, for instance? Do they look in different places than Huawei does? Do the HSBC and Deutsche Bank management teams look in different places for information that will give them competitive advantages? Where do organizations look for information to help them get an edge on their competitors? Do they dive into different sources than each other? Arguably, no. Do they hire different consultants? Most often, no. Do they draw on the benefits of different perspectives based on different experiences – from inside *and* outside the organization? I would argue, in too many cases, no. There is great interest in, for example, Google's, Facebook's and others' huge databases, and an idea that information and Big Data is the solution.

But although data-driven exploration is highly regarded, more and more researchers are now suggesting that such methods have obvious flaws, regardless of the amount of data.[1] Big Data needs 'thick' data. My take is therefore that it is time to complement traditional sources and methods for creating unique knowledge with true alternatives. Maybe we can discern tomorrow's opportunities in children's TV shows? This may actually help find more unique insights. Unique in the word's true meaning.

Several researchers now claim that it does not matter how much information an organization has access to in a database. The customer's needs are too individual, and it is basically impossible to generalize. This means that what is important is analysing and understanding the information. Several companies are therefore resorting to anthropological methods of analysis to study customers in their natural environment, as a complement to mathematical methods. It is not yet mainstream, but logically it will be, fairly soon. In addition, other researchers, for example in the field of modern *design thinking*, suggest that existing data cannot be used to address future needs. Organizations therefore have to build new data; new data that by default is imperfect, and when making decisions on such new and imperfect data mistakes are inevitable. What this means in practice, is that organization that want to achieve or create something unique first have to fail – a lot, to be honest. And learning from those failures to evolve is consequently a vital competency and behaviour for future organizations.

It is hard for organizations to find information that others do not have access to. How are we supposed to stay a step ahead if we look at exactly the same information, hire the same consultants and attend the same courses and conferences as the competition? When the same information is known to everyone, including competitors, how do we get better at adapting? The decisive factor in this case is finding methods to rapidly convert the information into knowledge and into competence. Speed is not about gathering the information quickly. Nor is it about making rapid decisions based on the information. It is about executing quickly on decisions once they are made and drawing lessons from the consequences that decisions have in order to learn and to develop.

This is why an organization must constantly question its own beliefs. This is also one of the arguments for not using homogeneous groups when working on strategy. Organizations need to harness diversity of behaviours, ideas and ways of thinking. Diversity from a behavioural perspective has nothing to do with gender, ethnic background, skin colour or religion. It is about different ways of seeing the world and different ways of thinking about strategy, markets, customers, new products, information gathering and the creation of knowledge.

One challenge that organizations face today is to separate valuable information from junk. In 2021, several hundred billion spam emails are sent each day. Over 70 per cent of all emails sent are spam. The originator of the term 'megatrends', John Naisbitt, allegedly said that 'we are drowning in information, but starved for knowledge'.[2] Organizations that want to be successful cannot let themselves drown in the information, they have to use the information to create new and unique knowledge that helps them compete. Many organizations today are in such a hurry that they don't have time to look at the results of what they are actually doing, let alone feed it back into the organization to improve their business. This does not create long-term success, by any means.

Information and the creation of knowledge

For a specific reason, the English language distinguishes between 'information' and 'intelligence'. This helps us understand the value of information, instructional value. 'Intelligence' means information that we can act on, and thus intelligence might be valuable. Information, to be honest, is just piled up data, not particularly useful if it is not 'refined'. Business intelligence, which began gaining currency in 2005, is an extension of this. Business intelligence serves as a basis for being able to make good decisions and provide input for new learning. Way back in 500 BC, the Chinese military strategist Sun Tzu told his emperor that it was possible to defeat an opponent by being better informed.[3] This is an old truth, and it is just as relevant today as it was then, if we learn to separate information from intelligence.

New knowledge or information that we can act on gives us a chance to identify opportunities for development. Without new information, we cannot create new knowledge. Without new knowledge, we cannot find creative solutions. If everyone has the same knowledge and thinks the same way, and if everyone knows the same things, we really don't know more than any given person.

Stockholm's Enskilda Bank, later SEB, is in 2021 one of the largest banks in the Nordics. Marcus Wallenberg was a leading figure in its development during the early 20th century, partly because he understood how to profit from information at an early stage. In 1903 the bank started the statistics department whose task was to gather and analyse information in order to create a competitive bank. Today, many organizations are good at gathering information, but to date relatively few have become good at transforming that information into unique knowledge and turning it into a competitive advantage. This issue has come to the fore particularly in the context of the increasingly heated discussions about Big Data. With all the information available in 2021, the need is even greater.

So how do we use information to create knowledge? To generalize, let's look at two fictional characters. One is Sir Arthur Conan Doyle's *Sherlock Holmes*, and the other is Antoine de Saint-Exupéry's children's book character *The Little Prince*. Sherlock Holmes makes use of something called the hypothetic-deductive approach, whereas The Little Prince uses an inductive approach. The hypothetic-deductive approach means that Sherlock Holmes proceeds on the basis of a finished idea, a hypothesis, that he tries to find evidence for. If he does not find evidence, he rejects his hypothesis, and if he does find evidence, this validates his hypothesis. The inductive Little Prince goes out into the world without any preconceived notions, looks at what is going on and then draws conclusions from what he sees in order to create knowledge. This applies to strategic thinking as well.

Knowledge and possible competitive advantages

Strategic issues are complex. Complexity makes the brain want to create structures, and it therefore resorts to generalizations in order to understand. The brain then seeks out the things that reinforce its own preconceived notions. We know that from the previous chapters in this book. This means that extra effort is required to find evidence of things that contradict our own conception. Recall Kahneman's Systems 1 and 2. It creates problems when an entrenched conception does not tally with reality. This is why it is important for organizations to create structures and processes that help them call their own preconceived notions into question, for example when important decisions have to be made.

We have to be critical of our knowledge. Asking ourselves 'What do I not know that I should know?' is a good start. It is important to question whether the things we take for granted are actually 'givens'. It is common to identify solutions to a problem based on preconceived notions. We should ask ourselves why the problem arose instead of solving it based on what we 'know'. A simple and powerful method that can be applied in order to identify the root of a problem is to ask ourselves at least five whys. Taking this kind of root cause analysis approach means that we do something to address the cause of the problem rather than the symptom and can then let the business carry on. *Carl slipped.* Why? *There was oil on the floor.* Why? *The machine leaked.* Why? *The gasket is broken.* Why? *We didn't change the gasket.* Why? *We have lost track of the maintenance plan for this machine.* Why? *Because it is relatively new.*

Organizations are good at coming up with a hypothesis and finding evidence for it. It's natural. Our brain is wired to look for things we recognize. But this poses a problem in organizations where those who make decisions have too many preconceived notions about how the industry and the organization work. Organizations that want to excel need to find ways to question the obvious. This can range from having internal or external advisors who challenge management teams to a decision-making process that ensures that several alternative solutions are evaluated. Everyone in the organization has a responsibility to generate new knowledge and encourage alternative ideas. It is the leaders' job to make sure this is possible.

So, what can we do with such unique or alternative knowledge? A long time ago I heard a story about Absolut Vodka, a Swedish brand, and their US launch. I don't know if it's true, but it does serve as a good example. Imagine having four images in front of you: a bottle of Absolut Vodka, an American flag, a picture of Leonid Brezhnev – the former Soviet leader – and a map of Afghanistan. What is the common thread? What is the connection between these images? How can you transform this information into knowledge, and into a competitive edge?

According to the story, the connection between the pictures is that Absolut Vodka launched its products on the US market in 1979–80. This happened when the Soviet Union, with Brezhnev at its head, was occupying Afghanistan. The reason that Absolut Vodka chose this period to launch in the US, or at least became established very rapidly at that time, was that the occupation of Afghanistan had caused the US to boycott a number of things Soviet. The Moscow Olympics in 1980 was one example, and Soviet vodka another. This caused several of the best-selling vodka brands on the American market at that time to be boycotted. Absolut, which was a new entrant, was seen as a good alternative spirit that was not Soviet, and it rapidly gained significant market share. In other words, it is important to keep an eye on our business environment if we want to be able to identify opportunities and, in the long run, stay ahead of our competition. We have to create competitive advantage out of knowledge that is gained from information. Otherwise, what's the use of information?

Innovation and long-term success

There is a relation between innovation and long-term success. Many organizations that have been good at actively gathering new knowledge, turning it into competence, and that have a mental climate that is generally open to different views are more prosperous. Over the course of history there have been a number of great inventors who created unique and world-renowned products and global companies. Classical companies such American conglomerate General Electrics and Swedish ball bearing company SKF are two examples. In modern times organizations like Tesla, Google and Linux have created unique products and services. All of these companies questioned the status quo, saw a better opportunity and identified new ways of behaving in order to cater to the market or to create a brand-new market. If employees are not allowed to express their ideas regarding a better alternative, development grinds to a halt.

Development is driven by what the Austrian economist Joseph Schumpeter calls *creative destruction*.[4] As soon as we find new and better production methods, new and more interesting products or services of superior quality, we jettison the old and divert our resources to the new. Not overnight, but in the long run. Just like the natural selection of species or behaviour. Whatever does not fill a role does not endure. There are many gods in Hinduism. The god of destruction is called Shiva. But Shiva is also the god of re-creation. According to Hinduism, all destruction leads to rebirth. This gives us an alternative lens through which to view change, rather than being intimidated by it.

I recently read that we are now able to produce super steel much tougher and than traditional steel, even tougher than the Grade 300 maraging steel used in aerospace engineering. And it costs only 20 per cent of the cost of traditional steel to produce. I don't understand how, but I realize that this is both a threat and an opportunity for many organizations that produce and use steel. I also read about a research director at a paint factory in Italy. They had developed a paint that made cars look black while not actually 'being' black. He thought the paint could be used on cars that we want to look black but without getting as hot in the summer, as black absorbs the heat from solar radiation better than bright paints. There is something called 'smart fabrics' in the MedTech sector. In the future, smart fabrics will probably make it possible to gauge someone's blood glucose level using their clothing. These fabrics could for instance help warn some 250 million diabetes sufferers worldwide when their blood glucose levels drop too low.

These inventions, and many like them, have come out of structures that reinforced innovation and the courage to make mistakes. There was no project geared toward producing a black paint that is not actually black. Sometimes organizations need to do what The Little Prince did by acknowledging that they do not know what they are looking for, but that they are going to find something.

> If we want to be truly innovative, it is not enough to find answers to the questions we have. What we have to do is ask the questions we have not asked before. And then try to answer them, collectively, and let individuals with many perspectives be present in the process.

In the middle part of the 20th century, Facit was a world leader in instrument engineering for office machines. From 1957 to 1970, sales grew by almost 500 per cent, reaching nearly €100 million in 1970 (approximately $120 million).[5] When instrument engineering gave way to electronics, Facit was not able to make the transition fast enough. They tried to deal with the threat by partnering with the Japanese company Hayakawa (Sharp), but the venture did not work out as well as they had hoped, and in 1972 the organization was threatened with bankruptcy. At the year end of 1972, the company was acquired by Electrolux for €8 million, i.e. significantly less than 10 per cent of the revenue from only three years earlier. What would have happened if someone had asked 'How should we address the threat posed by electronic machines?' a little earlier? The first electromechanical calculating machines were manufactured back in the 1940s. Shortly thereafter, they became fully electronic and were renamed computers. There was plenty of time to react.

It is possible to identify links between knowledge and profitability. In Japanese car factories on average nine improvements per employee per year are implemented. Any average US or European automobile factory, such as a GM and Mercedes plant, is far behind these numbers.[6] Profitability can be calculated in different ways, and it is not possible to isolate a single reason for profitability. However, there is scientific evidence to posit that an organization in which all employees contribute suggestions for improvement will achieve better results. In this example, we see a difference of about 10 per cent in the car manufacturers' respective profit margins over time.

Organizations therefore need to create a climate and a structure that causes all employees to actively contribute to identifying potential improvements in daily operations. One key behaviour and a measure of it (key behavioural indicator) that ties into this logic could be to measure the number of proposals for new ideas contributed by the employees. If the organization then goes on to identify ways of reinforcing this behaviour's frequency (quantity) and shaping its topography (quality), this is a very good start. Essentially, the managers' ability to reinforce the behaviour of questioning becomes crucial. This requires managers who have the courage to be challenged and who realize that others may possess more knowledge than they do themselves. Being a manager is one role and being an innovative thinker is another, just like being an accountant or sales manager is a third and fourth.

> Managers that want to create successful organizations realize they do not need to be the best at everything. They simply need to encourage and reinforce their employees to challenge and take charge over the development of the business.

Reinforcing the new

Each year, the business magazine *Fast Company* compiles a list of the world's most creative companies. Several of the companies that make the list are also companies that have been profitable and successful for many years. They have demonstrably learned to adapt to a changing environment.

It is quite natural for all organizations to adapt to the outside world. But the pace of change in 2021 requires a proactive approach to change if an organization is to adapt to the market fast enough. Some of the organizations that frequently make the list are 3M, IBM, Microsoft, HP and Google.

Many companies measure 'creativity' in some way, to be able to manage it. The number of patents applied for or granted is one way of measuring. Another is what fraction of total turnover is spent on research and development. A more direct and clearer way is to measure how many 'creative' behaviours individuals engage in. To reinforce these, we can then create an incentive system that is linked directly to that creative behaviour and to new business ideas that make the company money.

Many organizations have an individual bonus linked to a financial result on the organizational level, either the level you are responsible for or the overall performance of the organization. An alternative that supports innovative behaviour is to have bonuses tied to how much money a new business idea has generated. In such cases, the bonus is paid to the people who perform the behaviour that generates a new product or service that in turn generates a profit for the company. This is one way to create structured opportunities for employees to be creative. Another such created structure is to let employees devote a certain amount of time to 'innovative stuff'. At Google, working time distribution calls for employees to spend 70 per cent of their time on what they call the core competency. They are allowed to spend 20 per cent of their time developing their core competency and are free to spend the remaining 10 per cent on something called *marginal tasks*. Performing marginal tasks mainly comes down to doing things that are fun and generating new ideas. Many organizations have similar divisions of work time as the Google 70/20/10 rule.

Creativity in an organization is based on the creative behaviour of its employees – thinking new thoughts, coming up with new solutions, testing new ideas, failing and learning from mistakes. It is not based on decision-makers' arbitrary assessment of whether a new business concept can be profitable or not. Far too many creative ideas are stifled at the idea stage for lack of money or because someone with decision-making authority does not believe in them. Sometimes that is justified, but sometimes it is also due to prejudice, ignorance or lack of perspective. Organizations need to make sure that more people with different perspectives make important decisions that concern the products, services or offerings of the future. This reinforces that employees should contribute their ideas and views. The collective assessment of ideas is a better predictor of success than individual assessment.

Several years ago I worked with a start-up in the health business. As they grew, they recruited managers with a pronounced streak of thinking differently, who wanted to work across traditional department lines. This had helped them, initially, to create a good product, but the rate and speed of innovation and sales had stagnated and I was to help them create future opportunities. One part was a structure and process for creativity and idea management. What we did was to launch a fictitious internal stock exchange where everyone in the company had the opportunity to introduce (list) new business ideas in the form of a prospectus and a brief list of actions that had to be taken in order to move on with the idea. Initially this was just a white board with paper held up by magnets. Creativity and innovation need not be technically advanced.

All the employees at the company were then given the equivalent of €100,000 in pretend money to invest in one or more of the ideas – just like a stock exchange. Since it was a start-up, they all designed their own angel investor firms with logos and what not. When an idea cracked the top 10 list of the most highly valued ideas (most invested pretend money), it was taken up for more thorough analysis. The ideas that held water were given a real budget. Ideas that no one paid any attention to for three months – sometimes despite heavy pitching from the founder, joint ventures, mergers, acquisitions – were delisted from the fictitious stock exchange, as in the real world. The stock exchange was seen as a way of getting everyone to contribute their knowledge to help the company grow, and it really created interest in developing and finding the next 'killer idea'.

In this case a success factor was its 'democratic' foundation. The strength of the ideas was what made more, or fewer people want to support the venture. In that sense, it was the strength of the idea that determined whether it amassed a following or not.

I applied this principle in many organizations to increase their ideas, over the years, although often at a much smaller scale as well. If we as an idea creator – manager or not – have a good idea that we want to sell into the organization, we test it out on a number of employees. If they think that it's worth spending their time on our project, it's a go. We then look for a number of 'sponsors'. The sponsorship we receive takes the form of time to develop our idea together with others. Those who are good at generating ideas and selling these into the organization can make claims on others' time. This is what determines whether you are a leader, not a formal position. Later on, the most promising ideas became actual apps, products and services that made up the backbone of the organizational structure that also changed continuously as new ideas grew and old ones faded.

A lesson we can all draw from this is that true leadership in a knowledge society is not about power in terms of a role or position, or power based on knowing everything and not sharing or being the best at everything. The true leaders are the ones that serve their colleagues and realize their personal limitations, mandated to involve many others in solving the complex problems faced by organizations or developing great ideas.

Another structured measure to boost creativity is that everyone can be assigned an explicit responsibility to seek out and produce new knowledge relevant for the development of the organization. A paragraph about this responsibility can be written in every employment contract of the organization. This way of working seems to give rise to a new definition of commitment. In the health company, commitment was not about getting involved because you had to, because it looked good or because it was part of your job description. Commitment was described in behaviours like investing time (and, initially, fake money) in an idea they believed in, helping colleagues to improve their pitches and actually realize the ideas by giving customers a concrete offer. This was a particular example of conditions that positively reinforced the generation of new ideas, collaboration, the development of new products and successfully 'going the extra mile'.

Our next success will not be found by walking in the footsteps of others. New knowledge is required if we are to forge new ways. The more people that contribute, the more ideas the company has to choose between and the easier it is to elicit better ideas that end up being profitable.

Notes

1 See, e.g., V Charles and T Gherman (2018) Big Data and ethnography: Together for the greater good, in *Big Data for the Greater Good*, ed A Emrouznejad and V Charles, (pp. 19–34). Studies in Big Data Series, Springer-Verlag, Berlin

2 J Naisbitt (1982) *Megatrends: Ten new directions transforming our lives*, Warner Books/Warner Communications Company, New York

3 Sun Tzu (2005) *The Art of War*, translated by T Cleary, Shambhala Publications, Boulder, CO

4 P Schumpeter (1942) *Capitalism, Socialism and Democracy*, Harper and Brothers, New York

5 T Petersson. I teknikrevolutionens centrum: företagsledning och utveckling i Facit 1957–1972, Uppsala Papers in Financial and Business History, no 16, 2005, Department of Economic History, Uppsala University, Uppsala

6 See, e.g., C Yorke and N Bodek (2005) *All You Gotta Do is Ask*, PCS Press, Vancouver; J Liker (2004) *The Toyota way: 14 management principles from the world's greatest manufacturer*, McGraw-Hill, New York; M A Cusumano (1985) *The Japanese Automobile Industry: Technology and management at Nissan and Toyota*, Harvard University Press, Cambridge, MA

14

Smart and behavioural strategizing

From a behavioural strategizing perspective, at least two things are required to become high-performing, prosperous and successful over time. The first thing is a clear focus on one *generic strategy* – being big, best, fast or beautiful. The other thing is being smart. Being smart involves the application of behavioural and learning principles in order to realize strategy – i.e. the employment of behavioural strategizing. We need to incorporate change just as deeply into the core of the organization as sales or production or any given core process.

Behaviour is influenced to a greater extent by its immediate consequences, and to a lesser extent by activators. Traditionally, strategy is focused on activators. We therefore need to shift the focus of strategizing from the 'activator side' to the 'consequence side'. A behavioural focus contributes to this shift. By focusing on one generic strategy on the one hand, and by basing strategizing on behavioural psychology principles on the other, we can strike a balance between the activator side and the consequence side. The purpose of the strategy content (the activators) is to set priorities and start behaviours. The task of the realization process (the consequences) is to reinforce, refine and improve them. Become better, smarter.

As with anyone who wants to become masterful, employees in organizations must constantly work in a focused, active and meticulous way to learn to become high-performing. They practise and become skilled at driving through strategic changes. They develop what we might call a propensity for change, innovativeness or the capacity for learning and adaptation.

Dynamic capability is usually defined as an organization's ability to integrate, build, learn and adapt internal and external competencies so as to be able to deal with a rapidly changing outside world. In the long term, this leads to unique capability and competitiveness.[1] This is closely related to exploring smart as a competitive advantage particularly adapting and learning.

Galileo challenged the geocentric worldview. Picasso and other modernists challenged our conception of art. Einstein challenged Newton's physics. Miles Davis and David Bowie constantly challenged themselves to create ground-breaking music again and again. Innovative thinkers may have revolutionary ideas, but their goal need not be revolution. New knowledge that traditionalists see as the subversive beginning of a revolution is welcomed as enlightenment by individuals who realize that constant change is the only way to exist.

Organizations that draw on being smart as a competitive advantage challenge prevailing views. They proceed on the basis of what things could look like, not necessarily what they do look like. This type of foresight requires knowledge of trends within technology, demographics, legislation, lifestyles, etc. This entails an increased need for various kinds of information, to be gathered, assessed, sorted and transformed into intelligence, knowledge and competence. At the Walt Disney Company in the 1990s, the ambition was to look into the future by '*Imagineering*', drawing on imagination and engineering behaviours concurrently. This is one example of an ability that helps organizations to develop themselves.

There are always new ways of doing things better. If Henry Ford had given his customers what they wanted, he would have given them a faster and stronger horse. At least, so the story goes. Few were aware of the phenomenon of the automobile and therefore they did not ask for one. It thus seems more proper to ask what the customer really wants. Sometimes it may be a stronger and faster horse, but sometimes it's something different altogether – such as a car. Sometimes it is a drill, and sometimes it's a hole in the wall, to paraphrase legendary Harvard Business School marketing professor Theodore Levitt.

By listening carefully to the customer's needs, i.e. being customer-centric, we can find opportunities in the borderland between traditional industries, products or services. This is another way of utilizing the smartness that can come from behaviour strategizing.

The reason such constant challenging is hard to do is that it requires more effort to think in a new way than it does to think the same thought again. This is due to evolution and is not something we can influence. But we can learn how to handle it. The habit of repetition is negatively reinforced. By doing what I have always done, I don't have to think in new ways. The brain is designed to focus on what is most important. If something works, why change it? This is the brain's way of prioritizing. Many organizations stick with what they have always done because they do not know what else to do. Others do so in order to minimize the risk of failure. A strong culture is often nothing but 'habit' at the organizational level. Because habit wants to keep on doing the same thing, this means that a strong culture can be a threat to development and long-term success.

> It is by trying out new behaviour and sometimes failing that we can find new and better behaviour. This makes it important to reinforce behaviour like daring to forge new paths, questioning whether the existing way is the best one, encouraging problem identification, making sure we find the root of the problem and devoting time to learning from experience in order to become an adapting and successful organization – daring to succeed.

It requires more time to think in new ways than to think the same way we always have. Which makes it less 'attractive' in practical terms, as time is often in short supply in organizations. Many organizations are currently governed on the basis of short-termism. Their horizon often extends only to the next quarter or the next annual report. In tough times, it is natural to cut down on the amount of proactive change work. But doing so has a devastating effect on long-term success. Organizations that do not invest in their future rarely have much of a future at all.

Behavioural strategizing builds on philosophical assumptions that need to permeate the entire organization. It is not possible to get the full effect of an organization if we fail to invest in the behaviour that creates adaptable organizations. If we do not invest in top-quality raw materials, we will not get top-quality products. If we do not invest resources in developing competency that makes our organization smarter, we will not get a smart organization.

Exploiting smart as a competitive advantage

In studies on innovative companies, some of which are co-authored by one of the real heavyweights in innovation, Clayton Christensen, authors have identified a series of 'discoverer behaviour' that distinguishes excellent, successful and innovative companies from an average company:[2]

- They focus on the things that create long-term competitiveness and results.

- They challenge orthodoxies by asking provocative questions.
- They observe the world with curiosity in order to discover new and more efficient ways of doing things.
- They network with people who do not think the way they do in order to gain radically different perspectives.
- They experiment in order to test new ideas and to try out new experiences.
- They make use of several alternative ways to get input for strategy. For example, they ask their customers, employees, suppliers or people on the street.
- They seek out and openly acknowledge their limitations, and actively seek help in dealing with them.
- They recruit managers who see it as their role to serve their subordinate employees, not manage them.
- They set aside time to reflect, think in new ways and constantly improve themselves and their surroundings.

All of these behaviours, although not really pinpointed, create new ideas and allow the innovators to forge links between what was previously thought of as disjointed or unclear, by harnessing the perspective and competency of others. In so doing, they succeed in coming up with ideas that no one else has had before, and products that no one has ever heard of before.

To start a journey of harnessing the collective resources in terms of employee behaviour to try to exploit smart as a competitive advantage, the following principles are a good start:

- focus on learning and efficiency
- challenge current conventions
- involve more people in strategizing
- reinforce the positive rather than punishing the negative
- use several different reinforcers
- assign responsibility for change to everyone in the organization
- encourage new initiatives and provide opportunities to exert influence

Focus on learning and efficiency

Organizations that focus their energy and resources where they get the most out of them go further. Basically, focus should result in the most 'bang for the buck'. Focusing on a generic strategy – being big, best, fast or beautiful – is a prerequisite. Organizations that design their entire organization in such a way that its structure will create the organization's primary competitive advantage will find it easier to become successful. This involves setting goals, mirroring the chosen strategy and clearly defining the behaviour that drives the competitive advantage within a generic strategy. At companies whose strategy is to be big, this means striving after economies of scale and working to institute constant improvements. At those whose strategy is to be best, it means tailoring products and services to individual needs. At those whose strategy is to be fast, it means investing in ideation and innovation and getting quickly to the market. At those whose strategy is to be beautiful, it means investing in brand-building activities.

No organization has the time or money to invest everywhere. The world is developing far too quickly. In the future, strategizing is likely to be even more a matter of culling and rejection than of selection than it is in 2021. Those who specialize will outperform any generalist. A focus on reinforcing what the organization's employees actually do – behaviour – leads to us focusing on the things that have real significance for our business and that drive it forward.

Strategy formulation is sometimes considered to be easy to do in comparison with strategy realization. This notion originates from an image where formulation often delimits the entire process of 'discovery' and experimentation. Organizations neglect to involve the people who are to realize the strategy and do not invest the amount of intellectual resources needed in order to produce a strategy worthy of the name. It is easy to set goals when we proceed on the basis of a past result. It is harder to set goals when we need to find a way to sweep away the competition and simultaneously not make things too abstract and 'lofty'. When we discuss strategy in general terms, it is common to confuse *strategizing* with *strategic planning*. Real strategizing is not a planning procedure – it is a constant quest.

At organizations with a tendency FOR planning-oriented strategizing, the organization tries to exert control using conscious activators. Clear goals and strategies constitute 'rules' whose purpose is to influence employee behaviour. The goals, strategies and control systems that are set up often determine what behaviour the employees are to perform, often without regard to the knowledge they possess. Skilled employees are held back and those who do not do what they are supposed to, feel guilty. We also know that activators only have a limited influence on behaviour. Strategizing must therefore involve spending less time on delivering activators and spending more time on delivering consequences – less planning and more follow-up, feedback, and thereby also learning and development.

The flexible and informal character of this type of strategizing means that the strategy formulation process differs from that of traditional organizations. A traditional organization's strategizing is characterized by clearly defined steps that build on each other, and on rationality and logic. Behavioural strategizing trying to exploit smartness as a competitive advantage means that organizations are much more pragmatic and view strategizing as an ongoing effort where the organization evaluates what behaviour leads to what results. Based on the knowledge produced on follow-up, the organization then adjusts activities and goals so as to take prevailing internal and external circumstances into account. This process is characterized by continuous learning and the development of shared patterns of behaviour. Not planning, rationality or logic.

> Organizations who want to exploit smart as a competitive advantage need to find ways to systematize the delivery of positive work-related, social, emotional and symbolic reinforcers of the behaviours that lead to adaptability and long-term competitiveness; behaviours closely related to continuous learning.

Challenge current conventions

For organizations to compete on smartness a number of characteristics that distinguish them from traditional companies need to be in place. They need to be flat, with a flexible structure, and much of their communication needs to be done informally. They have an open atmosphere that encourages debate and conflict. They also have a greater tendency to involve external parties in their strategizing.

Vijay Govindarajan, one of the most renowned management thinkers alive, has pointed out five structural explanations for why companies have a hard time developing their innovative power, and thus risk losing competitiveness:[3]

1 Too much focus on existing business. Current decision-making processes and organizational structure impede innovation and future focus.

2 Low tolerance for experimentation and failure. Ninety per cent of all business plans become an end in themselves and allow no scope for innovative ideas.

3 Failure to highlight new ideas and innovations. There is no way to reinforce employees in the use of behaviour that can lead to the 'next success'.

4 Too much silo thinking. There is too little interaction between organizational departments and units, which is why they do not come up with any new ideas.

5 Lack of different perspectives. Despite having a globally viable product, there is no ability to understand local conditions.

Renewal takes place in the borderland between different disciplines, between ways of looking at things and work areas. Innovation is often created horizontally in an organization, rarely has a clear owner, and must therefore be one of the most structured processes. It is difficult to think in new ways and to question conventions without support and structure. What is required therefore is to establish structures and reinforcements to ensure that the organization generates and tests new ideas. Failure then becomes a crucial part of achieving success in the long term. Indeed, failure can be a good thing. Creating more contacts across different business areas, departments and units in order to foster an exchange of ideas and to induce employees to broaden their perspectives helps us to become more innovative. And, for that matter, outside stakeholders such as suppliers and customers can also be brought into *open innovation* and strategizing processes.

In addition, cultural differences can create brand-new ways of looking at things. Innovation in the West is usually associated with new products. Innovation in India, for example, is more about new delivery models and distribution channels to get products out to more customers.

At many companies, strategizing is often based on what already exists, such as last year's goals, budget and activity lists. Next year we need to make a bit more money than this year, have slightly more satisfied customers and improve our quality a tad. It is also common to have a plan that extends out three to five years. That is far enough away to make almost bold plans, but close enough that we feel we can influence the result. Very few dare to set up a *big hairy audacious goal* (BHAG) to be reached within three, or even five, years. Why not allow ten years, to make sure we dare to make a more bold move? In addition, people usually assume that the near future will look like today. But the world of tomorrow may not be identical to the one we have today. There may come a year when we can no longer raise the goals and be almost sure that we will achieve them. What is the most important thing at that point? To set higher goals than the year before just on principle, or to be sure that we achieve the goal and create a delivery culture?

Seeing constant growth from the current state as the starting point for strategizing without asking what could be possible necessarily has consequences.

To instead proceed from what could be possible is sometimes called *back casting* and can be seen as an alternative to traditional forecasting, which typically is the traditional method. If someone wants to do something completely new, why proceed from the status quo? Perhaps the goals should be even more ambitious?

In 1979, Canon set the goal of producing copiers for $1,000 each. Compare this to the cheapest model offered by Xerox, which cost around $3,000 at the time. The result of Canon's 'different' objective was a popular line of inexpensive copiers. The Polaroid camera came about when Dr Edward Land's daughter wanted to be able to see the pictures she took faster. Those are examples of not proceeding from the status quo.

Pioneering innovation need not be advanced, expensive or difficult to perform. Nor does it need to be linked to technology or a product. It is just as important to have the courage to engage in *management innovation*,[4] i.e. innovating how we manage organizations. What is needed, however, is new perspectives, the courage to challenge current conventions, and the daring to take a chance.

But opportunities and the willingness to learn and take independent initiatives are held back if we still don't derive any benefit from learning new behaviour. This means that there is no reinforcement for learning new things. Many organizations want to create an innovative culture that helps the organization to think in new ways. Organizations that engage in micromanagement or that are excessively structured do not allow for employees to perform 'newly learned' behaviour. In such organizations, learning is impeded, fewer ideas are generated, and an innovative culture does not come about.

Instead of building their future on preceding years, we should ask ourselves what we can accomplish, set a long-term ambitious goal accordingly, and define the behaviours needed to drive the organization toward that goal. If we then evaluate the impact of that behaviour on the goals frequently and continuously, we learn from experience and can make adjustments along the way.

Involve more people in strategizing

One common reason for difficulties in changing an organization is the composition of the management team. There we will often find people with similar experiences, people with a lot to lose if things change, and people who have invested both time and energy in the status quo. This probably also makes them those who have the greatest respect for the current situation. Where do we most often find the people responsible for developing strategies? At or near the top of organizations. At the risk of sounding a bit mean, we might say that the bottleneck that impedes development and change is often at the top.

Organizations are often 'pyramids of experience'. The higher up in the organization someone is, the longer their experience at the company. The longer the experience, the more difficult to think in new ways. One company I worked with had a management team made up of nine people. Eight of the nine people had been with the company since graduating from university – for just over 25 years on average. Five of them had the same degree from the same university – the CEO, the CFO, the COO and two of four EVPs. These five were all men and between 46 and 51 years old. The HR director was the only woman and the only person who was 'new' at the company. She had been there for four years. This sort of composition is not unusual, and naturally has consequences in terms of the thoughts that get thought and what actions are taken to create competitiveness. The more variety of perspective we have, the greater our chances of understanding the entire organization and the entire customer base.

Experience is valuable, but only up to a point. 2021's terrain is changing so rapidly that more and more people deem experience to be a less valuable component of success than before. Sometimes it can be downright crippling. If strategizing is beholden to past experience, it is hard to see an innovative strategy as long as those with the most years of experience or who have narrow perspectives are those developing the strategies.

Smart strategizing therefore brings more people on board to participate in the activities, e.g. meetings and workshops constitute the strategy process. They gather in more perspectives and integrate strategy formulation and realization. They make the strategy a 'living document' for real; a document that is evaluated and adjusted continuously. It thus needs to be integrated with monthly or quarterly performance reviews, or with whatever frequency the performance of the organization is assessed. This helps organizations to be challenged. It seems wise for experienced individuals to ask themselves: has my decade or two of expertise in the industry made me more or less inclined to challenge industry and company conventions? How can I get our customers and suppliers to share their views on the things we can do even better?

There are innovators at every company. But often there is no coherent process that lets them be heard. Their voices are often filtered through the hierarchy and the message is 'diluted' or not listened to. Those who come up with ideas that can help the organization get better are likely to expect some type of feedback. No feedback (e.g. reinforcement in the form of attention, praise or the opportunity to influence) leads to behaviour being extinguished. Smart strategizing involves taking care of innovators, asking for their views and listening actively to them. Advice to senior management is to ask themselves these questions: Do you know who the innovators in your organization are? Have they had a chance to make their voices heard in your strategy work? How can you harness their will to develop your business? If the innovators don't get the chance to challenge from within, there is a risk that they will challenge from the outside.

Tony Fadell left Philips as they did not believe in his idea of a digital music player. Steve Jobs recruited him, and he helped develop the iPod. John Warnock left Xerox to cofound Adobe. A number of individuals left Fairchild semiconductors to cofound Intel. AstraZeneca's stomach drug Losec and Ericsson's classical phones with a handset are the successful result of 'innovative' intrapreneurs who didn't wish to let the future be determined by 'obsolete' structures. The list could be much longer. Even innovators like Google lose significant talent as these types of 'mavericks', or bootleggers as 3M calls them internally, are often not allowed to prosper internally and are not reinforced in their behaviour to take part in strategizing to challenge conventions.

As much as innovators are needed in any organizations, innovators who don't get the support of management rarely accomplish anything in that organization. In most organizations, managers often have a monopoly on resources. I guess it is safe to say that a revolution rarely starts at the top, but an organizational revolution needs to be sanctioned from the top, in one way or another.

A top-down process often creates consensus with regard to purpose among the few who are involved and can ensure some form of compliance among certain subordinates. A bottom-up process, on the other hand, leads to a diversity of perspectives to choose from, a better chance of finding the best solution, and a heightened sense of shared responsibility throughout the organization. Consensus without diversity creates rules that impede development, and diversity without consensus leads to ambiguity and weak focus.

Strategizing is thus a process that involves both the top and the bottom of an organization that produces both diversity and consensus. By having responsible senior managers sit in quietly on discussions between secretaries, salespeople, carpenters, IT techs, middle managers, etc, they not only gain new perspectives, but also an understanding of what their employees think and feel, and what they are passionate about.

If a cross-section of the organization is participating, the strategy is lent the weight it deserves and will create the conditions needed for it to be realized. Senior executives should be curious about their employees' views, rather than being interested in hearing the right answers: more like the Little Prince, less like Sherlock Holmes. It is the managers' responsibility to stay close enough to the business that they are able to share their employees' views and understand the challenges they face. Because the employees are the ones who will be realizing the strategy, they should have a chance to express their own views on their future. If the goal is for the people with resources and the people with the smartest ideas to end up in the same place, they need to do the work together.

There are numerous studies that have looked at how you make sure strategy, change and innovation 'gets done', and most have come to the same conclusion. Involving larger parts of an organization in developing a strategy or in a change or innovation initiative increases the likelihood of it being realized, or if it's a bad idea it gets shut down before resources are allocated. Either way, it's a win.

> Strategy needs to be based on dialogue. Dialogue involves a free exchange of views. This means that I need to have the courage to lay bare my assumptions, my prejudices and my dreams, and need to be prepared to critically examine my own opinions. To draw on smartness as a source of competitiveness, this must be harnessed and reinforced.

Typically, three different categories of employee are heavily underrepresented in strategizing:

1 People with a youthful perspective. Most young people live closer to the future than older people. In a way, it is ironic that the group that is most affected by the future is not allowed to participate in shaping the strategy that is to lead them into that future.

2 People in the most remote parts of the organization (nationally or globally). The farther away we get from headquarters, the greater the opportunities to innovate. This is partly due to the fact that it is possible 'to do your own thing' to some extent, but it is also because remote parts of an organization often lack the resources available to headquarters and need to work more innovatively.

3 New hires. People with new thoughts, those who have not yet fully embraced the 'truths' that dominate in the industry or organization, can often contribute new and alternative perspectives.

How many 'new voices' were involved in your latest strategizing process? Honestly? How hard do you work to create opportunities to really be positively surprised?

One way to 'test' a strategy is to invite a cross-section of the organization and have a frank and honest discussion about the strategy before it is resolved and communicated. There is allegedly a concept used at IKEA called '*stationmastering*'. During IKEA's early years, after employees had put together a new set of assembly instructions for a piece of furniture, they would go down to the stationmaster at Älmhult station (the small village in the south of Sweden where IKEA was founded) and see if he could manage to assemble the furniture. If he was able to put it together, the instructions were considered good enough. Stationmastering our strategy – testing it on people who do not have as much insight into the issues, or who have a completely different perspective – is an easy way to ensure that the strategy is clear and unambiguous, and that it sets a direction. And it need not be complicated. A global technology group I worked with decided back in 2007 that, to drive their 'fast' strategy, everything they did, e.g. projects, acquisitions, divestments, etc, should lead to a more digital company as a whole, products with higher precision and that were cheaper for the customer. Every decision was compared to these 'strategy ground rules', and these ground rules were built mainly bottom-up. In 2021 the company is almost completely digital, has doubled its revenues, increased its profits by 50 per cent while simultaneously the products are on average 7 per cent cheaper to the customer. Everybody in the organization agrees that this would not have been the strategy for the company, if the management team had strategized exclusively.

Reinforce the positive rather than punishing the negative

In organizations we expend a lot of effort on fostering community, a sense of participation and work ethic, using goals, strategies, training sessions, value statements and policies. These can be seen as organizational activators that start various behaviours or establishing operations that influence the power of consequences. But the consequences are what determine whether a behaviour will persist. The behaviour that causes us to achieve goals and to work according to our strategies, values and policies needs to be reinforced, or else it will weaken and, in the end, extinguish.

All behaviour has consequences. Traditional organizations are often 'low feedback'. The organization only provides feedback on the results of employee behaviour – the actual organizational result – to management. At best, management makes an adjustment to the goals, strategies or working methods.

The result that gets fed back is also often of a financial nature, despite management teams often wrongly assuming that employees do not want to know the financial result that their unit has contributed to. In my experience, often they do not know of any real concrete alternative. But it can also be worse. Sometimes management teams feel that employees should not know the result – it is a secret. I get this, when it comes to issues with insider information, but that is not what I am referring to here. If employees do not understand how their work leads to different higher-level results in revenue and profit, how are they supposed to improve their behaviour and performance through independent initiatives?

Consequences should be fed back to the individuals and groups who are part of contributing to a result. Talking about the result and reflecting on why it turned out the way it did generates knowledge; knowledge is a powerful reinforcer for most people. This increases the likelihood of 'better' behaviour in the future, which in turn causes goals to be achieved with greater certainty, and possibly quicker.

An important learning under behaviour strategizing is to reinforce desired key behaviours. Focus on setting consequences for the things that create value for the business and the customers. Talk to employees, ask them about their work, and praise those who excel through their behaviour. Discuss the link between their behaviour, the results achieved by the unit or organization, and the underlying strategy.

If there is a frequent follow-up and adaptation process, and if the organization has an overall goal, it becomes less important to have goals and strategies looking out one, three or five years into the future. Strategy and goals in the traditional sense, as rules to steer behaviour, do not serve much of a purpose, to be honest. Instead, organizations that are contingency-shaped rather than rule-governed able to act faster in response to changes in the outside world due to competitors or customer demands. They do what works to get to where they want to go – not what it says in a one-year or three-year plan. Or, for that matter, what led to success over the past 50 years.

Agile has become an obvious buzzword in business. To simplify things somewhat, working agile means short work cycles, frequent evaluations and continuous feedback loops. Working in this way helps us get better at adapting to an ever-changing environment – we might say drawing on smart as a competitive advantage by employing behavioural strategizing demands to apply an agile competency or agile behaviours to the management of organizations.

Organizations that want to become efficient and successful need to provide feedback on consequences in a frequent, continuous process of follow-up in which key behaviour, its results and the contribution it made to strategy realization are discussed. With every follow-up that happens, minor adjustments are made to the activities to ensure that they make the maximum contribution to what the organization wants to accomplish today – not what they wanted to accomplish when the goals were set.

Use several different reinforcers

Monetary reinforcers such as salary and bonus account for only a very small part of the total quantity of reinforcers operating within an organization. Social reinforcers like pleasant conversations, a look, a smile, someone showing an interest, a friendly email, praise, working on a fun project with a good group, etc – all of that is of great importance. Cognitive reinforcers like a sense of developing and learning new things, getting to contribute, being part of a context and a sense of pride are also important, as are symbolic reinforcers like a diploma or a nomination. Along with work-related reinforcements – such as the opportunity to tackle new and developmental tasks, being given more responsibility or getting a promotion – these different types of reinforcers have a considerably greater impact on behaviour than financial reinforcers do. Organizations have to make use of many different reinforcements – a broad array.

We need to develop a system and a structure to drive the generation of new ideas. Questioning things in a positive way and suggesting alternative ways of getting the job done are important behaviours that need to be reinforced. A good start is to let everyone in the organization devote a certain amount of time – two hours a week, for example – to thinking about small improvements that could be made in their work. The more small ideas employees seek out, the more practice they get in generating ideas, which also improves the organization's chances of identifying the 'big' idea. This 'idea system' can later on be incorporated into the organization's ordinary business activities in the form of idea boards, idea meetings, etc, and then followed up on just as carefully as financials or sales, preferably in monthly combined reviews of the performance of the organization.

People want to share their ideas. They want to improve their work and be part of a winning team. It is important to tap into this. Everyone can contribute ideas, meaning that everyone can be a winner. Some questions that we should answer if we want to be smarter and more competitive are these: How does our organization handle ideas and innovation today? Do we have a clear structure for how we generate and reinforce new ideas? Who makes decisions about new ideas? How do we work to realize small improvements today?

Assign responsibility for change to everyone in the organization

In order to discover new opportunities, we need to look at the world in a new way. By contributing new perspectives, we can create new opportunities. Perspective is often worth more than intelligence. Seeing differences as levers for innovation and change, rather than threats to the status quo, is a new perspective for many people to adopt. This helps learning and adaptability. Another perspective is to realize that it is imagination rather than investment that determines an organization's capacity to be strategic and successful over the long term. This is not entirely true, but can function as a change of perspectives. Indeed, large organizations with big financial muscles can in fact buy smaller innovative companies instead of developing their own innovative capabilities. However, such a modus operandus is not possible for the majority of organizations, and just buying innovation rather than developing it internally is probably not good advice. And still, some kind of inovativeness is needed anyway, at least to determine what to buy that adds value to the existing corporation. Therefore, developing the skills needed to innovate and change is indeed crucial for most (if not all) organizations that want to be successful over time.

Organizations that want to create something enduring have the important task of encouraging and reinforcing new perspectives. If we want to do that, we need to devote time and knowledge to identifying truly innovative ideas and unconventional strategic opportunities. What we see from a mountaintop is not the same thing we see from the fields. Without being aware of different perspectives, we cannot contribute to innovation in the strategy creation process.

Research shows that management teams and senior executives generally assume two things about change. The first is that middle managers and subordinate employees oppose change. The second is that only a 'hero-leader' can force an otherwise lukewarm and backward-looking organization to see a brighter future. These assumptions are not true. People need stability – when everything is unstable, who has the energy to talk about new things? And who would oppose a change that actually makes an improvement? Humanity would probably not have accomplished what it has over the course of the last millennium if it had been doubtful about change, or if responsibility for change were vested in the political pinnacle of society. We need to understand how to benefit from our employees' willingness to contribute to the positive aspects of change and innovation.

Too often when management teams talk about change, they talk about terrifying changes, such as laying off 20 per cent of the workforce or relocating production to a country with lower labour costs. This type of change is not about creating new opportunities, but rather about correcting the mistakes of previous leaders and management teams. These types of changes should rather be seen as crisis management than change – paying off a '*strategy debt*' created by previous leaders. They are thus the results of past leaders and management teams not having taken the responsibility for changing and not innovating themselves and the organization in time. Future strategy debts can often be avoided through behavioural strategizing and the quest for utilizing smart as a competitive advantage.

> The goal for efficient and long-term successful organizations that want to explore smartness as resource is not to get employees to support change and innovation, but to assign them the explicit responsibility to contribute to the change and to want to take charge of their own future and that of the organization. For that to happen, organizations involve innovators, customers, partners and suppliers and any given stakeholder with 'good' input in conversations about a common future.

In behavioural strategizing, organizations invite their members to the table to discuss the future and frequently realize that the supposed resistance to change is not so formidable once everyone gets a chance to talk about it.

On one occasion, I helped a particular organization develop a strategy for a business unit in the telecom industry. We involved a cross-section of the organization, and their task was to work through the strategy without the help of the manager in charge. This is what the business unit president said when we decided to do that: 'And what if they come back with the wrong things?' After a second his face lit up in a smile. He laughed at himself and realized that there was no right or wrong, just that he was nervous about letting go. The second insight he had, and that he and I talked about for a while, was that if the employees did come back with something that actually was 'wrong', that meant that the new strategy was not his biggest problem, but rather that he had the wrong people in the organization. Or, indeed, that he was the wrong person in the wrong place. Managers or management teams who 'correct' new ideas because they feel that they know better are making a categorical error. Making corrections means punishing the behaviour that is the very purpose of developing a strategy in common – namely, getting more people to contribute their ideas on how the organization can get even better.

In his book *The Tipping Point: How little things can make a big difference*, Malcolm Gladwell describes what is required for something to become a 'social epidemic' – a change in society.[5] His arguments are based mainly in social psychology and he suggests a rule of thumb that says that at least 15 per cent of the population should be involved and convinced in order for a change to become real. More recent studies suggest 25 per cent.[6] That is the *critical mass* that needs to be achieved to have an impact. And, to be really safe, it needs to be 'the right individuals', not only a sufficient share. In a sense these right ones could be considered informal leaders. More specifically, they are people who push through changes, and these can be broken down into three categories. They are called *connectors*, *mavens* and *persuaders* and all have different roles in the actual change. The persuader sells the message, tells the organization where they are going in a convincing way and why it is such a good idea. Mavens find out what all the current conditions are and are able to answer questions and objections that could stall development. Connectors know people in several different circles and make sure that the ideas are disseminated properly.

Applying these thoughts to changes in an organization, and to ensure realization of strategy since that entails changing an organization, and inviting people to take responsibility for the future, are concrete ways of involving the *key stakeholders* we need to have on our side in order to bring about a real shift in the organization.

Encourage new initiatives and provide opportunities to exert influence

Employees generally care about their organization and would like to improve it. At least that's my opinion. But not everyone waits for permission to act. Some individuals take initiative, start doing things to get something to happen. There are, of course, initiatives taken that should not have been taken. However, in order to spark actions, we need to invite people to participate, and reinforce them when they take new initiatives. Organizations underperform and flounder because employees do not have an opportunity to speak up without risking their hide. Innovative thinkers and change activists need to be reinforced, or else they will leave. If no one steps forward when more energy is spent on defending the old order than on creating the future, where does that leave the organization in the long run?

Although there are cultural differences, studies[7] show that the employees of tomorrow want to have more than 'a job'. They want influence and they want to be involved. They want greater responsibility earlier on in their careers. They are more loyal to their own development and less loyal to employers. The employees of tomorrow don't join a company and stay for 40 years. They rarely stay in a position for more than a couple of years. In order to attract and retain the talent of tomorrow, organizations must increasingly begin adapting to their wishes. This requires greater focus on individual and organizational development, and faster learning and development processes. It requires an understanding of and a competency for the big picture and for adapting to the outside world. One way to do this is to let several people participate and take responsibility for the future of the company. Another is to reinforce initiatives, all initiatives that employees take. An assessment of the initiative's quality can be done later. Positive reinforcement is the only way to increase a behaviour. If we want more initiatives, we must not let our eagerness to improve, adjust or correct the suggested or taken initiative act as punishment as this will decrease the behaviour in the future.

Why smart as a competitive advantage is rare

Far too many organizations are not strategizing with a focus on behaviour, learning and adaptability. They don't utilize the principles of smartness to build competitive advantage. By analysing the cause from a behaviour analysis perspective, we can get answers to why, while at the same time generating ideas as to how we can actually achieve this in our organization.

When behaviours are in deficit, we have learned that this depends on *lack of knowledge, skill or competence* or *lack of reinforcement*. The rarity in this case is due, on the one hand, to a lack of knowledge, skill and competence. No one wants to be deliberately unwise. The principles that apply to human behaviour are not taught at the courses where many future managers are trained. Business schools, technical colleges and internal corporate leadership programmes do not teach how behaviour is actually influenced. They don't teach *applied behaviour analysis*. In other words, there is a gap between the collective knowledge that can help organizations and the competency possessed by the employees and leaders of an organization. On the other hand, it is also due to a lack of reinforcement. Behavioural strategizing and exploiting smart as a competitive advantage require discipline and meticulous work. For those who were trained in old management principles, it is a big change when we start applying the principles advocated in this book.

The greater the change, the greater the effort required. It is easier to continue along the course we have staked out and to train new managers in the methods we ourselves have been using for 10, 20 or 30 years. The methods may even have worked quite well.

> Traditional ways of leading and managing organizations are neither right nor wrong. They are just not enough in today's world. They don't focus enough on learning and adaptability, and they are too abstract as they rarely address particular behaviours as creators of organizational performance and success.

We already know that immediate consequences are what govern our behaviour most strongly. Habit causes many people to get stuck in a rut. A new way of running our business brings major changes. When the new way also contradicts what people call their 'gut feeling', or experience or intuition, it becomes even harder to justify a change.

For many organizations, transitioning to behavioural strategizing as an alternative to traditional strategy formulation processes involves a number of immediate and negative consequences for all included. Creating and leading an organization through behavioural strategizing requires more discipline and somewhat more effort than leading by gut feeling – at least initially. On the other hand, the results often turn out far better, and, as we learn, more time is spent on delivering and less on learning how to strategize properly.

So, it is safe to say that behavioural strategizing has consequences. To begin with, it means that we have to change our way of looking at people. People are not simply a certain way. They do any number of things. People are not static but can always change their behaviour. We are accustomed to using generalizations, which makes it harder to change our view of people. This change involves an immediate, negative and certain consequence that causes me not to abandon my current way of looking at people. Instead of using cookie-cutter templates like 'We need to be customer-focused', I need to make an effort to identify what behaviours an employee performs that are signs of them being customer-focused and find ways to reinforce them.

Behavioural strategizing must therefore permeate the entire organization if it is to have full effect. If I am to develop competitiveness by being smart, this means that I need to be prepared to apply the big-picture perspective, see facts, distribute power, reinforce people who challenge me. For an organization, this can mean having to tear up existing structures, review the organization and different entities of financial responsibility, and force managers with responsibility for cost, revenue, earnings or financial return to collaborate. All of these, and these are just some things, involve a tremendous amount of work and are perceived as negative, immediate and certain consequences of changing and working according to the new methods. No wonder people hesitate. I guess I would as well.

For many people, being meticulous is reinforcing. We don't want to make mistakes. When we have more opportunity for planning, we receive positive cognitive reinforcement thanks to the perception that we are more on top of things. Being meticulous is incompatible with daring to take chances and investing in something totally new. Walking in the footsteps of others means that we will never come first, but it also means that we will not be the first to take a hit. Being first almost always means failing every now and then. Of course, that's risky.

We know what we have, but not what we will get. There is a fear of making mistakes in many organizations. Those who make mistakes are often kicked out or are exiled to a far-off corner of the organization. Those who try new things are typically punished more often than they are rewarded. It is risky to try new things. If we are to hit our quarterly or monthly numbers, we cannot afford any mistakes today. And as long as the short-term perspective is considered more important, slow processes such as innovation, change, learning, etc will be on the losing end. On the other hand, if we are to be able to meet the challenges of tomorrow, we need to dare to try new things, and that can mean making mistakes today. Indeed, as

B F Skinner put it: 'A failure is not always a mistake; it may simply be the best one can do under the circumstances. The real mistake is to stop trying'.[8] That statements resonates well with an entrepreneurial mind.

This widespread uncertainty in organizations means that senior managers and decision makers receive plenty of reinforcements from 'conventionalists'. I have never heard of an employee who got a promotion because they were 'questioning things all the time'. Nor have I heard of anyone who got fired for just being 'one of the herd'. All organizations need naysayers on the inside. They exist on the outside anyhow. But this means that managers and management teams need to be prepared to accept negative social consequences in the form of criticism when there are a variety of contending opinions. That requires courage; unfortunately, this seems sparse in many organizations. Our brain spontaneously thinks it would be much easier if everyone felt the same way and believed the same things.

Organizations are generally built on the basis of aversive (negative) reinforcements. To a large extent, people simply do their jobs to avoid being yelled at, being scolded, being fired, or losing their salary. I often ask myself: What does 'doing what is necessary to avoid stress from above' have to do with becoming a successful organization in any type of business or market?

By inviting more people to share in strategizing, we give up power. More perspectives entail 'risks' of dissidence and seeing our ideas come under fire. Seeing our strategic ideas come under fire may well be perceived as a form of punishment. On the other hand, it also presents an opportunity to gain more perspectives and to build a stronger strategy, which ought to be great.

The positive consequences of strategizing in a learning-oriented manner focusing on behaviour are that we get an organization with the courage to think in new ways, one that adapts to the market, develops products and services that no one has seen before, applies ways of working that no one has heard of before and, in the best case, supplants the competition thanks to having succeeded in something completely unique. Many trailblazers have been unsuccessful – yes. Yet Microsoft, Spotify, IKEA, VISA, DuPont, Tesla, Avanza bank and many more have all had the courage to think a bit differently and now hold strong positions, so it is not just a fairy tale.

But all the positive consequences of behavioural strategizing are relatively uncertain and distant. If we do not succeed in making the positive consequence more immediate and certain in people's minds in a sufficiently clear way, it becomes too risky to throw in the new. As with any change.

Negative, immediate and certain consequences exert 'stronger governance' than positive, future and uncertain ones do. Transitioning from leading an organization in a traditional way to leading it in a new way means having to give up tonnes of existing reinforcers that are immediate and certain in the hope of gaining future, positive ones. In my view, this is why organizations that work with management innovation or have a genuinely alternative way of managing themselves are relatively few. We end up talking to the usual suspects when providing advice and showing examples.

> This book is an attempt to lay a groundwork that makes it reinforcing for employees and managers in organizations to pick themselves up by the bootstraps and create their own and the organization's future, no matter how tough it may be. It is an attempt to illustrate the long-term positive consequences that make it worth accepting the negative, immediate ones.

Physical exercise to get better at something is hard for everyone to do, regardless of their initial level of fitness, since you push yourself to the next level. But doing so, however hard it may be, has positive consequences in terms of improved performance in the longer term. So, clichéd as it may sound, 'No pain, no gain' is also true in strategizing.

Aligning behavioural strategizing

A governance model can be regarded as a description of the factors whose purpose is to create a 'governance effect' – i.e. to influence behaviour – in an organization. When we want to develop an organization, the governance model helps us to analyse what in the organization we can, should or must make changes to in order to bring about behaviour that contributes to the goals we want to achieve.

American researcher J K Galbraith created something called the *Star Model*, which can serve as a governance model.[9] The Star Model can be used as a tool to ensure that the various elements that an organization needs to change are interconnected and aligned. It is a tool for understanding an organization and its five primary elements: strategy, structure, process, incentives and human capital. These five components are tightly interlinked and are interdependent. In simplified terms, this means that if a change is made to any of these, it will have impact on the others. For example, if we adopt a new strategy or a new way of strategizing, this will have consequences in terms of what our structure should look like, how our processes should be designed, which behaviours should be reinforced by the incentive structure, as well as the competency that our employees need to have. The full effect of certain behaviour in an organization arises when all the parts of the governance model reinforce behaviour in the same direction – when the governance is rigorous, and the elements are aligned.

The purpose of an organization's strategy is to set a direction and to help employees prioritize their work tasks and behaviours. We want to ensure that their behaviour contributes to increased competitiveness and, in the long term, success. We have also mentioned that change and innovation are becoming more and more important to long-term success. This means that strategy also becomes a tool for driving change. Both innovation and change are held up as cornerstones of the future success story in many organizations.

> Strategy without change does not contribute to long-term success. Nor does change without a tie-in to strategy. Strategy and change are closely interlinked and are impossible to keep apart in practice.

By asking questions about innovation and adaptation based on the Star Model's five elements, we can understand whether innovative and adaptive behaviour is being reinforced. Do we have a strategy that includes innovation and change? Does the existing structure strengthen innovative and adaptive behaviour? Do we have processes set up for how we integrate learning and change into strategizing, daily business operations performance evaluation and feedback to the organization? Are strategy and change an integral part of everything we do to create long-term success? Are the organization's incentives linked to learning, adaptation and change? Are members of the organization encouraged and reinforced to test more or less uncertain new ideas? To learn something new? Do employees have the competency needed to drive change and innovation? Is our culture allowing the failures associated with innovating and change?

In short, our governance model reinforces the behaviour that makes us perform or not perform, succeed or not succeed. Do we have a clear strategic focus? Are we challenging our organization's and industry's current conventions? Are we involving enough different perspectives in our strategizing?

Are we focusing on reinforcing good behaviour rather than punishing bad behaviour? Are we assigning responsibility for innovation and change to everyone in the organization?

If we want to create momentum with regard to an issue, we need to think through how the entire governance model affects this. The organization needs to make clear choices and to accept the consequences of these choices. It's not really that difficult at the planning stage. Realizing it is going to be exacting, but it is not complicated.

In order to become a successful organization, the power of the entire organization must be harnessed to reinforce behaviours that build competitiveness through learning and adaptation: focusing on learning and efficiency, challenging current conventions, involving more people in strategizing, reinforcing the positive, assigning responsibility for change to everyone in the organization, reinforcing new initiatives and providing opportunities to exert influence.

Notes

1 D Teece, G Pisano and A Shuen. Dynamic capabilities and strategic management, *Strategic Management Journal*, 1997, 18, 1319–50; C Helfat and M Peteraf. Understanding dynamic capabilities: Progress along a developmental path, *Strategic Organization*, 2009, 7, 91–102

2 See, e.g., C Christensen and M Overdorf. Meeting the challenge of disruptive change, *Harvard Business Review*, March/April 2000, https://hbr.org/2000/03/meeting-the-challenge-of-disruptive-change (archived at https://perma.cc/P6GS-YR9X); J H Dyer, H Gregersen and C Christensen. The innovator's DNA, *Harvard Business Review*, December 2009, https://hbr.org/2009/12/the-innovators-dna (archived at https://perma.cc/8DCB-D66E)

3 See, e.g., V Govindarajan and C Trimble (2005) *Ten Rules for Strategic Innovators*, Harvard Business School Press, Cambridge, MA

4 See, e.g., J Birkinshaw, G Hamel and M Mol. Management innovation, *Academy of Management Review*, 2008, 33, 825–45

5 M Gladwell (2000) *The Tipping Point*, Little Brown, New York

6 D Centola, J Becker, D Brackbill and A Baronchelli. Experimental evidence for tipping points in social convention, *Science*, 2018, 360 (6393), 1116–19

7 A Turner. Generation Z: Technology and social interest, *Journal of Individual Psychology*, 2015, 71 (2), 103–13; K K Myers and K Sadaghiani. Millennials in the workplace: A communication perspective on millennials' organizational relationships and performance, *Journal of Business and Psychology*, 2010, 25 (2): 225–38

8 B F Skinner (1971) *Beyond Dignity and Freedom*, Bantam Books, New York

9 J Galbraith (2001) *Designing Organizations: An executive guide to strategy, structure, and process*, Jossey-Bass, San Francisco

15

The future of competitive advantage

Given the increasingly scarce resource base of skills to draw on, coupled with the ever-faster pace of technical and societal development, it is reasonable to believe that the future will be about adapting, finding new ways of solving problems and learning how to learn new things. Competitiveness will increasingly come down to who is able to embrace the rapid pace of change in the outside world.

People who can help organizations change, whether they are consultants or internal innovators (e.g. intrapreneurs, mavericks, bootleggers), will be in demand as a competency in the future. In 2013 some of the world's largest companies, including Citibank, hired global chief innovation officers (CINOs) with responsibility not only for product or technological innovation, but also for creating an organization that behaves innovatively and demonstrates a propensity for change. IBM hired its first CINO in June 2013. Since then, others have followed. Innovation, thinking in new ways and change are considered so important that someone needs to be put in charge of the issue for the entire corporation. But in many, many organizations they have yet to appear. Who is accountable for ensuring your organization constantly adapts to future demands? Do you have a chief strategy officer? What type of view on strategy do they have? If you don´t know, look at your strategy, and your management and control processes. If more attention and resources are invested in planning than evaluation, there is your answer. And, in that case, there is room for improvement if you want an organization that continuously develops.

In the early post-war period when strategic management 'grew up', 'big' or 'best' were the only two possible generic strategies. They were then complemented in the 1980s with 'fast' as more information was accessible. And later, during the late 1990s, 'beautiful' came along and we learned how to capitalize on customers' will to be a part of something and demonstrate individual uniqueness. Fast and beautiful, however, were initially simply considered a 'necessity' in addition to being big or best. Over the years, knowledge and brand issues have then become so important that being fast and beautiful can be regarded as their very own generic strategies.

In 2021, being smart, i.e. learning and adapting, is considered a 'necessity' to all organizations, in addition to being big, the best, fast or beautiful. However, I would not be surprised if in a couple of years from now we consider 'smart as a competitive advantage' a unique generic strategy of its own besides big, smart, best or beautiful. Time will tell, but it comes down to one question: Can an organization down-prioritize their focus on economies of scale, on tailoring products and services, on research and innovation to gain temporary monopolies, on building and exploiting a strong brand – and focus chiefly on being the quickest to learn, to adapt and in that sense always surf the next and best wave? I certainly think so. But, to me, an even more interesting question then follows: If such organizations can exist, what would they look like? What industries and types of businesses would they engage in? What would their resource base look like? What would the organizational structure look like? How will they employ individuals, e.g. 'giggers', to get their hands on the sharpest minds? Again, time will tell, but my best guess is that these organizations will bear very little resemblance to a traditional organizational hierarchy.

I have yet to come across such an organization, and if you know of one, please do let me know.

KEY POINTS

Part Five: Smart as a competitive advantage

How is behavioural strategizing related to the ability to compete?

Organizations that actively seek out information that they can use as a competitive advantage will endure. Behavioural strategizing entails harnessing the vast amount of information that is generated and using it to become nimbler. This demands a structured process for using the information, reflecting on it, making sure that it is transformed into intelligence, knowledge and the ability to compete. The new knowledge is used to identify ideas and suggestions for improvement that allow the organization to better adapt its business to the conditions in the outside world.

What is the focus of behavioural strategizing?

Organizations that employ behavioural strategizing focus on what creates results – behaviour and its consequences – not on activators. They spend time on influencing what they can influence and what actually creates results – behaviour is efficient.

Behavioural strategizing demands that we identify key behaviours that create results in the business and understand what influences this behaviour. By continuously measuring this behaviour, it is possible to say with more precision what the current state is and where to go from here. This leads to a greater adaptability.

Why is innovation an important part of behavioural strategizing?

The outside world is constantly changing. Organizations that fail to think in new ways and to adapt to prevailing conditions die.

In behavioural strategizing, organizations make sure that more people can make their voice heard during the course of strategizing. They make use of innovators and a cross-section of the organization, as well as its customers and suppliers, when strategizing.

How do we create organizations that utilize smart as a competitive advantage?

In order to perpetuate behaviour, we need to create structures that reinforce behaviour, that make up a competitive advantage by learning, adapting and its way of strategizing. The entire governance model of an organization – the strategy, the structure, the processes, rewards and employees – needs to be interconnected and aligned so as to reinforce the behaviours like thinking in new ways, learning new things, innovating, taking chances, failing quickly, adapting to changing environments.

INSPIRATION AND POINTERS
TO FURTHER READING

I am not young enough to know everything.

J M BARRIE

If I were to list everything that gave me inspiration when writing this book, that would probably turn into a whole new book, possibly an even longer one – and in all likelihood more boring. So, I will settle for mentioning those that have had the greatest influence. Several of the books exerted an influence going beyond the particular part under which they are sorted. To the best of my ability, I have tried to place them where they had the greatest significance for me, and to provide pointers for further reading.

Part One: A theory of everything

Cyert, R and March, J (1963) *A Behavioral Theory of the Firm*, University of Illinois at Urbana – Champaign's Academy for Entrepreneurial Leadership Historical Research Reference in Entrepreneurship

Damasio, A R (2005) *Descartes' Error: Emotion, reason, and the human brain*, Penguin Books

Darwin, C (1959) *On the Origin of Species by Means of Natural Selection, or the Preservation of Favoured Races in the Struggle for Life*, Natur & Kultur

Felin, T, Foss, N and Ployhardt, R. Microfoundations for management research, *Academy of Management Annals*, 2015, 9, 575–632

Hambrick, D and Crossland, C (2018) A strategy for behavioral strategy: Appraisal of small, midsize, and large tent conceptions of this embryonic community, in *Behavioral Strategy in Perspective (Advances in Strategic Management)*, ed M Augier, C Fang and V Rindova, 39, 22–39 Emerald Publishing

Hawking, S (1987) *A Brief History of Time*, Bantam Books

Isaacson, W (2008) *Einstein: His life and universe*, Simon & Schuster

Levinthal, D and March, J. The myopia of learning, *Strategic Management Journal*, 1993, 14, 95–112

Lovallo, D and Sibony, O. The case for behavioral strategy, McKinsey & Co, 2010, www.mckinsey.com/business-functions/strategy-and-corporate-finance/our-insights/the-case-for-behavioral-strategy (archived at https://perma.cc/KH28-GJFD)

Moxley, R. Pragmatic selectionism: The philosophy of behavior analysis, *The Behavior Analyst Today*, January 2004, Cengage Learning

Nörretranders, T (1991) *Märk världen – en bok om vetenskap och intuition*, Bonnier Pocket

Powell, T, Lovallo, D and Fox, C. Behavioral strategy, *Strategic Management Journal*, 2011, 32, 1369–86

Skinner, B F (1976) *About Behaviorism*, Random House USA

Skinner, B F (1976) *Walden Two*, Macmillan Publishing

Skinner, B F (2002) *Beyond Dignity and Freedom*, Hacket Publishing Company

Thorndike, E. Animal intelligence: An experimental study of the associative processes in animals, *Psychological Monographs*, 1898, 1911, 8

Part Two: Arbitrariness is over

Bourne, M, Mils, J, Wilcox, M, Neely, A and Platts, K. Designing, implementing and updating performance measurement systems, *International Journal of Operations and Production Management*, 2000, 20, 754–71

Burns, T and Stalker, G (1961) *The Management of Innovation*, Tavistock

Chenall, R. Integrative strategic performance measurement systems, strategic alignment of manufacturing, learning and strategic outcomes, *Accounting, Organizations and Society*, 2005, 30, 395–422

D'Aveni, R, Dagnino, G and Smith, K. The age of temporary advantage, *Strategic Management Journal*, 2010, 31, 1371–85

Kahneman, D. The big idea, *Harvard Business Review*, June 2011, 50–60

Kahneman, D (2011) *Thinking, Fast and Slow*, Farrar, Straus and Giroux

Kaplan, R and Norton, D. The balanced scorecard, *Harvard Business Review*, 1992, 70, 71–79

Melnyk, S, Bititci, U, Platts, K and Andersen, B. Is performance measurement fit for the future? *Management Accounting Research*, 2014, 25, 173–86

Morgan, G (1986) *Images of Organization*, SAGE Publications, Inc

Pfeffer, J and Sutton, R I (2006) *Hard Facts, Dangerous Half-Truths and Total Nonsense*, Harvard Business School Press

Senge, P (1990) *The Fifth Discipline: The art and practice of organizational learning*, Doubleday/Currency

Simon, H (1957) *Models of Man, Social and Rational: Mathematical essays on rational human behavior in a social setting*, Wiley

Simon, H (1997) *Administrative Behaviour: A study of decision-making processes in administrative organizations*, 4th edn, The Free Press

Skinner, B F (1966) *Science and Human Behavior*, The Free Press

Walsh, J. Managerial and organizational cognition: Notes from a trip down memory lane, *Organization Science*, 1995, 6, 280–321

Part Three: Unexpected simplicity

Baer, D, Wolf, M and Risley, T. Some current dimensions of applied behavior analysis, *Journal of Applied Behavior Analysis*, 1968, 1, 91–97

Bandura, A (1977) *Social Learning Theory*, Prentice-Hall

Braksick, L (2007) *Unlock Behavior, Unleash Profit*, McGraw-Hill

Collins, J and Porras, J. Building your company's vision, *Harvard Business Review*, Sep–Oct 1996, 65–77

Daniels, A (1989) *Performance Management*, Performance Management Publications

Daniels, A (2000) *Bringing Out the Best in People*, McGraw-Hill

Ericsson, A, Krampe, R and Tesch-Romer, C. The role of deliberate practice in the acquisition of expert performance, *Psychological Review*, 1993, 100, 363–406

Johnson, C, Redmon, W and Mawhinney, T (2001) *Handbook of Organizational Performance: Behavior analysis and management*, The Haworth Press

Locke, E A and Latham, G P (1984) *Goal Setting: A motivational technique that works*, Prentice-Hall

Skinner, B F (1969) *Contingencies of Reinforcement*, ACC, Meredith Corporation

Sulzer-Azaroff, B and Meyer, G (1991) *Behaviour Analysis for Lasting Change*, Wadsworth/Thomson Learning

Sundel, M and Sundel, S (1999) *Behavior Change in the Human Services: An introduction to principles and applications*, 4th edn, SAGE Publications, Inc

Wadström, O (2019) *Quit Ruminating and Brooding*, Psykologinsats

Part Four: Strategy is behavioural change

Andrews, K (1987) *The Concept of Corporate Strategy*, McGraw-Hill

Ansoff, H I (1965) *Corporate Strategy: An analytic approach to business policy for growth and expansion*, McGraw-Hill

Beer, M and Nouhria, N (2000) *Breaking the Code of Change*, Harvard Business School Press

Campbell, A, Goold, M and Alexander, M. Corporate strategy: The quest for parenting advantage, *Harvard Business Review*, March 1995

Csaszar, F. What makes a decision strategic? Strategic representations, *Strategy Science*, 2018, 3, 606–19

Garud, R and Van de Ven, A (2002) Strategic change process, *Handbook of Strategy and Management*, SAGE Publications

Grant, R. Strategic planning in a turbulent environment, *Strategic Management Journal*, 2003, 24, 491–518

Hamel, G and Prahalad, C K (1994) *Competing for the Future*, Harvard Business School Press

Hofer, C and Schendel, D (1979) *Strategy Formulation: Analytical concepts*, West

Johnson, G, Langley, A, Melin, L and Whittington, R (2007) *Strategy as Practice: Research directions and resources*, Cambridge University Press

Krüger, W. Implementation: The core task of change management, *CEMS Business Review*, 1996, 1, 77–96

Mason, R and Mitroff, I (1981) *Challenging Strategic Planning Assumptions*, Wiley and Sons

Mintzberg, H (1993) *The Rise and Fall of Strategic Planning*, The Free Press

Mintzberg, H and Waters, J. Of strategy: Deliberate and emergent, *Strategic Management Journal*, 1985, 6, 257–72

Mintzberg, H and Westley, F. Cycles of organizational change, *Strategic Management Journal*, 1992, 13, 39–59

Mintzberg, H and Westley, F. Decision-making: It's not what you think, *Sloan Management Review*, 2001, 42, 89–93

Mintzberg, H, Ahlstrand, B and Lampel, J (1998) *Strategy Safari: A guided tour through the wilds of strategic management*, The Free Press

Nickerson, J and Argyres, N. Strategizing before strategic decision making, *Strategy Science*, 2018, 3, 592–605

Ohmae, K (1982) *The Mind of the Strategist: The art of Japanese business*, McGraw-Hill

Peteraf, M A. The cornerstones of competitive advantage: A resource-based view, *Strategic Management Journal*, 1993, 14, 179–91

Pettigrew, A and Whipp, R (1991) *Managing Change for Competitive Success*, Blackwell Business

Porter, M. What is strategy? *Harvard Business Review*, Nov–Dec 1996

Prahalad, C K and Hamel, G (1996) *Competing for the Future*, Harvard Business School Press

Quinn, J. Strategic change: Logical incrementalism, *Sloan Management Review*, Fall 1978, 7–21

Sun Tzu (2005) *The Art of War*, translated by T Cleary, Shambhala Publications

Wadström, O (1995) *Att förstå och påverka beteendeproblem*, 4de uppl, Psykologinsats

Whittington, R. Strategy as practice, *Long Range Planning*, 1996, 29, 731–35

Part Five: Smart as a competitive advantage

Abernathy, W (1996) *The Sin of Wages*, Perfsys Press

Bartlett, C and Goshal, S. Changing the role of top management, *Harvard Business Review*, Nov–Dec 1994, 79–88

Birkinshaw, J and Gibson, C. Building ambidexterity into an organization, *MIT Sloan Management Review*, Summer 2004, 47–55

Crossan, M and Apaydin, M. A multi-dimensional framework of organizational innovation: A systematic review of the literature, *Journal of Management Studies*, 2010, 47, 1154–91

Dachler, H and Wilpert, B. Conceptual dimensions and boundaries of participation in organizations, *Administrative Science Quarterly*, 1978, 23, 1–39

Drucker, P (1985) *Innovation and Entrepreneurship*, Harper & Row

Drucker, P. The discipline of innovation, *Harvard Business Review*, 1985, 63, 67–72

Finkelstein, S and Hambrick, D. Top-management-team tenure and organizational outcomes: The moderating role of managerial discretion, *Administrative Science Quarterly*, 1990, 35, 484–503

Floyd, S and Wooldridge, B (2000) *Building Strategy from the Middle*, SAGE

Grant, R. The resource-based theory of competitive advantage: Implications for strategy formulation, *Knowledge and Strategy*, 1991, 33, 3–23

Hambrick, D and Mason, P. Upper echelons: The organization as a reflection of its top managers, *Academy of Management Review*, 1984, 9, 193–206

Hamel, G (2002) *Leading the Revolution*, Plume Books

Hamel, G (2007) *The Future of Management*, Harvard Business School Press

Pettigrew, A. On studying managerial elites, *Strategic Management Journal*, 1992, 13, 163–82

Rogers, E (1962) *Diffusion of Innovations*, Free Press of Glencoe

Schumpeter, J (1942) *Capitalism, Socialism, and Democracy*, Harper & Brothers

Simons, R (1995) *Levers of Control: How managers use innovative control systems to drive strategic renewal*, Harvard Business School Press

Wagner, J. Participation's effects on performance and satisfaction, *Academy of Management Review*, 1994, 19, 312–30

INDEX

Italics denote information within a figure.

CPSIA information can be obtained
at www.ICGtesting.com
Printed in the USA
JSHW010024300322
24434JS00006B/21

9 781398 604827